Sean Mooney's Practical Guide to Running a Pub

Sean Mooney's Practical Guide to Running a Pub

Sean Mooney
with
George Green

Nelson-Hall nh **Chicago**

Library of Congress Cataloging in Publication Data

Mooney, Sean.
    Sean Mooney's Practical guide to running a pub.

    Includes index.
    1. Hotels, taverns, etc. I. Green, George, 1925- joint author. II. Title.
    III. Title: Practical guide to running a pub.
    TX950.7.M66   658'.91'64795   78-27436
    ISBN 0-88229-400-8 (cloth)
    ISBN 0-88229-681-7 (paper)
Copyright © 1979 by Sean Mooney

Manufactured in the United States of America

10   9   8   7   6   5   4   3   2   1

To Curt Gentry, author of Helter Skelter, *whose idea it was*

Contents

Appendixes

Foreword

One Sunday morning in June of 1973, I found myself in a charming cafe on Paris's Left Bank, in the company of Sean Mooney, noted San Francisco publican and raconteur. We had just arrived from the United States, and were softening the effects of jet lag with some Cognac and coffee, when Mooney suddenly remarked (his voice rising above the sophisticated chatter of the Parisian families surrounding us), "No one can run a bar like Americans. I could teach these people a thing or two if I had the chance!"

I was not in a position to argue with him, as this was my first trip abroad, but hoping to quiet him down before we were overheard, translated, and evicted, I suggested that if he knew so much, perhaps he would be willing to share his knowledge by teaching a course for me at San Francisco State's Extension Program.

Stunned, Mooney fell strangely silent. I pressed on, flushed with my own off-the-cuff creativity, and we soon had a rough outline for a course which became reality the following September.

Simply put, the course, *Bar Management and Bartending*,

conducted in a specially equipped classroom at Mooney's Irish Pub in San Francisco, was one of the most successful extension programs ever presented by San Francisco State. Accompanied by full media coverage, with scores of students clamoring for admission, Mooney embarked on his newest adventure. Over two hundred students, twenty-five per class, completed the course. The press of several dramatic new business opportunities combined with fatigue caused the early retirement of Professor Mooney, but the work which had been accomplished in preparing for his teaching career served as the foundation for this book.

Mooney is one of a kind, as is his book. If you have ever thought about, dreamed about, or seriously considered buying your own bar, this book will either push you further along, or stop you in your tracks. I know, because I read it, and I'm now part owner of a modest establishment in California, with all the headaches that go with this business.

PETER DEWEES, *Associate Dean*
Continuing Education
San Francisco State University

Acknowledgments

We could not have written this book without the help of our friends. Cliff Todd, who conducted the course on "Bar Management & Bartending" for San Francisco State University at Mooney's Irish Pub after the original professor abdicated, contributed materially to a number of chapters in the book.

Roy Page, publisher of *Beverage Industry News*; Fred Corti, Deputy Director of the California Department of Alcoholic Beverage Control; George Reilly of the California Board of Equalization, and Cooke O'Neal of the National Association of Credit Management allowed us to reprint some of their material as did Paul Dufek, executive director of the National Licensed Beverage Association from their *Compendium of State Beverage Alcohol Laws*.

Vic Burnham gave the manuscript its final editing as he typed it.

1

So You're Thinking
of Buying a Bar?

The mortality rate in the bar business is one of the highest of any type of enterprise in the United States. "Mortality rate" is a silver-tongued expression for going down the tube, losing your shirt, or going broke. The extraordinary fact is that practically everyone you meet wants to own a small, friendly bar.

Recently an acquaintance of mine, successful in the fertilizer business in New York City, who has been making over $100,000 a year for twelve years, confided in me his desire to drop his business and become a governor. Not a governor of a state, but the governor of a pub. Granted he was a little in his cups—we had been drinking for two hours—but no amount of Irish Logic could dissuade him from reaching his inevitable goal.

When I challenged him as to his sobriety, he said:

"I'll tell you what. Stay with me at my home in Westchester tonight. I'll show you the place I'm going to buy. I think you'll be convinced."

The following morning, sure enough, we visited the establishment in question. I certainly would have loved to own the place myself. It was finished in Tudor style, immaculately whitewashed, with neat leaded windows, and highly polished oak furniture throughout. It had a rugged, well-worn floor, shining brass, beamed ceilings, and a fireplace complete with the most powerful set of irons to keep the home fires burning.

My friend was beaming and I could sense the longing that was craving at his guts to quit the fierce competition of Manhattan and retire to this little bit of tranquility in Westchester.

After a couple of Bloody Marys, I figured I had the right to ask the portly, silver-haired, ruddy gentleman tending the bar a question.

"Excuse me, sir, do you own this place?"

A whimsical look came on his face. He answered:

"I wish I did. I've been here only six months and love every minute of it. The owner is in the hospital. He's an alcoholic."

This fiftyish bartender was pure music to watch. He never missed a move, and was friendly with all twelve customers. In the space of one hour he had three brandies. Had he the wherewithal to purchase the premises he so dearly loved, chances are that he would have finished in the same place as the owner.

We left; I tried to reason with my friend.

"That could never happen to me," he said. "The only reason I drink is on account of the pressure of business."

He left; I shook my head. If only he knew. I decided then to put my fifteen years of experience tending the plank as a proprietor onto paper, telling everything I learned, in the hope that at least, like my friend, some wayfarer may not enter the glamour of the bar business without having both of his eyes open wide.

My advice to you, browsing curiously through this first chapter, is to drop the book like a hot brick. Go home. Take your wife out for dinner, and find satisfaction with your present job. If you are still reading, you are not convinced and are obviously on the threshold of changing your life. By following a few simple rules, there's hope for you. Many pitfalls can be avoided if your foundation is sound. Reluctantly, I'll tell you the reward you can expect.

Popularity. Something everyone craves, and no amount of money can buy. Think of yourself walking down the street, greeted every ten yards by total strangers whom you are convinced you have never seen before. Yet they call you by name, and smile delightedly when you acknowledge them. It's embarrassing to a fault, isn't it, not knowing the names of these friendly faces, who obviously like and respect you?

Read on, my friend. You know my name and I'll never know yours.

I've met very few publicans who were not alcoholics. Bar owners generally abstain totally or hit the liquor bottle to excess. The chances are that you fall into one or the other of these categories if you are determined to finish reading this book. The total abstainers, I might add, are usually reformed drunks.

So plunge yourself and your family into the hazy world of booze. If you start drinking late in life, at, say, thirty years of age, your chances of going through your next thirty years with the perpetual shakes are high. On the other hand, you who started imbibing young, at, say, sixteen, know the hazards by the time you reach the legal drinking age and tend to become wary of the continual hangover.

The Sure Way to wreck a happy marriage is to allow your spouse into your bar for one or two pops before s/he goes home to put the potatoes on. The divorce rate in this racket is frightening. To top the moral anguish, when the split occurs it usually necessitates the sale of the premises to pay the attorneys. Both of you end up with exactly nothing.

Partnerships are another form of marriage, and unless you are extremely lucky, or very tolerant, your enthusiastic partner at the offset is liable to be at your throat before the first year is out. From there on it is a downhill battle pending the inevitable split.

Your first question will be: "If you're so smart, why are you in this business and why aren't you a millionaire if you are?"

The answer is simple. I don't take my own advice.

If you do take my advice, you might just well end up a millionaire (or close to it, our currency being what it is).

My character fault is just that which I advise you against, and which publicans easily fall into: *You live like a millionaire when you aren't actually one.*

2

You've Made Up
Your Mind to Do It

If you are going to run a pub, where are you going to find a spot that will match your dreams? The first consideration in choosing a location is whether it is a good place to make a living, that is, will the neighborhood support a bar or another bar, especially of the type you propose to run. Finding a place compatible with your personality is the second consideration. My two latest ventures in saloonkeeping are good examples for illustration.

Eight years ago I was a half-partner in an elegant small bar-restaurant located on Lombard Street in San Francisco. Lombard is one of the most un-San Franciscan streets, known as "motel row." Our place, however, became extremely popular with locals, and was to become considered an archetypal San Francisco dining house. The customers dressed well and behaved properly, and they did so with a lot of joy and satisfaction. The reason I sold out to my partner was because I have a restless nature and like always to be trying new ventures.

I had located a place which was just the antithesis of that restaurant, a gay joint on Upper Grant Avenue named Poopsey's.

My partner and everybody else I confided in said I was totally daft, that this was the craziest plan I'd ever had—and I've had plenty of crazy plans, I assure you. Upper Grant Avenue, under the western slope of Telegraph Hill, is one of the most notoriously unkempt and disreputable locations in Christendom. As long as there has been a San Francisco, this area has been overrun by successive hordes of bohemians and barbarians. It is designated a prime "trouble area" by the San Francisco Police Department. The area and its habitues are raffish eyesores.

The premises had been host to numerous failures in the bar business, and were now occupied by what is oddly called a "gay" bar, that is, a homosexual bar. My friends all told me I couldn't have chosen a surer loser if I'd tried.

I reasoned otherwise. North Beach is filled with interesting people. A great many of them like to drink. The physical layout of this place was dynamite. The price was extremely low, due to its dismal history. There was no parking, but the Hill is covered with a drinking population within easy walking distance. Most important, there were six gay bars in four blocks, and no well-known straight place within two blocks. There was no so-called Irish pub within miles, while a quarter, perhaps, of the local bar-frequenting population consider themselves Irish.

The joint has been a small gold mine to me.

But I got restless again three years ago and felt I had to get out of North Beach to God's clean country. I located a small hotel, 110 years old, in the Mother Lode town of Jamestown (population 950). It was one of four bars there. (The California licensing authorities figure a ratio of one bar per 2,000 inhabitants is about right.)

This bar had been redecorated and refurbished so many times that it was a mongrel, only vaguely resembling its original state, to which I proposed to restore it.

The principal problem here, I was universally assured, was that the local population bitterly resented city slickers coming into their town and mucking about with its historical buildings.

Well, my partner and I restored it so that it won historical society awards. We were proud of it. My partner, an attorney who had given up his lucrative Chicago practice, moved into the hotel and did all the work of restoration with his wife. The natives were mocking and highly suspicious—at first. We had it all put back nicely, when it was gutted by fire. My partner, who had been appointed the town's only judge, got a letter from Jamestown's citizenry sympathizing with his heartbreaking loss and offering all the rebuilding materials and all the townspeople's services—totally free of charge—to chip in and rebuild the hotel. The hotel reopened a year later.

Both these places, in San Francisco and in Jamestown, were ideal choices of location for me. They probably would not have been ideal for somebody else. They suited my personality, while my neighbors at both places seemed to like my personality. Let me emphasize: one of the most important criteria in choosing your place is to be sure that its location and population are compatible with your nature and character—your personality.

I would size up alternative locations as a general would evaluate possible sites of battle. I would get out of my car and walk around the course, looking, listening, and questioning. A methodical person could make up all sorts of comparative graphs, charts, and projections, but that's not my nature, and it tends, to me, to overkill.

The suitability of the location depends to a large extent on the type of operation you have in mind. It wouldn't make good sense to locate a swinging singles discotheque in the heart of a conventional residential neighborhood, or a workingman's bar in a metropolitan financial district. Those would be obvious mistakes. You will have to make a much finer evaluation of your potential clientele than that. Citing again from my own experience, "Sauce for the goose is *not* sauce for the gander."

Several years ago three young men got together and bought several old railroad boxcars, hitched them together, furnished them with delightful, genuine, old railway artifacts, and planted them in a dark, unfashionable location near San Francisco's waterfront. They came round to me and asked me if they could measure the size of the booths in my place so that they could copy them. They assuredly had more going for them than correct booths. Now they are a public corporation with scores of branches patterned after the original one. The total worth of the chain is $37 million. Victoria Station has been one of the most resounding successes in the history of the bar and restaurant business.

A couple of years ago I had to tear out the booths in my place because nobody would sit in them.

That might sound like the vagaries of chance, but I'm sure that their meticulous planning had a lot to do with it. They had gone into much nicer calculations about the wants of their potential customers than I had. I suppose I had just thought those booths looked great and were comfortable. They figured their operation was going to attract a young, romantic crowd who would want to drink and dine in the relative privacy of booths. My crowd, had I reflected in advance, comprised serious drinkers and raconteurs who like to hang in groups at the bar in the daytime, and at night younger customers who come in primarily to look at and listen to loud live music. Booths, no matter how comfortable, are unnecessary to the first and an obstruction to the second.

This is not as serious a mistake as locating a beer garden in an Italian neighborhood, but it is costly. Were I scouting locations, I would carry round a clipboard and a checksheet with as many questions listed as I could think up in advance. And I would case the opposition to observe what they are doing, right and wrong.

Some remarkable individuals have the quality of being able to impose their personalities and tastes on a locality and effect a change on that locality. Most of us, though, will find it much more expedient to adapt ourselves to the location, rather than the location to ourselves.

The geographical location you choose for your bar should give you a good general idea of the clientele you can expect to attract. Unless you have a preconceived idea of what you want your place to look like—say an English pub—you would do well to study the nature and habits of your potential customers, in keeping with the thought that it will be easier for you to adapt your bar to its neighborhood than to adapt the neighborhood to your bar.

For example, you will have to determine the ratio of bar stools to booths and tables. You could have a long bar with fifty stools, but only one or two tables, or you could have places at the bar for only ten persons, but room to accommodate fifty at the booths. If you are in a locale where most of the trade will come in singly, the first arrangement will make you more money because people seated laterally at a bar tend to mingle easier. Different separate groups at the bar are not set apart as much as those at tables or booths. It is much easier to make casual conversations and acquaintanceships. A customer can talk to a pretty girl seated next to him or a few stools away and if she cuts him he doesn't lose face. On the other hand, in a place which is heavy in tables, if a man walks from one table to another to talk to the pretty girl and is turned down, he feels a fool, thinking that everybody is watching and laughing at him as he trudges back to his own table in defeat.

But if most of your trade is married couples or groups who come in together, the table arrangement is better because it discourages an outsider's crashing a private group or twosome, gives more privacy to the group, and encourages intimacy within that group because they are face-to-face rather than side-to-side.

People who come in twosomes, foursomes, or larger groups tend to be conventional middle class. For them, to sit at a table or booth is considered proper, but to sit at the bar is not quite respectable.

Younger customers generally prefer booths or banquettes. There is more privacy for handholding and such. Older customers prefer tables because they have lost the agility to squirm in and out of booths.

Operating conditions vary widely in the fifty states, so I have taken California, particularly San Francisco, as my example. In California there are 27,741 licensed premises allowed to sell some combination of spirits, wine, and beer for consumption on those premises (on-sale licenses). The number of licenses has been set by the Department of Alcoholic Beverage Control (of which more later) and are transferable within the county in which they are issued, but not outside that county. The number was determined by a population formula. It is so difficult to obtain a new, or original, license that the methods of doing so are outside the practical scope of this book. We then assume that you must purchase an existing license from its current owner with the approval of the Alcoholic Beverage Control (or its equivalent in your state). The licenses, therefore, have considerable monetary value.

In San Francisco County there are 625 licensed public premises which can sell liquor by the glass as well as beer and wine. (Five hundred twenty-six more bars are attached to restaurants, a related but different subject not covered in the present book.) The licensing formula obviously took more into account than simple population figures because in Los Angeles County, with ten times the population of San Francisco, there are 1,197 public premises, or roughly only twice as many.

First, then, in California at least, you must determine the county in which you wish to operate. Do not think, though, that you can just plonk your bar any place you wish in that county. The licensing board is chary of "undue concentration" of bars. If there are four bars in one block in a sleazy part of town, they are not going to be too keen on having another one open, especially if the others have suspicious reputations. The worst prospect of all is in moving another bar operation into an ABC and police "problem area." North Beach, the neighborhood in which my saloon is located, is a prime example of that designation. It is highly unlikely that you will be allowed to buy the license from a bar located in a nice, respectable residential neighborhood and move your operation to a trouble area such as North Beach. You will have to find an owner presently operating in that same area and buy his license from him. This is the principal reason why licenses vary so much in value and price even within a specific county.

You must, then, ascertain in advance from the licensing authority whether you will be permitted a license to sell alcoholic beverages in the location of your choice.

3

On the Verge of Your Deal

Just because you have found a location you feel is suitable does not mean you necessarily can open a bar there. In life few people get exactly what they want. If it is an existing bar, the owner may not be interested in selling. If he will sell, you may not find his price reasonable. If your chosen spot is a premises occupied by some other type of business, the authorities may not allow you to convert it into a bar. (Licensing is a complicated subject as indicated in Chapter 2. Details will be discussed in a later chapter.)

But if you do find the right spot and obtain the license, you will need to sign a lease with the owner of the property and building. Generally you will buy this lease from the current lessee and have it transferred to you. This lease is a valuable consideration and legal instrument. I would *never* sign a lease without an attorney's studying it carefully. It's too easy for a layman to overlook even the most obvious provisions, or absence of them. If your attorney does not specialize in this branch of law, you should ask him to consult a specialist in this type of practice for the same reason—his familiarity with such leases.

One of the most important provisions of the lease will be your monthly rent. You won't necessarily pay the rent to the same party from whom you bought the lease. You may negotiate the transfer of the lease with a departing lessee while you pay the rent to the landlord.

While it varies from place to place, the general rule of thumb in the bar business is that your rent should be 10 percent of your monthly gross sales revenue. An average monthly sales of $10,000 worth of drinks for example would make $1,000 an appropriate monthly rent.

It is most important to know how long the current lease has left to run at what stipulated rent. If the lease has only a short time left before its expiration, you could be evicted or have your rent sharply raised after its expiration. Either of these contingencies could be disastrous for you. You might be able to rewrite the lease with the landlord so that you will start with a full term, say ten years. Your lawyer also should check closely any options to renew the lease and any graduated increases in rent it might contain.

Either the lessee or the landlord may decline to close the deal because they have doubts about your ability to meet long-term financial obligations.

If you are buying an existing on-sale general licensed premises, most likely you will make a package deal with the current operator. You will usually buy his liquor license, his lease on the premises, his equipment and furnishings, and his good will (sometimes this includes the name of the establishment). You will usually make a separate deal to buy his liquor inventory. Or you may buy just one or more of these items.

What is it worth? This is the most important question in this book and the hardest to answer. There is no fixed answer or formula because the sale is the result of bid-and-ask negotiations and each deal is an individual situation with different conditions. One thing is sure, the seller will try to get the highest price obtainable at the time, and you, the buyer, will try to pay the lowest figure.

Securities analysts set price-earnings ratios to stocks, but these ratios do not hold equally for different types of stocks and are usually disregarded in the actual market. If these ratios were heeded, there would be little price fluctuation. If the handicapper for a racetrack were always right and heeded, there wouldn't be any horse races.

Six seems to be the magic number in figuring rule-of-thumb price ratios for bars. The theoretical price should be six times the average monthly gross revenue of the bar. If a bar's daily gross sales average $500, for example, that is approximately $15,000 a month. Therefore:

$$\$500 \times 30 = \$15,000 \times 6 = \$90,000.$$

Another formula is to pay an amount which you figure you will amortize from the operation's profits in six years. How you come up with this figure ranges from the wildest surmise to a detailed calculation of all the known probabilities.

The first method is based on gross sales, and the second on profit, but both by the figures of the current operation you are thinking of buying. How do these figures relate to your projection of sales and profit figures you estimate for your proposed operation? At the time you conclude the deal, the only actual figures you will have are those of the current operation.

You will want to see the seller's balance sheet, financial statement, and tax returns.

How do you know these records are accurate? You can't be sure, so the degree of faith you have in the seller is important. If his bookkeeping is not exactly accurate, it will most likely be in your favor. The commonest way a publican cuts corners illegally on declaring taxes is by buying liquor outside the proper channels and then fiddling the tape on his cash register. The effect of this is to show less gross sales on which to pay sales tax and less reported profit on which to pay income tax.

By any formula or ratio you use, the lower the sales and profit are, the lower the value of the business.

(There is a possibility that an owner might deliberately overstate his sales. He might be extremely anxious to sell and so overstate his receipts figuring it would be worth paying the extra sales tax, usually around 6 percent, in order to make his business appear greater than it actually is, thereby driving up his alleged value. Some old professionals are very skillful at judging a bar's business simply by casing the place. I know one man who can hang around a bar for a week or so and, as he says, figure the gross almost to the dollar just by counting the cigarette butts on the floor. That's a little exaggerated, of course, but a practiced eye can really do an uncanny job of judging a bar's gross sales.)

"Anyone who acts as his own counsel has a damned fool for a lawyer." I by no means advise hog-wild expenditures for expert advice, but to sign a contract such as a lease, which might well determine the course of your future, without the best legal advice would be the height of folly. Find out how much it costs before you sign anything. Ask the lawyer what his fee will be—in advance.

I most assuredly am not giving out legal advice in this book, but I am trying to tell you to obtain it. Your lawyer will counsel you, but it is usually out of his province to advise you exactly what the value of the property you propose to buy should be.

There is a specialized sort of real estate agent who may be of help. He deals in business opportunity situations, sometimes exclusively in liquor licenses. He makes his living by expertise in this field. He is a negotiator because he receives his commissions only when a deal is consummated, and to do that a price acceptable to both the seller and the buyer must be arranged.

You may make queries of a number of these business opportunity agents who specialize in bar, tavern, restaurant, and cafe leases, but once you start solid negotiations on a specific property you must continue these negotiations to their conclusion with the same agent, who will probably have a 30-, 60-, or 90-day exclusive option on the sale of the premises.

With all this talk of licenses, leases, rents, and attorney fees, you are likely wondering how much money does it take to open a bar? Depending upon its size, location, and so on, it will cost at least $10,000. You might buy a small place and have a small income for the rest of your life. Or you could buy a bar for $350,000 and go broke. There's no guarantee in this business, but it is one of the few businesses in the United States which you can get into very reasonably, be your own boss, and buy yourself a job.

There are several different ways of raising the capital to enter the bar business if you don't have the cash. You can borrow from a bank if you have good credit. You can establish your credit with a bank by borrowing and promptly repaying loans in progressively larger sums (even if you don't really need the money). This is a classic way of getting a bank to trust you. The subject of bank loans is thoroughly and exhaustively covered in innumerable books and articles. You can easily get a list of basic references by asking your public librarian.

Because the procedure in applying for a loan is essentially the same no matter what the nature of the business, I won't dwell on it in detail. It is obvious, though, that the prospective publican will have a harder job prying a loan out of a banker than will the prospective proprietor of a different sort of business. Bars are still not considered totally respectable.

A great number of individuals and segments of society consider the sale of liquor, in toto, an immoral and disreputable affair, which definitely should not be encouraged. Further, the stability and trustworthiness as well as the morals and ethics of anyone engaged in this business are rated rock bottom by most of these same people, many of whom are the bankers and other capitalists to whom you must apply,

That is a matter of their opinion. What is indisputable, however, is the mortality rate in the bar business, which I saw fit to emphasize in the very first paragraph of this book. Bankers rightfully consider ours a high-risk situation.

Anyone applying for a business loan should never show up at a bank without preparation, but, because of the above facts and opinions, it behooves you, especially, to prepare your presentation carefully. Three documents are essential:

1. *A personal resumé of your life and career.* The more detailed this is, the better. The most important part is your business background and experience. Usually they will not even consider your application unless you have had at least two

years' experience in the type of business for which you need the loan.

2. *A profit-and-loss statement.* This should be a two-year projection. You won't have any hard facts because the business hasn't even been started. A "business projection" is a calculated, reasoned, and detailed estimate of future operations. It is a probability report. The banker will be more impressed by a sober, closely calculated evaluation of *probabilities* than he will be by glittering *possibilities*.

3. *A breakdown of exactly what you want the money for.* You want so many dollars for the lease, so many for capital improvements, so many for inventory, and so forth. The sum of these categories is the amount of your loan application.

The federal government has an agency called the Small Business Administration (SBA) whose purpose is, in part, to aid, counsel, assist and protect the interests of small business concerns. (See Appendix A.) In its lending function the SBA does not compete with privately owned lending institutions, but rather develops rapport between them and small businesses in need of capital. The SBA, by the direction of Congress, has as its primary goal the preservation of free, competitive enterprise in order to strengthen the nation's economy. Almost all bar operations, with a few exceptions such as large chain operations, would qualify as a small business under the SBA's definition.

By law, the Agency may not make a loan if a business can obtain funds from a bank or other private source including the private resources of the principals or owners. You, therefore, must first seek private financing before applying to SBA. This means that you must apply to your local bank or other lending institution for a direct loan from them first. See your banker, ask for a direct bank loan and if declined, ask the bank to make the loan under SBA's Loan Guaranty Plan or to participate with SBA in a loan. If the bank is interested in an SBA guaranty or immediate participation loan, the banker will furnish the necessary forms and instructions.

In all cases of guaranty or participation loans, SBA will

deal directly with the bank. This type of loan may appeal to the bank where a direct loan has been refused because SBA can guarantee 90 percent of a bank loan up to $350,000 (or $500,000 in certain special situations). This reduces the bank's risk enormously, enabling them to place many loans they wouldn't ordinarily. If they will still not make yours you have a remaining option. Obtain written refusals from *two* banks and you can be considered for a direct loan from the SBA. You would then contact your nearest SBA office, listed in Appendix A(1), to discuss your proposal and obtain the necessary forms and instructions. Direct loans can be made up to $150,000 (or $350,000 in certain special situations).

The order of attempt then is:

Direct bank loan

SBA Loan Guaranty Plan or Immediate Participation Loan

Direct SBA loan*

In order to qualify for a loan to establish a new business you yourself must put up equity capital, usually 40 to 50 percent of the total, and SBA must be convinced you have genuine repayment ability. They will take a close look at what is known of your character and review other credit factors.

Vietnam veterans and certain minorities who are considered either economically or socially disadvantaged may qualify for relaxed credit criteria, and have to put up only a reasonable percentage of the equity capital. Severely physically handicapped persons may be eligible for a special low-interest direct loan.

If the above fails, you will have to go to the "public sector" for capital. This usually means a private investor or investors who will probably want a percentage of the business. This, in effect, means a partner or partners.

I would call on as many branch bank managers as I could for advice. Often they will know of sources of private investment capital and may direct you to them. Again, I would come prepared to both the branch manager and the investor, and I definitely would want to make as favorable an appearance as I

---

* See Appendix A (2)

could. Somebody said that Confidence is the Cornerstone of Credit.

By this late date even the most diehard conservative Republican businessmen have given up on publicly trying to dictate such matters as hair length and mode of dress in others. But you can be sure they haven't forgotten about it. And just whom do you think you are going to be facing across that loan desk?

It's pretty generally conceded now that you can wear your hair any old way you want. You should recognize, though, that somebody else is also entitled to his opinion of the seemliness of your appearance.

Some months ago I took a trip East to try to sell a leading department store chain a very, very large order of a new perfume made by members of my family in Ireland. I'm as independent as anyone alive about the way I choose to dress and look, which is far from conformist, but you can be damn sure I looked in at my barber and my tailor before I left. (I got the order, incidentally.)

If you can raise some part of the capital by bank borrowing, you may raise some more from a jukebox and cigarette-machine concessionaire. Shop around these vendors to find out which is the most generous in your town. Tell them, "I have my location picked out. I want to go into the bar business. How much will you give me in a capital loan if I put your jukebox and your cigarette machine in my establishment?" This is a common practice. They might say, if they like the location, that they will give you about $3,000. You reply that three is no good to you, that you need closer to six. They might say that they can't give you six, but will take another look at your place. These people are experts in the bar business. If they like the look of your location and if they think that you are stable, they may lend what you ask and a lot more when you're established. When you're brand new, for putting in their jukebox and cigarette machine it is not too difficult to borrow. You will have to sign a contract with them and they'll probably have you locked up for life. It is difficult to get out of one of these contracts once you have signed.

Normally, a jukebox franchise operates in one of two ways. You and the vendor can split it down the middle so you get 50 percent of its revenue. If you make a really good jukebox deal, you can pay a weekly rental.

From the cigarette-machine sales, concessionaires will give you approximately ten to twenty percent of the price of each pack sold. If you have taken an initial loan from them, you might want to tell them to take *all* the money from the machines to pay off the loan. You've never seen that dough, so it is a painless way to pay it back. I have always found all these distributors to be completely honest; they have never tried to beat me out of one penny.

Many bars pay all their monthly rent out of their percentage of the receipts from the coin devices. These machines can give you not only a source for borrowing but an important source for continuing profit.

When you first buy a bar it's almost impossible to get any credit. To establish your credit, you have to establish yourself with one or two particular liquor distributors. When you start paying your bills promptly, these sellers will recommend you to other liquor wholesalers and trade suppliers as a good risk. The mortality rate in the bar business is extremely high. One of the surest ways of going broke is by overextending your credit, particularly at the beginning. Once you have established your credit, though, there will be no shortage of distributors coming to your door and almost begging you to buy from them.

Juggling around with your credit is an interesting subject. Say you owe one liquor company $1,000 and you haven't got it to pay them, so you buy another $1,000 worth from another liquor company, and so on. This whole cycle starts catching up on you forty-two days later when the first bill becomes overdue. Quickly it becomes almost impossible to pay off *any* of them. Then you must buy everything COD, so instead of buying fifteen or twenty cases of one particular thing, you buy two cases and you have to give the salesman a check each time for the amount of liquor that is coming in on the COD. The salesman doesn't bring up the matter of the old bill. He wants the new COD order, but interest is still mounting up steadily on that old bill.

There are a lot of different ways you can juggle around so you will always have enough liquor, but you will always owe an awful lot of money; still, you're making all kinds of friends with people. When you owe liquor people money, they are much nicer to you than when you are paying your bills. When you are paying them you never see the boss; when you stop paying the bills he will drop by your place for a few drinks. He wants to take a look and see that his investment is protected.

After you have chosen your location, you should then determine as accurately and carefully as you can, on the basis of all the facts which you can assemble, how much capital you will need to buy your license and lease, to pay the rent, salaries, overhead and other expenses and to have a cash cushion during the crucial initial period of operation. Then you must determine how you are going to raise this sum and set about doing it.

4

You've Bought Your Bar

This book was written in San Francisco. While federal law regulating the sale of alcoholic beverages remains constant and standard throughout the fifty states, state laws and regulations vary widely. I have used California's regulations in this book. If you plan to open a bar in another state you should check with their regulatory bodies to find out that state's variance from California statute.

The regulatory organization in California is called the Department of Alcoholic Beverage Control (ABC). Here, I paraphrase the NOTICE which concludes the ABC's Notice For Persons Submitting Applications For Alcoholic Beverage Licenses: *The following information is of a general nature. Specific or unique situations or problems should be discussed with the local office of the Department of Alcoholic Beverage Control.* Doing this is particularly pertinent in other states, whose regulations can differ greatly from California's.

The Twenty-first Amendment to the United States Constitution, repealing prohibition, vested power to the states in licensing and controlling the sale of alcoholic beverages. Subsequently the states have adopted various forms of internal control in the matter. The statutes vary widely, but fall in two general types. First, some states—such as California—license and regulate the sale of alcoholic beverages. Others actually sell these beverages themselves, through a state monopoly. To date, no state has engaged in the manufacture of these beverages.

Some states are local option. That is, the sale of alcohol is determined and controlled by the municipality or county rather than by the state.

Licensing laws are so different, arbitrary, and capricious that they often seem specially designed to confuse the public. Erratic as they are, they do not approach those of England, Scotland, and Ireland for sheer willfulness. If you want to engage in this business, this is just one of the vexations you will have to face.

These bodies issue a wide variety of licenses: to manufacturers, vintners, importers, wholesalers, retail stores, and so forth. The specific license which concerns us is on-sale public premises, or a bar licensed to sell spirits, wine, and beer. There are two other similar but different licenses, on-sale general (bona fide public eating place also serving spirits, wine, and beer) and on-sale beer and wine. (Off-sale licenses are establishments which sell the beverages in sealed containers to be consumed outside the premises where they are sold, that is, retail stores of several varieties.)

The ABC has a dual function and dual responsibilities, licensing and enforcement. They must investigate and approve all applications for licenses. Then they share the responsibilities for enforcement of the laws with local police forces. Generally speaking, they leave the day-to-day enforcement to the police, who have more manpower, although officials of the ABC are peace officers and can and do make arrests.

An encyclopedia could be compiled of governmental regulation of the alcoholic beverage industry. All I try to do in this chapter is give, first, a brief highlight of the more important points regarding *obtaining* your liquor license in California, and, second, the more important points in *retaining* your license. That is, I shall first deal briefly with the ABC in their role of a licensing authority, and second in their role of an enforcement authority.

Appendixes at the back of this book give somewhat more detailed information. Please note that these appendixes are not comprehensive texts of laws and regulations. They are *excerpts* from laws and regulations as they apply specifically to on-sale public premises.

Appendix A. Federal Laws and Regulations.

Appendix B. Fuller Highlights from California ABC Rules and Regulations.

Appendix C. Brief Highlights from Rules and Regulations of Other States.

Appendix D. Addresses of the 50 State Regulatory Bodies. (Apply to this regulatory body of your state for complete information.)

The following is excerpted from *Instructions For Persons Submitting Applications for Alcoholic Beverage Licenses*, issued by the ABC.

Any person wishing to obtain an alcoholic beverage license should apply at the nearest office of the Department of Alcoholic Beverage Control. All parties concerned should be present. It is not feasible to accept applications by mail since considerable detailed personal information is required, including fingerprints.

On-Sale means a license to sell alcoholic beverages for consumption on the premises, such as a restaurant or bar. On-sale applications require the publication of a Notice of Intention to Engage in the Sale of Alcoholic Beverages. The form of this notice is provided by the department.

For on-sale public premises license, the applicant is to submit a diagram indicating what part of building is to be designated as the "public premises," and drinks may only be served in the area so designated. Post at or near each public entrance a clearly legible sign reading "No Persons Under 21 Allowed." Another sign shall be maintained at a prominent place in the interior. Keep one exterior entrance unlocked at all times while any member of the public is in such premises. Furnish, sell, or serve no meals of the variety and type served in a bona fide eating place. Sandwiches, beverages, salads, desserts, and similar short orders of food products may be sold and served as an incidental part of the principal business.

If only a barroom is designated as the "public premises," no service is permitted outside that room since that would be a sale at a place not licensed by the department.

A new "public premises" license may not be issued except on a showing of substantial public demand. Therefore, *such licenses may be obtained only by transfer.*

Under some circumstances, temporary retail licenses are available where licensed premises are changing ownership. Caution: It is illegal for an unlicensed person to exercise control of the licensed business unless or until a temporary license is issued in his name.

If there is any purchase price or consideration in connection with the transfer of a business operated under a retail license an escrow must be established with some person, corporation, or association not a party to the transfer.

The full amount of the purchase price or consideration must be placed in escrow. Escrow agreements must provide for payment only after the transfer of the license is approved by the department.

Consideration includes cash, checks, promissory notes, or other thing of value which has been agreed to be paid to the transferor for the license, inventory, fixtures, household interest, realty, good will, covenant not to compete, or other property connected with the licensed business. At the time of filing, the applicant shall present a copy of the Notice of Intention to Transfer which shall be certified by the county recorder.

Every application filed for transfer shall be accompanied by an affidavit indicating the actual consideration for each asset to be transferred, including but not limited to (1) transfer of the license; (2) good will; (3) realty or interest therein; (4) fixtures; and (5) inventory. The act requires a 30-day posting period. Because of these requirements and other necessary procedures, the department ordinarily needs a minimum of 45 days to process an application. Do not make inquiries regarding the status of an application until this processing period has elapsed.

The department lists the various documents required for application, and then a schedule of fees of different sorts.

At one time it was necessary to be a United States citizen to qualify for a license, but that is no longer necessary. However, all applicants, as mentioned, are fingerprinted. The department gets back a rap sheet from the police and FBI. Generally speaking, conviction of a felony will disqualify an applicant, but this is not a hard and fast rule. The department will use discretion. They look for the *ability* of the applicant to obey laws. If he has obviously reformed, he will not be ruled out. However, if he has a string of misdemeanor convictions as well as a felony rap, they will not approve his license. The prospective licensee does not have to pay cash for the license. In the escrow he may submit a promissory note showing that he is going to pay for the transfer of the license and lease by installment. The department will want to know where he intends to get the money to pay. They will not discuss the subject, but it is said that they wish to prevent money from alleged Eastern crime syndicates from being used to buy California liquor licenses.

The department offers its services in helping all prospective buyers of a license as well as all present holders of a license. Members of the department told me that they try their best to be fair and reasonable. They are interested in compliance with law and regulation, not in imposing hard penalties. They know that most violations are inadvertent. They have the power to suspend or revoke a license, but often they take an offer in compromise in lieu of suspension. This usually amounts to a fine of 20 percent of the gross sales during the period of suspension. What they are concerned with primarily is willful, continual disrespect of the law. The penalties of suspension and revocation of license are not criminal law action, rather administrative procedure and there is a right of appeal.

When the final action, revocation of license, is imposed, it is usually because the department wants to close down a notorious location. If the premises, per se, are not bad in their opinion, and violations are caused by the ownership, they will usually permit the operator to sell his license to another party whom the department feels will clean up the act.

You will see ads for liquor licenses with their price and the note "clean." This word is ambiguous in this context. Many people have the impression that, if you buy a license that has a black mark against it, the ABC will be on your back right away. Actually, though, if you buy a liquor license that has two counts against it—for prostitution, or gambling, or serving minors, or watering drinks, and so on—immediately that license is transferred, it becomes a "clean" license. The transfer itself "cleanses" it; the ABC says in that sense the word is meaningless. Their interpretation of a "clean" license is that the license alone is for sale, with nothing attached to it—no lease, no inventory, nothing else—only the license. The first thing you should determine in any negotiation with a seller is his meaning of the word "clean" in order to avoid talking at cross purposes.

In California the sale of liquor has quite effectively been separated from organized crime, largely due to the efforts of statute and its enforcement.

By the mid 1970s, there were about 52,000 licenses in effect. San Francisco, city and county, held about 7 percent of those. Within that group, about 20 percent were public premises licenses of the type concerning us, and about 15 percent were general licenses (bar and restaurant).

The department has nineteen district offices in the state. The San Francisco office has only twenty-one field investigators to check all this licensed liquor activity, so mostly they check on "referrals," as they term complaints. Most of these originate from the police department, but many come from the public. The ABC cannot keep a constant surveillance on all the bars in the city, so they pay special attention to those which have been subjects of referrals. That's why I think it is so highly imperative to keep strictly within the law. It's similar to the Internal Revenue Service. They usually leave the little fellow alone unless they pick up some flagrant violation. Once you get audited by them, you never seem to get off their blacklist. Do all you can to avoid that *first* audit or referral.

Because the ABC does not have a large force of peace officers empowered to make arrests, they concentrate on operations where they suspect an intentional flouting of the law and public interest. I feel that they do far more to promote my interests than to harass me, so I take good measure not to give them just cause of suspicion of me.

5

Essential to Remain
in Business

The first person you pay is Uncle Sam. By that, I mean all taxes, federal, state, and local. It doesn't matter if you're starving to death, you pay your taxes first, because not to do so is the one way to finish up behind the other kind of bars. You pay your employees second, your bills third, and yourself last. If you do this, you're not likely to get in any trouble.

In the bar business there's a constant large cash flow coming in every day. You don't want to presume it's yours because it's not. Possibly 20 percent of it is yours.

Unless you are trained in bookkeeping and are willing to spend an appreciable amount of time on your accounts, I strongly recommend engaging the services of an accountant to handle your books. Usually he or she will do this on a part-time basis because few saloon operations are large enough to afford a full-time bookkeeper (although many restaurant-bars are). The accountant will usually charge several hundred dollars per month, depending on the amount of work done.

Apparently only a few old-time professional bar owners, even in "sophisticated" San Francisco know that they *must* buy and conspicuously post a $54 Federal Occupational Tax Stamp.

It is not a license to do business, merely a required tax stamp. Failure to have one could result in two years in a federal slammer or a fine up to $5,000.

For some reason, the feds haven't made the effort to publicize the necessity of this stamp or to follow up and check for compliance. Most owners don't even know about this, giving rise to the suspicion that it is some sort of trap laid by the Treasury Department, so that they have leverage on most bar owners, unbeknown to the latter, and when they want to get the owner for something or other, they can always nail him on this omission. Otherwise, why the secrecy about this tax?

In 1955 the Board of Alcoholic Beverage Control was created, leaving the sole responsibility of the Board of Equalization in matters involving booze to collecting the sales tax, which is a flat 6 percent of gross sales (6½ percent in San Francisco, the extra nudge to pay for the mass transit system).

Of course, you will open a checking account at a convenient bank. I suggest that you take the bank manager and his assistant manager to lunch and get to know them and their services. You may usually arrange to have two separate accounts at your bank. The bank may automatically transfer 6 percent (or whatever your state sales tax may be) into the second account in much the same way they would transfer deductions for life insurance or mortgage payments. You could make your own calculations and put this percentage into the second account yourself, if your bank does not have this service. Withholding taxes for your employees should be treated in the same manner in the same account. Remember that this is not your money. You're merely acting as a collector for Uncle Sam.

This puts your tax deductions on a daily basis so you don't get caught short in a cash squeeze situation as do so many people who handle a large cash flow and make the false assumption that "all is mine, mine!" It's surprising how quickly 6 percent adds up. Quickly enough, indeed, so that things might get tight enough to make you lag behind on your other bills, if they should fall due at the same time. You will also be above board on any audits, which will surely score you points with the government types who do the collecting.

Some bar owners put this tax money aside in a savings account in order to let the money work for them collecting interest. If you can make a few bucks on money earmarked for Uncle, the bite is somewhat softened.

It is difficult for a bar owner to cook his books in order to reduce his taxes. The board's auditors have been around this game a long time and are on to all the tricks. They know from the distributors just how many bottles of what you have purchased. They covertly observe the size of the drink you and your bartenders pour and they know what you charge for it. A simple calculation from these facts gives them an accurate figure for your gross sales. (You must purchase your liquor from an accredited distributor within the state. If you are caught buying it elsewhere, you will be in deep trouble with the Alcoholic Beverage Control.)

The California State Board of Equalization generally allows a 5 or 10 percent variation to cover spillage, mistakes, and free drinks. (See Chapter 16.) It also states that any owner who lets more than this be passed out in free drinks is not in touch with current bar economics. State law does not prohibit giving drinks to customers within reason, but if there is a wide discrepancy between the tax which should be paid and the tax which is actually paid, the board will investigate and has the authority to level crippling penalties.

Nobody loves a tax collector, it is said. Despite this, George Reilly of the California State Board of Equalization is one of the best-liked and respected men in San Francisco.

Why, then, do so many owners like and respect George Reilly?

"We provide a valuable auditing service for them," he said. "Most of the discrepancies we note are caused by an honest mistake, overpouring. The house policy is, say, a one-ounce drink, but they only come up with twenty paid drinks from a quart of whiskey. Usually that means the owner or bartender is consistently pouring about an ounce-and-one-half.

"If the owner has any business sense he will want to know

about this before he loses his shirt. We don't *want* to put anybody out of business. You can't collect on a dead horse, you know. We advise the owner so at least he'll be aware of what's going on.

"The bartender who is consistently overpouring should want to be advised of it because he's needlessly jeopardizing his job."

Mr. Reilly is inferring that nobody likes to pay taxes, but if one has to, he'd like to get something out of it. Such as an impartial auditing service.

Throughout this book I have scrupulously attended to correct legal procedure and to accepted business ethics, for whatever those are worth. This is not because of especially lofty morals, but because an Irishman, especially one who drinks, is almost always somewhat paranoid. I don't wish to aggravate this lurking tendency by the legitimate fear that I am being watched or pursued by the law. There's good profit to be made in a totally honest bar operation if you follow the advice in this book. There are, to be sure, innumerable ways of cutting corners. You will hear of many of them before you have spent a month in the business. If you want to adopt any of these practices, it is none of my concern. I elected to be a publican, not a priest or a policeman.

Remember, though, that the authorities have been in this game one hell of a lot longer than you have and that you are most unlikely to come up with a new dodge that they aren't on to in some guise. You must, then, have a sales tax permit from your state as well as a Federal Occupational Tax Stamp. If you have even one employee you must obtain from the Internal Revenue Service an Employer's Identification (EI) Number, which must be used when submitting federal income and Social Security taxes on all employees' salaries. You or your accountant must figure out and make deductions from their salaries and pay the necessary taxes.

Many states have similar withholding taxes as well as unemployment and disability insurance premiums which require payroll deductions and prompt payment. I deduct a flat 25 percent from the weekly paychecks I give my employees. At the end of the month my accountant figures the exact amount owed for withholding taxes of the various sorts, and he pays them. There is usually a small refund due each employee each month because the total of these taxes comes out to about 23 percent.

Psychologically it is better to take a little too much, then give it back, rather than take too little and then have to ask for another donation. I read in *Reader's Digest* many years ago that there was a store in New York selling salted nuts which had two salesladies. One sold tons of these nuts, while the other did just an average business. The owner came round and started investigating. The woman who did so well had the habit of putting too few nuts on the scale initially and then adding to the pile. The one who didn't do so well put too many nuts on the scale and then took some of them off. The customers of the first saleslady thought they were getting a bonus, while the customers of the other figured they were getting shortchanged. The customers weren't looking at the scale but at the pile of nuts.

Then you will have to fulfill local governmental requirements. Before engaging in business, you must contact the appropriate county and city officials to find out if a local business license is required and what the fee is. The city or county assessor's office undoubtedly will require you to pay property taxes on your equipment and inventory. Find out when the flooring tax on your inventory is due. You should allow your liquor inventory to dwindle to the bare minimum just prior to the annual inventory count for taxation purposes.

When the name of the bar is not your legal name, you must make a fictitious name registration with the city or county clerk. This DBA (Doing Business As) name statement must be advertised in a local publication of general circulation.

You will need a permit to operate issued by your local health department. If you are in a rural area, your state health department often assumes this responsibility. Very likely you will be inspected by your fire department, who will require some sort of permit to be posted. You will probably receive a visit from electrical and building/structural inspectors. All your coin-operated amusement machines will probably need a license from the local police department.

In California a lighting inspector has to determine that the intensity of the interior lighting shall not be less than one-half foot-candle when measured by a foot-candle meter at a point thirty inches from the floor wherever patrons are sitting or standing within the premises.

Since I have a relatively small operation I give my accountant minimum responsibilities of keeping my books, paying all taxes, and answering all governmental forms and inquiries from information I give him. The owner is responsible for errors and omissions on his accountant's part, but having one gives the owner a plausible excuse if any such sin happens. The taxing bodies are willing to give the owner the benefit of the doubt, because they want to keep him in business so they can continue taxing him.

Simply to reduce expenses, I assume the following fixed monthly obligations, which could be delegated to the accountant: (1) rent, (2) wages, (3) gas, (4) electricity, (5) telephone, (6) water, (7) maintenance, (8) accountant, (9) garbage, (10) current bills due, and (11) insurance premiums.

If, for one reason or another, you decide not to engage an accountant, relatively simple bookkeeping and tax record books are available and inexpensive. These simplified system books of less than 100 pages, including specimen pages and informational pages, can give a perfectly comprehensive and accurate bookkeeping record because they were designed specifically for taverns and cafes. To be of any use they must be filled out accurately, on an almost daily basis. I wouldn't advise anyone with a hangover trying to enter this information, though. It takes a good deal of concentration on the part of a person not trained in bookkeeping. Just to show you how much detail is required to be recorded in even a small business if you want to be accurate, here is a list of the entries you must make.

  a. Income—Cash Receipts
  b. Income—Quarterly Summary
  c. Payments—Cash and Checks
  d. Distribution of Expenses
  e. Payments—Quarterly Summary

 f. Distribution of Expenses—Quarterly Summary
 g. Bad Debts
 h. Depreciation
 i. Contributions and Other Deductions
 j. Monthly Summary of Business and Statement of Income
 k. Balance Sheet (yearly)
 l. Accrual Basis Schedule
 m. Payroll Record—Social Security & Withholding Tax Record
 n. Payroll Summary
 o. Workmen's Compensation Report Summary
 p. Proprietor's Account
 q. Furniture & Fixtures, Machinery & Equipment, and Buildings
 r. Loan and Note Record
 s. Inventory
 t. Insurance Record

I guess it's evident why I so strongly suggest hiring a bookkeeper or accountant. In either event you should have a handy Weekly Time Book to keep track of all hours worked.

It would be foolhardy to open your door without adequate insurance. No matter what you think about personal insurance, don't skimp or cut corners on business coverage. Surplus limits are relatively inexpensive. A limit of $1 million won't cost much more than $100,000 would, because your carrier will reinsure the excess coverage. Remember that a jury will tend to treat a saloonkeeper harder than they would another type of businessman. Premiums will vary according to your location, building construction, fire-prevention systems, neighbors, and so forth, but a competent business insurance broker in your town knows what you will need and will shop around for the lowest premiums. Your basic insurance package will include:

Storekeepers Liability to cover premises, products and contractual liability, and, usually, auto liability. It also pays claims for bodily injury and property damage arising from normal business operations.

Personal Injury to protect the bar owner against claims for
   injury due to false arrest, detention, libel, slander, or
   defamation.

Fire and Extended Property Damage to pay for damage from fire
   and specified perils like lightning, windstorms, explosions
   and riots. The policy usually covers the building, inventory, fixtures and equipment for actual cash value or
   replacement costs.

Glass Insurance to pay for replacing show windows, mirrors,
   and structural interior glass broken accidentally or malici-
   ously (by vandals or thieves), for actual cash value or replacement cost.

Business Interruption to reimburse the owner for lost profits and
   continuing expenses resulting from a business halt due to fire
   and other insured hazards.

Burglary and Robbery to insure against loss of money or
   merchandise from theft, either inside or outside the bar.

Workmen's Compensation to pay all medical expenses and
   reimburse lost wages for employees injured on the job.
   Coverage, mandatory in California, must be obtained as
   soon as staff is hired.

Dram Shop Liability to protect bar owners held responsible for
   injuries to third parties as a result of negligent sales to
   minors or obviously intoxicated customers. Since this type
   of protection is not usually included in most insurance
   programs, bar owners must consult their insurance agents
   about the coverage.

These "Dram Shop" or Civil Liability Acts fall into the
murky realm of tort law. A "tort" has never been clearly defined, but, in general terms, it is an injury which one person
inflicts upon another, which, however, is neither criminal nor in
breach of contract. In the Civil Liability Acts, the issue is
further confused by differing opinions on fault and negligence.

Under common law a seller of intoxicating beverages was
not generally liable for injuries committed by one of his intoxicated customers upon a third party. Common law held that the
proximate cause of any damage, such as injury or death result-

ing from an auto accident caused by a drunk driver, was the drinking of the liquor, not the selling of it. (An exception was New Jersey, where in such a case the saloonkeeper was deemed negligent if he sold liquor to an obviously intoxicated person.)

Some fourteen states have now superseded common-law rule by statute which imposes strict liability, without negligence, upon the seller of intoxicating liquors when the sale results in harm to the interests of the third party because of the intoxication of the buyer. These various state statutes vary significantly as to who may bring the action and the type of conduct that will give rise to liability. Appendix E gives the gist of the statute in New York State, formerly Section 16 of the Civil Rights Law and now part of the General Obligations Law.

Because of the dire damages which might result from a successful lawsuit against him under these statutes, every bar owner and prospective owner must obtain expert legal advice on this matter as it is construed in his state, and to insure himself liberally against the contingency. Whether you think these laws are fair or not is beside the point. If they exist in your state, you, as a prudent man, should protect your interest by adequate insurance.

Note: A prudent man, yes, but perhaps not a particularly affluent man. Recently, I got word from my insurance broker that my total premium had jumped from several thousand dollars for a three-year period to a little over that amount for *one* year. Our friends, the lawyers, are becoming increasingly aware that there's big money for them in encouraging this sort of litigation. There is grave danger that the law profession may see a gold mine in this, similar to malpractice suits in the medical profession.

An insurance executive in the financial district thinks that this is not exclusively an insurance problem. In his opinion, there will have to be major changes in court procedure. Judgments are getting out of hand in their astronomical amounts. There is no solution in sight. This increase in Dram Act Insurance is going to put a whale of a lot of bars out of business; then the big hotels are going to come under the gun. Premiums will be prohibitive. At the moment the hotels can afford it, but one

Judge Drewes Sues Over Car Accident

Presiding Superior Court Judge Robert J. Drewes and his wife, Caroline, yesterday sued the driver of a car that struck them last September 28. They also sued three businesses they said sold liquor to the driver—William Thomas Gilson, 43, of Petaluma.

Both the judge and Mrs. Drewes were seriously hurt in the accident and Judge Drewes' mother, Claire D. Ringland, was killed,

Those who were named as defendants besides Gilson are the owners and operators of Mario and John's Place, 428 D street, Petaluma; The Green Mill Inn, 10201 Old Redwood Highway, Cotati, Sonoma county, and Four Mile House, 5251 Third street, San Francisco.

The suit charges that Gilson negligently and recklessly operated his car so as to cause it to collide with Drewes' auto.

The businesses were accused of selling quantities of liquor to Gilson so that it affected his mental and physical faculties and made him incapable of safely driving his car.

The suit asks for unspecified general damages, plus medical and funeral expenses, loss of wages and cost of the litigation.

February 18, 1976
Here's another reason for what's been happening with regard to your insurance!

Gentlemen,

As you were advised, your insurance carrier made a mass cancellation effective March 19, 1976. This resulted mainly from the heavy losses they've suffered through the bar and restaurant program.

Antincipating this, I've already submitted your account to between three and ten different insurance companies for quotes. Once your complete quote file from the various companies has been assembled, you'll hear from me. We can then decide which is best for you.

I'd like to sincerely thank the many of you who've already called (as I requested in prior correspondence) regarding receipt of your cancellation notices. It's important for me to know your cancellation date.

Sincerely,

Harry B. Krier III
117 Newton
Burlingame Hills, CA
94010

major judgment against them will, in my opinion, force serving of alcoholic beverages to room guests only. This is not too far away, and the day of 75-cent drinks has already passed.

Prices will rise; you are going to have to put more effort into your business. People will continue to drink, but you will have to do more to get them into your bar.

The only bright spot on the horizon is the internecine warfare which is shaping up among lawyers. Coming right on top of their giving the doctors the monumental shaft, and now rounding on barkeeps, they are starting to fight among themselves. Their chickens are coming home to roost. In the last several weeks in California, clients who have lost a lawsuit are hiring a *second* attorney to sue their first attorney for losing the initial lawsuit because of *legal malpractice*. Unless these legal eagles bring down the whole temple on our heads first, they may get so embroiled fighting themselves that they may leave us alone.

You should discuss with your attorney the pros and cons of forming a corporation under the laws of your state. The advantages of being a corporation relate to tax rates and limitation of personal liability. I don't think it's legal for me to give out any advice on this subject because I'm a member of the wrong bar association. I can say that you ought to find out about it.

6

Organizing a Bar Properly

Any licensed premises you are likely to operate will contain, along with various optional components, three *essential* components. The bar itself where the customers sit or stand is called the *front bar*. Behind and underneath this bar, where the bartender does his work facing his customers is the *work station*. Behind him is the *back bar*, where bottles of liquor and glasses are kept.

The arrangement of the front and back bars varies widely from place to place because in these areas appearance is an important factor. Work stations, where efficiency is the prime consideration, are much more standardized, based empirically upon logic and experience.

A large operation with a long bar may employ two, three, or more bartenders working at individual stations, each in some cases with his own cash register. Described here is a single typical, efficient work station. (To employ two bartenders on one shift both working from the same station would invite confusion, animosity, delay, and inefficiency, so your bar will need a separate station for each bartender, while the register, sink, refrigerator, and other fixed equipment could be used commonly.)

A standard fixture at each mixing station is the "speed rack," a shelf holding frequently used bottles of liquor and mixes, which is suspended about or below waist level. An ice bin with areas around it for holding more bottles is set below bartop level and just above the speed rack. If your bar uses a mixing gun (a nozzled hose dispensing various charged mixes) in place of bottles of your widely used mixes, this gun will be in a holder attached at bar level above and to the side of the ice bin. Completing the individual mixing station is a level space set in the well, or interior indentation, of the bartop. Sometimes it is a metal grate or a piece of rubber with short, protruding knobs, or it may be just a folded cloth towel. This spot is where the glasses are placed during the mixing of the drinks.

Working at a mixing station which is properly set up, the bartender doesn't even have to look where he's going for a bottle. He just reaches out and grabs it. The speed rack that is set up right in front of the bartender has the bar's bottles of most popular drinks in it, for example, Scotch, bourbon, vodka, gin, tequila, vermouth. They are arranged in an order and each has its definite place in the sequence. Bars aren't set up identically; they should be set up for their particular area. However, in any area you will always find a Scotch, bourbon, gin, and vodka. In Maryland you will also have rye whiskey. In El Paso you will have tequila. It depends on the demand. But whatever you have, each bottle should be in its definite place. Then you don't even have to look down when you're picking up a bottle. You know exactly where it is. You reach for it and start pouring.

The drinks from bottles in the speed rack are called the *well drinks*. (The *call drinks* are from bottles on the back bar.)

If a customer asks for a Scotch-and-water without specifying, or "calling," the brand, you will make it from the bottle you have in the well, because the drinks in the well are normally the least expensive drinks in the house. These are the liquors you got the best discount on, not necessarily the cheapest obtainable, but the best at the price at the time.

While the well drinks usually cost ten or twenty cents less than the call brands, they provide the volume of your business, so it is essential to provide a correctly set up speed rack for each of your bartenders because this is where the bulk of your revenue will come from. The faster he can pour these drinks, especially at your peak traffic hours, the greater the chance of success for your operation.

A sink area with two or three large sinks that may be filled with running water should be behind the bar, adjacent to the mixing stations. The first is filled with hot water and detergent for washing glasses; the second contains hot water and disinfectant; and the third is filled with plain hot water for rinsing them. If you can afford an automatic glasswasher, you will not require the third sink.

Your sinks will not be stoppered with plugs but with pieces of pipe about a foot in length. This allows the faucet to remain running while the water level remains constant at one foot. The sink will not overflow, but spill into the top of the pipe. This is where you dump the dregs from used glasses. The liquid goes down the drain. The ice melts and goes down the drain, too, instead of chilling the water in the sink. There will be lemons and limes in many drinks. The funnel will retain this fruit so that it neither clogs the drain nor contaminates the water.

Do not empty ashtrays into this funnel. Tobacco swells when wet and will surely clog your drains. Have metal containers into which to empty the ashtrays, especially near closing time. Never empty ashtrays into wooden or cardboard containers. This is how fires in bars usually start.

Your method of washing glasses will be an object of close scrutiny by the health inspectors. There should be drainboards on both sides of the sinks. On one you set the dirty and used glassware. On the opposite drainboard you place the clean glassware to drain. An area of drainboard is used for such housekeeping tasks as cutting fruit for garnishes.

Either under the bar or behind it in the back bar you should have two or three refrigerated cabinets for beer, bottled soft drinks, mix, fruit, and everything else which needs cooling. Unless you carry and sell a lot of beer, this storage area doesn't have to be large, but it is necessary and should be close to the stations.

If you serve tap beer, a two-keg beer box can also serve for refrigerated space. This beer box will be bulky and should be integrated into the bar setup in such a way as to be unobtrusive, not always an easy task.

One afternoon shortly after I opened my operation a brewery deliveryman started trundling one of those heavy metal kegs through the crowd in my barroom. The entrance to a back bar is almost always at the end of the bar farthest from the front door for security reasons, so when there is any crowd at all, everybody is inconvenienced and has to make way for the deliveryman's hand truck and bulky burden. Then he has to squeeze and jam it along the narrow passageway behind the bar and manhandle it into place, effectively preventing bartenders from working while he is at the operation. Naturally all this doesn't put the deliveryman, either, in too good a humor.

I stuck up my hand and said:

"Hold it, neighbor!"

He didn't know who the hell I was and was about to blow his cork.

"I've saved you some work," I said quickly. "Drop your keg right there at the front end of the bar."

He couldn't believe it; he'd never seen this before. I'd had a carpenter cut a doorway through the lower part of the front bar and fit in two hinged doors swinging outwards. This is only four steps from the front door. The deliveryman slid the kegs into place from the outside of the bar, saving one hell of a lot of time and fuss and momentarily displacing just the two or three customers at stools in front of that beer door.

Prominently displayed on the back bar are the call brands of well-known liquors and liqueurs. Often there are several shelves of them, their display enhanced by overhead lighting or mirrored walls to help an impulse buyer choose his more expensive drink. It takes a bartender a bit more time to turn round and select a call bottle than to reach automatically for a well bottle, so what you're selling the most of should be closest to hand, and what you're selling the least of should be farthest away. Again, this should be determined by the tastes in your area and of your clientele in particular. The bottles you use every day should be on the front, or closest shelf. Normally the liqueurs go on the top shelf. Not being used much they are the farthest away. However, in a dinner house they might be in front because such houses sell a lot of after-dinner drinks, while a saloon normally sells few of them.

It is essential to return the well bottles to their correct places after they have been used because, as stated, your selection of them will be automatic, not visual. Having once made a Margarita (these are popular enough in my neighborhood to warrant tequila in the well) with vodka rather than tequila, similarly colored liquors in similar bottles, because I had previously replaced the bottles incorrectly, both my customer and I can stress the importance of getting into the correct replacement habit.

It is not essential, but it is important also to replace the call brands in their original places on the back bar immediately after using them. Some bartenders leave out bottles of the call brands their customers are drinking at the bar. While this may save a second or two at the time, it can be a problem if more than one bartender is working. If there is only one bartender, he will know the bottles are always in their right places, and he won't have to scan mentally where they may be when drinks are being ordered. Keeping an orderly work area helps to keep an orderly and clear mind. Having to search for a certain bottle in the middle of an order can easily make one forget the remaining drinks, forcing him to ask for the order again, doubling his work and perhaps irritating the customer.

The next chapter considers equipment which is as essential as proper organization of a well-run pub.

7

Fixtures and Equipment

You cannot function efficiently without the proper equipment. Recheck all the equipment you may have purchased with your lease. These are the tools of your trade. Make a checklist to determine if you have everything necessary, and provide for back-ups of essential equipment.

The equipment you will need to open and operate a bar efficiently can be broken down into four categories:

A. Indispensable small tools of the trade. These are similar to what would be used in a home bar, and their use and necessity are self-evident. With the exception of the mixers, which most people now have at home, too, these items are inexpensive. They also, unfortunately, seem to be expendable, so must be replaced often when they disappear. (Glassware is treated in a later chapter.) This list is the basic minimum for a small bar. The larger and more elaborate operation you plan, the more of these items you will need in number and variety.

2 ice picks
3 paring knives
2 cutting boards

4 17-oz. glass cocktail mixers
3 20-oz. metal (milkshake) mixers

2 salt shakers
2 pepper shakers
2 under-bar sugar bowls
1 juice extractor, arm
    winding type
2 lime squeezers
3 ice strainers
1 box long straws
1 box short straws
3 water bottles
3 long-handled mixing
    spoons
3 doz. pouring spouts
3 boxes cocktail napkins
2 boxes toothpicks
2 fruit tongs
7 metal fruit bowls

2 doz. cloth bar towels
3 ice tongs
2 large ice scoops
1 bucket for moving ice
2 wooden muddlers
3 bottle openers
2 small funnels
3 large round serving trays
3 corkscrews
4 boxes paper matchbooks
6 barman's aprons
2 sink brushes
24 ashtrays
1 Osterizer-type electric
    mixer
1 milkshake-type electric
    mixer

B. Larger, expensive, fixed equipment. Some types of this equipment are necessary to operate a modern bar realistically. Here you are faced with numerous choices and decisions, some of them potentially costly or disastrous if made wrong.

   a. back bar
   b. refrigerators or iceboxes
   c. ice machines
   d. beverage dispensing system (mixing gun)
   e. sinks and their appurtenances for each work station
   f. automatic glasswashing machine
   g. cash register
   h. front bar

C. Equipment and machines not necessary for the basic function of making drinks. These are nevertheless desirable or necessary for attracting customers and producing revenue.

   a. cigarette machine
   b. jukebox
   c. amusement devices

D. Furniture and decorations.   As noted earlier, you will almost always purchase by transfer an existing liquor license. Usually it will be part of a package deal in which you also purchase from the previous owner the lease on his premises, his equipment, his furnishings, and separately, his inventory. In most cases where you buy a liquor license "clean" or of itself, you intend to move into on-sale premises vacated by another licensee. When a man sells you his license by itself, his bar equipment is not going to do him much good without that license, so chances are that he has made a deal to sell his lease and the rest to yet another licensee (a third party) who wants to move into his operation.

In these cases, you will either use the equipment you have acquired as is; remodel or refurbish it; supplement it; or sell and replace it. Because of these options, I shall assume the last, or most drastic (which would also apply in case you intend to build your place from scratch or remodel from a different sort of business). Following, then, is the *total* basic equipment you will need, noting that you will likely have most of it in operating condition.

A back bar, 21 feet by 2 feet, vinyl plastic top and exterior, 6-foot, three-door refrigerator, mirrored back, and locked drawers will run a few thousand dollars. You can probably buy a used one for about a third less at a distress auction of a bar's furnishings and equipment.

On the other hand, a 65-foot back bar which came round the Horn from Belgium before 1885 has been the prominent fixture at Breens, a famous old San Francisco saloon. It is made of rosewood, with the top part supported by four carved caryatids, and is worth far in excess of $20,000, the figure which was recently declined. Before the 1914 war, this bar was tended by five barmen, now by three.

Another famous pre-Prohibition San Francisco landmark, the back bar at the Templebar, which also survived the 1906 fire, is the more reasonable length of 25 feet. It also is of rosewood, not the more usual mahogany, and was made in Brunswick. Its owner estimates its fair present value at $25,000.

You can probably pay anything in-between these two extremes.

You may buy your expensive equipment either new or used, or you can lease it. If the latter, investigate a purchase option lease where a certain portion of your monthly payments are credited to an option to buy at the end of the lease term. Check the warranty and maintenance provisions on any deal you make. A bar is in serious trouble if its refrigeration or ice-making machine goes on the blink. We're not in the British Isles. Virtually everyone in this country wants chilled beer and ice in his drink.

While traveling in Ireland in May of just this year, I dropped in at a bar in a small village in Cork. When I asked a young barmaid to please put a little ice in my Irish-and-Water, she looked at me as if I were daft and said:

"Now, sir, where would you get ice in the month of May?"

You may probably save on initial purchase price if you buy used equipment at an auction of a defunct bar's fixtures. I would want to take along someone who knows something about mechanics to give me somewhat-expert advice because you will not get any warranty here.*

The refrigerators or iceboxes are the operative part of your back bar, the rest being furniture. As mentioned, it is vital that you know they are in good working condition and large enough to keep an adequate supply of beer, white wine, mixes, fruits, and cocktail glasses properly chilled. Make sure that there are accurate temperature controls. Have a mechanic check the compressor. Can the boxes be cleaned easily and are the interior racks adjustable?

As mentioned, if you plan to carry draft beer, perhaps its dispensing system will provide a part of your refrigerated space. Check with the representatives of the brewery distributing

---

* Guidelines to help purchasers understand the new warranty law have been prepared by the Federal Trade Commission. The law affects warranted products manufactured after July 4, 1975, which sell for $5 and more.

Included are explanations about when the manufacturer may charge for repair or replacement of a defective product and other limitations of a warranty.

Questions not covered by FTC rules and regulations—such as what is a reasonable time to wait for repairs—will still have to be decided in the courts.

companies before you make a commitment here. Some things to take into account are whether it is a carbon dioxide or an air pressure system; if the coil length between the barrel and the spigot is matched to the quantity of beer on tap; the number of barrels that can be tapped at one time; whether the pressure ensures an even flow; whether temperature controls are adjustable; if any exposed lines are insulated; and whether the coils can easily be cleaned.

You can't run an American bar without lots and lots of ice, and you can't ever afford to run out of it. In large cities you can arrange for daily ice delivery, but most bars buy or lease an ice-making machine. The majority of the ice you use will be cubes, so check whether the machine produces cubes, cubelets, shaved, or cracked ice. Is the machine air- or water-cooled, and is the flow of ice continuous or regulable?

I know of a fellow in Los Angeles who bought a bar which was hooked up only with electricity. He bought an ice machine which ran on natural gas. It was for sale at a bargain price. He had to dump it right away at a loss and start all over again looking for an electric machine. If you don't have a friend who knows something about machinery, ask your utility company to send a representative to counsel you. You should compute the cost of a new machine, a used model, and ice delivery. You will want a machine in the long run, but perhaps you can buy ice at first and defer this capital investment for a while. You will probably want a 450- to 600-pound model.

Sometimes the physical setup of a bar dictates where the ice machine has to be, due to space available and where the electrical wiring (or gas outlet) is located. Given a choice, the closer the machine is to the work stations the better.

Often the ice machine is found clear across the room from the work stations, resulting in wasted time and confusion every time the ice bins get low. At a peak period this time is never really made up, meaning money out of the owner's pocket.

A shaved ice (actually finely ground ice, often called snow) machine can be placed anywhere, because the bartender makes the snow out of the regular cube supply when the station is being set up prior to service.

A large quantity of snow, determined from previous usage,

should be ground and placed in a bin with easy access to the blender. Placing Martini and Manhattan glasses in a section of this bin of snow looks inviting and chills the glasses thoroughly, but the shaved ice is primarily a necessity for blended drinks such as Grasshoppers and Daiquiris.

The beverage dispensing system, or mixing gun, is another costly tool which may either be purchased or leased. This system is a group of plastic hoses with a nozzle with from four to seven finger-pressure valves connected to large bottles of syrups and a CO_2 tank. According to which button is pushed it will pour out a different mix, all except plain water, charged by carbon dioxide for effervescence. (Early models had a common dispensing hole, so after several uses the mixes all acquired the predominant taste of Coke, so make sure you don't buy one of these pioneer models.)

The seven-valve system naturally costs more than one with fewer valves. How many valves you need will be determined by the drinks you serve in volume. With a four-valver you will probably want soda water, Coca-Cola, ginger ale, and 7-Up. You might also want tonic water, sweet-and-sour mix, or just plain water.

The obvious reasons for using the gun are speed and elimination of messing with cases and cases of bulky cumbersome bottles and empties. Some old-time owners and customers dislike the gun intensely, but it's still a moot point whether anyone except a connoisseur of soda pops can tell the difference in taste. My guess is that about 90 percent of San Francisco's bars have converted to the gun. The holdouts are not cheapies usually, but the finest quality bars serving high-priced drinks to a conservative, well-heeled clientele.

A number of places, mostly hotels, service bars, and chain operations, have installed automatic beverage dispensing systems for liquor. I am totally against these things, which depersonalize a bar and demean the bartender, and I have never taken a drink in a place which uses one. Herb Stansbury made this statement, which sums up my opinions perfectly, on automatic liquor dispensing systems in his *Bear Flag Republic* wining and dining newsletter.

Keep Your Eye on the Bartender's Gun. The next time you're on a bar stool, you may be surprised to see him squirt his whiskey from a hand-held, chrome-plated "gun". It's the latest concept in booze dispensing. The gun is attached by long hoses to bottles in a locked liquor station. Its appeals to prudent bar management are: (a) elimination of spillage, (b) no overpouring, and (c) speed. Its appeals to customers are difficult to determine. Sitting on a bar stool, contemplation of the pretty labels and having the barkeep mix, *hand pour* and serve your drink is part of the total emotional drinking experience.

The days of generous over-pours and "have one on the house" are going, but we pray that our favorite bartender will be the last to find interest in things like shot programmers and counter boxes coupled with multi-button selector packs and solid-state logic.

The gun has lots of buttons. Each controls a different booze selection. One typical model has seven buttons for liquor (the promoters claim it will handle 85% of the bar volume) plus a "long button" and "short button". "Long" might be pressed for Martinis, Manhattans and drinks on the rocks. A typical long pour would be 1½ oz. "Short" could be used for Whiskey Sours or light drinks at ¾ oz. The normal pour might be set for one ounce, and used for most cocktails and highballs. It all sounds dismal. When it comes to creature comforts, let us hope solid-state logic is not overdone.

I don't think the owner of a modest operation will want to even consider these devices. However, one cannot stand in the way of progress, and in a situation where the bartender is stuck away in a service area and is not seen in an establishment catering up to 1,000 people at a clip, the savings in labor, liquor, and time are really extensive. But such establishments are not the subject of this book.

In the average bar each work station will require sinks and their appurtenances. A typical unitized sink-drainboard-ice-bin-speed-rack combination features one-piece die-stamp tops, faucet, continuous waste assembly, basket type drains, removable stainless steel undershelf, and stainless legs with adjustable bullet feet. One of a similar arrangement will be necessary for each work station. Even smaller bars usually have at least two work stations.

A drain in the floor behind the bar, under the duckboards, comes in mighty handy in swamping. If there isn't one there, you should want to have one installed if the cost isn't ruinous.

If you are expecting to do the volume, think seriously about buying or leasing an automatic glasswashing machine. The machine keeps the bacteria count low and leaves the glasses sparking clean. It will also probably prevent potential problems with the local Health Department, which will love you for having one. (This book predicts that they will be mandatory in many locales quite soon.)

You will need at least one cash register. (The cash register is discussed in Chapter 15.)

Finally, you will need your front bar. Here the considerations are the same as with the back bar. The price varies immensely. On the West Coast, antique bar furniture of excellent wood and fine workmanship has been in tremendous demand, naturally driving the price sky high.

Among profitable but nonessential equipment, there are three types of coin-operated machines usually found in bars: cigarette machines, jukeboxes, and amusement devices. These are rarely owned by the bar, and as I explained at the beginning of the book, they are often a vital source of revenue as well as credit. Many bars cover their monthly rent from their cut of the revenues of these machines, which are owned and maintained by distributors and placed in the bar under contract.

You will have to buy a permit for every one of the coin-operated amusement devices located in your place from municipal or county regulatory bodies. A few old mom-and-pop wineshops and bars sell cigarettes loose over the counter because there is much better profit in it than by vending machine. In a bar with any volume, and with employees, this creates an impossible inventory-control situation. You make about 10 cents a pack from the vending machine and maybe 20 cents handling them yourself.

Cigars also are a nuisance, but it might be necessary to have a box or two of Old Ropos on hand, although I like the sign I saw in a saloon: "Cigar Smokers Will Be Shot."

When I was last in Ireland I went into the joint which had been the largest volume place in Dublin, out in Ballsbridge. The last time I had been there maybe four hundred people were in the establishment. Now there were maybe fifteen. I asked for a pack of cigarettes, and the owner told me they didn't carry them anymore. I went in the joint next door because I wanted a weed. This place, which previously had done nothing, now was jammed. The owner there said the fellow next door couldn't be troubled to carry tobacco because he didn't make any money off it. He laughed and added, "I sure as hell make a bloody fortune off his *not* carrying it."

The surgeon-general says that smoking is bad for the health. So is drinking, perhaps, but I've never yet held a funnel in anyone's mouth and poured the booze down it. Neither have I jammed a cigarette in anyone's mouth. Probably the thing most injurious to the health is being alive in the first place.

The jukebox is a more-or-less necessary evil. I mentioned how the jukebox and cigarette machine lessor can be a vital source of credit and revenue. A fine, old, men's bar can scorn the jukebox, but most places are stuck with it. My machines bring in my monthly rent. The music that plays on these things gives me a headache, but I'm running the bar for my customers, not myself. Frankly, I can't tell the difference between the noises available in contemporary music.

I put a pad on top of the jukebox requesting connoisseurs of this music to request their favorites. Your bartender or cocktail waitress may know something of your customers' preferences. If so, then they should select the tunes. If you or your bartender roll dice for the tunes, then you have quarters marked with red nail polish to inject in the machine. You get these back off the top of the weekly take.

Pinball used to be considered an amusement confined to the lowest of the lowbrows, but recently the game has become popular with highbrows. An article recently in the *New Yorker* stated that Fun City's two leading pinball experts were a well-known novelist and a featured writer for the *New York Times*. These machines bring in one awful lot of money monthly. The King Cole Bar at the St. Regis Hotel in New York probably isn't ready for them yet, but don't reject them out of hand because of your personal aversion before you check on how much they can earn you.

Regarding furniture and decoration, the choice is so immensely varied that it would be futile and presumptuous to try to set down rules or standards. It's all a question of space, taste, and pocketbook. Obviously you will have to have a front bar and furniture to suit the theme, if any, of your place, as carried through in your tables, chairs, and carpets. (It has been illegal for years in San Francisco to have sawdust on the floors. First, it was ruled out for being a fire hazard, then when fireproof sawdust was developed it was deemed unsanitary. The real reason is that women dislike it, considering it overly masculine and reeking of the old-time saloon.)

There is a similar history to bar stools, which you will have to have. In our early days men sat at tables in taverns (so called because "inn" sounded too British). They drank beers, wines, and rum drinks. When American whiskey became popular in the nineteenth century, the tavern gave way to the saloon (a misspelled version of the French word for "front room"). The saloon had a bar and brass foot rail, but no stools, the theory being that when you couldn't stand up any longer it was time to quit drinking and go home.

During Prohibition a number of curious places called "American bars" sprang up in Paris and other European cities. They had little resemblance to a real American bar. Women frequented them, so they provided high bar stools.

When the speakeasies sprang up at home, many of them copied the format of the Parisian "American bars," complete with females and stools.

After Prohibition ended in 1933, most states made bar stools mandatory. The reason was that if a man were seated, he would be less likely to circulate round the bar talking to strange women. This is a prime example of the contention that laws prohibiting and restricting the use of alcoholic beverages are really anti-fornication laws. The reformers don't really care much about a person's getting drunk, per se. What they want to prevent is sexual promiscuity.

It is too late to do anything about these matters. You will just have to accept the fact that all bars now contain women and stools.

(Themes, including decorative styles, are discussed in the final chapters of the book.)

It's annoying and inconvenient for the bartender and other customers to have hats and parcels laid on the bar, while it's a waste of valuable space when hats and coats are placed on the barstool next to the owner.

Very few bars, unless they are part of a hotel or restaurant, have a cloakroom; none that I know of has a cloakroom attendant. But all bars should have an adequate place to hang hats and coats and to place packages in order to keep them off the bar and the stools and chairs. Usually pegs for hats and coats and a shelf or two for packages is adequate. This facility should not be hidden away, but should be in plain sight of the bar and away from the exits to make it difficult for anyone to abscond with somebody else's property.

One of the principal banes of a bartender's life is purses and handbags on his bar. Not only are they a nuisance and obstruction, but, next to drunks, they are the principal cause of spilled drinks. But what is the poor woman going to do? She certainly doesn't want to place her valuables and personal necessities out of her reach and sight, and it's a nuisance for *her* to hold her purse on her lap when seated on a bar stool.

I have never seen this any place. My wife just suggested it to me, and I'm going to do it in my bar. Screw a large brass hook under the bar in front of each stool so the ladies can hang their purses from it.

A bar owner is not *absolutely* liable as insurer for the safety of the property of his customers, but he is liable for negligence as bailee, where he accepts the property for safekeeping either in a checkroom or elsewhere on the premises, and fails to return it when called for. He is also liable for losses caused by lack of adequate supervision of the premises. He is *not* liable for loss of an overcoat or hat left on a chair or hung on a hook by the customer himself. He is well advised to post adequate notices in conspicuous places stating that he will be "Not Responsible for Personal Property Unless Checked with the Management." If the customer disregards these notices, it indicates contributory negligence on his part.

Finally, you will have some sort of sign outside the front door. Avoid the neon Martini glass, the surest indication of No Class Inside. Of the 116 bars along the two main drags of San Francisco's grungy Tenderloin, one of the most unsavory districts in the world, 64 have lighted neon cocktail glass signs and eleven more feature unlit cocktail glasses.

The next worst sort of sign you can have is a tin one furnished by a soft drink bottler also advertising his beverage.

The size and positioning of your outside sign will probably be regulated by your state liquor control board.

Remember that your sign is an important part of your long-term advertising program. It should be an extension of the personality of your bar because it is often the only way a passerby has of determining whether he will step inside for a drink or not.

8

Liquor Inventory

Since you are going to make your money selling liquor, it is most important that you stock the kinds and brands your customers want. This depends on your location, but here is an extremely modest, basic selection which will hold good for most regions and neighborhoods, because American tastes have been standardized nationally by rapid communications.

Don't overbuy when you're starting out. You can buy a quantity of something a salesman has sweet-talked you into because of some great discount, then find that all it does is sit on the back bar and evaporate over the years and that you will probably leave some of it in your will to your children.

If an item or brand shows a good demand, you can always order it, but there isn't too much you can do with an excess of something nobody wants. Don't get stuck with nonmoving items just to save a few dollars on a discount. You won't get stuck on the following quantities, liquors, and brands.

Basic Bar Stock*

A. Well Stock:
    1. 1 Case Each
        a. Scotch
        b. bourbon
        c. vodka
        d. gin
        e. brandy
        f. rum
    2. 3 Bottles Each
        a. white creme de menthe
        b. green creme de menthe
        c. white creme de cacao
        d. dark creme de cacao

B. Call Stock (½ Case Each):
    1. Whiskey:
        a. Scotch ½ case:
            (1) Cutty Sark
            (2) J & B
            (3) Dewars White Label
            (4) Johnny Walker Black Label
            (5) Chivas Regal
        b. bourbon and blended ½ case:
            (1) bourbon:
                (a) Jack Daniels Black Label
                (b) Early Times
                (c) Jim Beam
                (d) Wild Turkey
            (2) blended:
                (a) Seagram's V.O.
                (b) Seagram's 7 Crown
                (c) Canadian Club
                (d) Crown Royal
        c. gin and vodka:
            (1) gin:
                (a) Beefeater
                (b) Tanqueray
                (c) Bombay

---

* Note: The basic price of liquor changes over the years. The basic volume one requires does not. We therefore have not included cost estimates.

        (2) vodka:
           Smirnoff

  2. Aperitif and Miscellaneous approximately ½ case:
    a. aperitif
      (1) Dubonnet
      (2) Campari
      (3) Harvey's Bristol Cream Sherry
      (4) Dry Sack Sherry
      (5) Cinzano, red
      (6) Amer Picon
    b. miscellaneous
      (1) Christian Bros. Brandy
      (2) Bacardi Rum, White Label
      (3) Tequila
      (4) Paddy Irish Whiskey
      (5) Old Overholt (rye whiskey)
      (6) Southern Comfort
      (7) Triple Sec
      (8) Sloe Gin

  3. Brandy and Liqueur ½ case:
    a. brandy:
      (1) Courvoisier Cognac V.S.
      (2) Hennessy Cognac
      (3) Metaxa Brandy
      (4) Benedictine & Brandy
    b. liqueur:
      (1) Galliano
      (2) Kahlua
      (3) Drambuie
      (4) Grand Marnier
      (5) Cointreau
      (6) Tuaca

C. Wine—1 case gal. (4 gallon jugs to a case):
  1. Burgundy
  2. Chablis
D. Beer (3 or 4 different brands)

This representative selection may be supplemented with local favorites. From this basic stock, the fast-moving, frequently ordered items are replaced (in larger quantities to take advantage of volume buying with quantity discounts), while seldom-ordered brands are phased out.

Well stock or "house brands" should be ordered in larger quantities. Some owners change their well stock often to take advantage of brand sales promotions (discounts).

The amount of money tied up in liquor behind the bar and in the storeroom depends on the volume you do. If your gross sales are $10,000 a month, you should have $3,500 inventory, by a rule-of-thumb ratio of 3-to-1 sales to inventory. You can have a smaller inventory, but it is a great annoyance because you have to order so many more times little piddling things you need, and you have to be there for the deliveries.

I keep a large healthy inventory. Often my friends in the business are amazed when they come in and see how much booze I've got. One owner asked me why I keep so much liquor around the place. I told him I couldn't be bothered sitting around waiting, maybe for two days in a row, for a $300 delivery. Some distributors will not deliver less than one case. Many will split cases. Some will deliver even a single bottle when accompanied by a larger order.

Detail men, the local sales representatives of the liquor distributors, are anxious to sell you the brands their firm represents. They are quicker with their order pads than their teamsters are with their deliveries. (We owners aren't blameless, usually waiting until the last minute to order.)

When ordering, many bar owners rely solely on the advice of their favorite detail men. These salesmen are in a highly competitive business, so their advice is hardly impartial. They will certainly let you know about the discounts offered on their firm's brands, but they can't be expected to advertise the competition's discounted wares.

A more comprehensive source of information on wholesale pricing and availability comes from the beverage industry trade press. Here in Northern California, the trade bible is Beverage Industry News (BIN-Merchandiser), a thick magazine mailed to trade subscribers each month. Publications servicing other parts of the country are listed in Appendix F. Among other valuable information, these publications inform you just what you can buy from whom, at what price.

Bar owners normally deal with twelve to seventeen suppliers when purchasing liquor, bar accessories, and groceries. The Yellow Pages of local telephone directories also list services in the immediate vicinity. These supply houses conduct routine credit checks on prospective customers. Before establishing an account, the bar owner will want to shop around for those companies that offer reasonable rates and promise speedy delivery. Generally speaking, suppliers fall into three categories: those for liquor, wine, and beer; those for glasses and tools; and those for cocktail mixes, beverages, and groceries.

State laws require on-premise licensees to deal only with companies that have wholesaling privileges. This regulation is hardly limiting, however, since there are many liquor, beer, and wine wholesalers.

Full-line wholesalers offer an extensive selection of liquor types but one somewhat limited in brand names. Thus, they stock a complete range—vodkas, bourbons, Scotches, and gins—but carry only two or three brands of each. To acquire a complete selection of liquor, bar owners establish accounts with six to seven full-line wholesalers. While full-line suppliers also carry beer and wine, many tavern owners prefer to deal with separate wine and beer wholesalers who carry greater selections of imported and domestic brands and varieties.

Licensees may order either by phone or by mail. In addition, wholesaler representatives often visit their accounts to fill orders and introduce new brands. Most wholesalers are equipped to handle rush orders. Most liquor, beer and wine wholesalers deliver two or three times a week, although many barmen require only weekly visits. A retailer in a serious crunch may pick up his stock from the local warehouse, but most avoid this back-breaking chore, preferring to rely on scheduled truck deliveries.

California law demands full payment for purchases within

thirty days of delivery. If the full amount is not paid at the end of this period, the bar owner must pay cash for future orders. If payment is not made within forty-two days, a charge of 1 percent a month is levied on the unpaid balance.

The law requires distillers, wineries, and brewers to post minimum case and bottle prices for retailers and consumers. These schedules are published monthly, and individual wholesalers usually provide on-sale licensees with discount schedules.

Some brands are always on special discount, others only once or twice a year. Appealing bargains may pressure bar owners into buying larger amounts of liquor than needed. The result: too many cases of slow-moving brands stashed in the storeroom for months, tying up cash, occupying space, and requiring repetitive inventory counts.

If you do buy five cases on special discount, you might get a dollar off per case; if you buy ten cases you might get two dollars off a case; and if you buy twenty you might get three dollars off a case. So, watch for discounts in your monthly trade catalogue. These discounts are called post-offs. Brands switch constantly in the well due to post-offs and owner dissatisfaction with a certain distributor. Those bars which do keep the well brands constant invariably pour a name brand from the well.

From time to time, it is inevitable that you will make an unwise or unfortunate buy in a call brand. A bar I knew had an excellent customer who drank an obscure, but expensive, Kentucky straight bourbon whiskey. The owner got tired of buying a bottle at a time, so laid in a case. Exactly two days later this man's doctor put him on the permanent wagon. In an event such as this, where nobody else is inclined to call that brand, you can put it in the well. It will cut your profit on it, but at least it won't be a loss. Some bars invent a "house drink" made around the unwanted items in inventory. Usually these concoctions are terrible because all the good drinks have already been invented. Also, there is a slight danger that the drink might catch on for awhile, and you would have to buy more of the stuff you had been trying to get rid of. You can be sure that at that time the fad will pass over, and you will be stuck with twice as much of the stuff as you had originally.

You will also need what is called in the trade "groceries." A basic list follows. It will be a nice touch if you can see fit to squeeze your own fresh orange, grapefruit, and lemon juice. This is not a gimmick because there is a world of difference between the freshly squeezed and the processed juice, be it canned or frozen. It is, of course, a lot of trouble and the effort is wasted on many customers, but some discriminating people will patronize your bar simply because of fresh juice. If I want a Screwdriver (vodka and orange juice), I will walk blocks out of my way to get one made with real orange juice.

Basic Groceries

Superfine sugar	Cinnamon sticks
Milk and cream	Cloves
Eggs	Ground nutmeg
Cherries	Tomato juice
Olives	Grapefruit juice
Pearl onions	Orange and lemon slices
Worcestershire sauce	Limes, sliced and quartered
Tabasco sauce	Lemon peels
Salt and pepper	Aspirin

"Marrying" is the term used to describe pouring the contents òf one bottle of liquor into a bottle of the same type of liquor, for example, transferring a quarter of a bottle of Jack Daniels Black Label into a half-filled bottle of Jack Daniels Black. There is nothing dishonest about this, but it is prohibited in California, and, I daresay, every other state. It is, however, an extremely widespread practice, even in first-class places, because it saves so much shelf space. "Marrying" is illegal because it can lead to "dumping." This means transferring inferior booze into bottles with prestigious labels, which is almost as dishonest as watering the booze. Unfortunately, this also is a widespread practice, especially in slow bars. I base this statement on two observed facts. Some bars buy one awful lot of practically unknown brands which are similar to, but far less expensive than, popular, famous brands. You almost never see bottles of this off-beat stuff behind the bar, and practically nobody ever calls for it. Where does it go? Second, you often see a bottle of very popular liquor behind a slow bar with a worn label, obviously years old. Nobody can tell me that a bottle of, say, V.O. lasts five years without refilling in even the slowest of bars.

9

Security, Precautions, Protective Maintenance, and Inventory Control

You cannot make your bar absolutely burglar-proof. A top professional burglar can get in practically anyplace. But if you make your security as tight as possible, the professionals will be likely to break in someplace easier, while the amateurs probably won't have the skill to get in, or, if they do, they will likely be caught.

The first essential is good, stout doors with double-action locks. In addition, I use a chain and heavy padlock. The windows should be protectively taped to set off a burglar alarm if they are broken or cut. There are many different kinds of burglar alarm systems. I think the best is of the type which the burglar can't hear ringing, but which flashes an alarm in the local police precinct station.

You should try to keep as little cash on hand as possible, especially overnight. Ideally the money should go into a safe. The only type of safe worth having for a bar is the round type sunk into concrete in the floor. It should be in a conspicuous place, if possible in full view of the street through a front window. At night window shades, curtains, and drapes should be left open so the police patrolmen and casual passers-by can see in. Very few burglars welcome an audience.

After removing the money from your cash register, you should leave the drawers open. If they are closed, a burglar can easily damage the register severely in jimmying it. If you leave it open and empty, he won't go to this trouble, and you won't have an expensive repair bill for the machine.

Here's another tip. I take all my liquor bottles out of the cases they come in and put them on shelves. If I am unfortunate enough to have burglars, they can take only three or four bottles of liquor because they have nothing to put the bottles in. If they want to start packing it, they're welcome, because, believe me, they're going to take so much time and make so much noise that they're going to get caught.

Most important, you or the last employee to leave should search and double check *all* the premises before locking up. I mean every place—attic, broom closets, washrooms, furnace room, everywhere. The majority of burglars will hide in the premises and do their work after everyone is gone. This saves them the trouble and danger of breaking in. It isn't too risky for the would-be burglar. If on your nightly check you find a man, say, locked in a stall in the women's bathroom, he will say he just passed out. He hasn't done anything *yet*, so there isn't too much you can do about it. You know he's lying, but how do you prove it and get it to stick in court?

Fire is another ever-present danger which requires serious precautions to prevent or contain. Before you open your operation, you can be sure your fire department will inspect the place carefully. Local regulations vary, so there isn't much point in my going into requirements here, especially since your fire department will tell you what you have to do to comply with their minimum regulations. You have no choice. You do as they say, or you don't open. If you have purchased an existing bar and aren't going to make significant changes, chances are that it will be at least close to standard. If you are remodelling or making important changes in the setup, check with the fire department *first*. You don't want to put in new, expensive wiring, say, then find out it doesn't meet fire regulations for some reason or another, then have to tear it out and start all over again.

Here are several important pointers, though. I mentioned earlier that you should have metal containers to empty ash trays into to prevent fires. Paste the telephone number of the local fire house on the cash register. Make sure all employees know where this number is. Even if it is not mandatory in your locality, all your exit doors should open *outwards*. The doors should be of the "required exit" type, furnished with "panic equipment." That's the metal bar which when pressed throws the doors open outwards.

There was a fire in a large theater in Canada recently. Three hundred people died. They panicked and rushed the exit *en masse*. The doors opened inwards. The press of bodies against them made it impossible to get the doors open.

You should have at least one lighted fire exit sign.

All employees should know exactly where the fire extinguishers are and should be able to get right to them, even in the dark. Have them serviced at least once a year, and have a new tag attached attesting to the servicing. When the fire inspectors make their periodic inspections, this is the first thing they'll look at. You'll score points with them, if you have had it done before they have to tell you to.

You hear about panics over fires in theaters and auditoriums. Bar habitues are something else, at least those in my bar. Last year a smoky fire broke out in the wiring under my back bar. I tried to retain my wits, and told everyone to leave the bar quietly, while I went downstairs to check and cut off the circuits. First I phoned the fire brigade. When I came back up about two minutes later, everyone was still at his place at the bar chattering away about the thrill of it all. I again ordered everybody out and got busy trying to douse the fire and keep my eyes open for further breakouts.

In a few minutes the firemen burst in with hoses and axes and all sorts of exotic equipment. They quickly put it out. The battalion chief came up to me and asked furiously why in the goddamn hell I hadn't got all these people out. I explained why, and the firemen literally had to push everybody out. I have no explanation why anyone would hang around and risk the chance of roasting to death. It wasn't as if anyone were trying to help me put out the fire. It was just a good show, I guess.

This prompted me to do something I'd put off for a long time. I checked the neighborhood and found an old retired Italian maintenance man who knows quite a bit about most sorts of machinery and handy work and is ingenious with his mind and hands. He comes round once a month and checks everything out, especially the electrical wiring and equipment. I'd suggest you try to make some such arrangement, if you can find such a man in your neighborhood and if the fee isn't exorbitant. Usually preventative maintenance is far cheaper in the long run than repair bills.

There is quite a bit you can do yourself with a little effort and without much mechanical expertise. You can check for small things such as screws coming loose in the hinges of the doors of your refrigerator. The constant opening and closing of the doors can work these loose on even brand new equipment. The locks that snap the door shut get especially heavy wear. If you tighten the screws periodically, you won't lose any small parts, which are usually quite difficult to replace. Wash your refrigerator out with a strong detergent then a mild disinfectant every two weeks. Not only will this keep it clean and smelling good, but it will prevent the formation of rust patches.

Keeping your drains clear is a problem, especially because you are using toothpicks, straws, limes, and lemons which tend to get caught in the sink drains. A number of years ago I found a power gun which I estimate has saved me over a thousand dollars a year. Although the initial cost seemed high, little did I know how much money I was going to save by this investment. I've used it to clear drains and toilets as often as three times a day. Now, how much would a plumber cost right there? The gun is a cylinder about two feet high with a hand pump on top. The nozzle of the hose is placed on top of the opening of a drain or inserted in a toilet bowl. You hand pump it to a prescribed tautness, then squeeze the trigger, and presto! The drain is free. I lend it to everybody in the neighborhood. It has created a lot of good will for me. You could charge a small fee to amortize the initial cost.

Know exactly where your fuse boxes and breaker switches are and which circuit each controls. You can be sure that if anything is going to blow it will blow at your busiest time, so have extra fuses on hand. By solving the problem right away, you will not lose business. You should have a powerful flashlight next to the cash register. Check the batteries periodically.

Also you should have a long extension cord with a caged light at the end, so if one circuit does go out you can temporarily switch to another. Be familiar with the location of all your plug outlets in case of one of these emergencies. (Normally you won't have 220-volt power in a bar unless you have a glasswasher, and it will be on a circuit breaker, anyway.)

Whatever needs attention, do it right away. Don't procrastinate if you find a loose tile or curling linoleum or chipped plaster or flaking paint. It will just get worse and more expensive to fix. It certainly isn't going to get any better by itself.

Your stockroom, or liquor room, should be secure at all times, day and night. You should retain the only key to it; no one should be authorized to enter it without your express permission. Persons who wouldn't dream of stealing anything else often will "borrow" bottles of liquor. You should restock the bar yourself from your storeroom, or if you delegate the task to somebody else, it should be on a time-to-time basis. I wouldn't give anyone the discretion to move my liquor about at will. If something is missing, then there's only one person to blame—yourself.

If you're fortunate you'll have plenty of space in the storeroom, hopefully enough for your office space where you keep your checkbooks and bills and receipts and other bookkeeping adjuncts. It should be well lighted.

I mentioned I take all bottles out of their cases and get rid of the cases. I place the bottles on shelves in an orderly manner so that the liquor room looks like a sort of filing system. All the Scotches are together by brand, as are the other types of liquors and liqueurs. The beers and mixes I do keep in their cases, but piled according to type and brand. I can tell at a glance when I'm running low on something and should reorder.

It's also simple this way to take physical inventory, which I do once a week. It takes only a few minutes this way. Incidentally, I have a simplification on taking physical inventory of the stock behind the bar. With all opened bottles, if they are half full or more, I count them as full bottles, and, if less than half full, count them as empty bottles. When I have a total bottle count for all the liquor, I multiply by the median price of a bottle of liquor to get the dollar inventory (Two bottles of aperitif wines count as one bottle of liquor.) This eliminates gauging how many ounces are left in each opened bottle, then looking up the price of each brand and multiplying it separately, then adding up all the totals. It boils a long, tedious task down to a brief fifteen-minute job. I have found that I will come within $10 error in a $1,000 inventory.

The purpose of taking a physical inventory is this: You should know what you have purchased. It either should be in stock or have been converted to cash. If it is not in your physical inventory or in your cash register or bank account, something is amiss. The sooner you find out that something is wrong, the easier you can correct it; therefore, the need for frequent physical inventories. To have an accurate control system, you then need to know three things.

1. Exactly what has been purchased and received.
2. What is still in inventory.
3. What has been sold and converted to cash.

Here is how you can keep track of what has been purchased and received. Your aim should be to set up the maximum practical controls without the system costing more to operate than it will save. In other words, the control system should be simple. Avoid complicated systems that produce duplication of work.

The control begins with the inventory. All merchandise should appear on the inventory book and the cost value should be calculated and extended. The inventory book is the first book in which all items must be recorded completely and accurately before the doors can be opened for business. The inventory book should be the fundamental record of a system called perpetual inventory. All movements or changes in inventory are entered in the book each day. Such an inventory book will let you know at all times the stock in the house of any given item.

When orders are delivered, the person responsible for receiving the merchandise must check the items on the invoice. He should not sign the delivery sheet until he is satisfied that the goods billed have all been delivered and that they check with the purchase order (PO). Written purchase orders represent the ideal method of purchasing. Often in small operations POs are not possible. Then, any telephoned order or one given to a salesman verbally should be made and kept in a predetermined place. Thus, when the person who placed the order is absent, whoever is responsible for receiving the goods will know exactly what was ordered.

With the least practical delay, the items received should be posted in the perpetual inventory. The invoice should be marked to show that the inventory posting has been made, and then be given to the accountant for further accounting procedure.

Controls have to do with money—money paid out and money received. You know at all times the amount you pay out and for what, because you get an invoice, a receipt, or you have a check stub with the record of the payment.

The records or the analysis of cash received is somewhat more difficult to obtain. But cash control can be obtained without a very complicated procedure.

The cash register is the best assistant control agent yet devised, as explained in Chapter 19.

10

Employer-Employee Relations

From the San Francisco State University Course "Bar Management and Bartending."

> *Professor Mooney:* Can anyone tell me why you're taking this course?
> *Attractive Girl:* I want to travel.

You can get a job as bartender anywhere in the world, but you don't make any dough outside the United States. In Europe it's not unusual to see a bartender who's twelve years of age. Everyone here will be qualified to be a bartender *when he finishes this seven-hour course* (I'm not promising you that you'll get a job, but you'll be qualified). In Europe, though, it's a seven-year apprenticeship, starvation wages all the way through, and sixteen hours a day.

It's not easy to get a job in San Francisco, but, on the other hand, it's not really difficult if you're trying. For example, you'll find that most people who own bars are slaves to the business, and it's not unusual for them to be walking around their place with a broom in their hand. This happens to me two or three times a week. Somebody comes up to me and says, "Is the boss around?"

"No, he's not." So that's the end of him. "Why did you want to talk to the boss?" "I'm looking for a job as a bartender." "Oh? Well he's not in today. He's in Florida."

I got a job in a furniture store one time when I first came here. I approached a man who was sweeping the floor, and said:

"Excuse me, sir, do you own this establishment?"

"Yes, I do," he said.

"I'd like a job," I said.

"You're hired," he replied.

It's amazing the number of people who presume that because you're in your shirtsleeves and a bit dirty that you're just a flunky around the place.

A bartender is often compared to a priest or a psychiatrist. He listens to everybody's troubles and nobody wants to listen to his. Everybody wants to tell a bartender his troubles and get his advice. People never take any notice of the advice, but they all want it.

You can count on it that when you get busy you're going to get somebody who really becomes attached to you. If you got an orangutan and gave him a shave and put him behind the bar and taught him how to smile he would have twelve regular customers in three days. Most of them just want to talk. You don't want any long talks; you want to pour drinks. So you have to be severe and you have to be polite. If somebody says:

"I heard a great story the other day that I'm going to have to tell you . . ."

You say, "Will you just hold it for one second. I'll be right back."

But smile and be polite. That's how you build up a steady ·clientele. You must get the customers to like you.

But there is no such thing, in my opinion, as a following for a bartender. It's a fallacy. People who drink are creatures of habit. They drink in certain spots, and, usually, at certain times. It's almost impossible for a bartender to take his following with him when he moves. It happened to me. When I moved over here I thought I'd get all my old customers from my old neighborhood. I got them . . . once. The people who drink in Flatbush don't like Park Avenue, and the people who like

Manhattan don't drink in Brooklyn. People circulate in their own area. I live in a little village here in San Francisco. If you have a very hot bartender that everybody just adores and if he moves six blocks away, everybody presumes that your business is going to go down the tubes. The customers will visit him maybe once or twice, but then they'll revert to their old habit again. They go back to their old bar, and they get to know the new bartender, and away you go again.

So a bartender's following is mostly illusory. Customers may follow a bartender for a couple of blocks, but they won't follow for any substantial distance. The owner need never be afraid that if a bartender quits he's going to lose any business.

Regarding staff in general, I have never had any difficulty with any employee I have ever had. I think that's because I tried to be a good employee myself. I respect the people who work for me and I think I always respected the people I worked for. The particular bar I run is a very loose situation. My bartenders and cocktail waitresses run my place. If anybody is going to take off time, they arrange it among themselves as to who's going to work. If anyone wants to take a vacation, he doesn't even have to ask me. I know there's going to be somebody here. We have a very good relationship and always have had.

A lot of owners will hire a bartender, and, no matter how good he is, will fire him in three months. The owners go in for this because they're convinced everybody working for them is a thief. I don't think that I've ever had anybody that stole any dough from me. I think it is a fallacy to believe that most bartenders steal. I have never found this to be true, and I have checked in many places, big places and small places; and while I have seen bartenders stealing, I found that if they are stealing, they are stealing an awful lot, and if they're not stealing, they're not stealing at all. Invariably when you go back a month later the ones who were stealing are not there any more, because if the bar has any kind of inventory control at all, and if you know exactly what percentage you're working on, it is almost impossible to have appreciable shrinkage in the bar business. Many people won't agree with me here, but I am sure it is true.

However, if you do have good reason to suspect that an employee is swinging with your bread, most cities have an employee checking service whose service you may hire. They send trained operatives incognito into your place to observe the suspect employee; then they give you a written report.

Never pay an employee in cash. Pay by check, taking out the necessary deductions. Then cash the check for him or let him do whatever he wants with it. I find it a wise procedure to pay myself a salary each week, just as if I were an employee. I pay myself by check, taking out the 25 percent deduction I take out for my employees. This prevents me from just dipping into the till at random for cash to pay my expenses—one cardinal way an owner can get himself into deep trouble. He starts to lose track of what he has taken, and often says the hell with it and gets his cash and accounts more and more mixed up.

Pay whatever you can by check. Who can remember the cash he laid out on a rainy day a year ago?

A lot of bars insist that you pour with a shot glass. If you learn the one-ounce shot glass, you've got the bartending business whipped, and you can make some money. If you don't learn this glass, you're never going to learn the bar business. If you know how to pour exactly one ounce of liquor, then you can pour one-and-one-half ounces of booze, and you can pour two ounces of booze, and you know exactly what you're pouring.

In my first class I gave each student a one-ounce shot glass and a pourer (the plastic or metal device bars put into the mouths of bottles to control the pouring flow) and told them to practice at home so they could pour exactly one ounce every time. If a bartender can do this, he can get a job anywhere and he's going to make money for the owner.

You're also not going to do anybody any favors by overpouring. Let me illustrate. One of the worst things that can happen to somebody in the bar business is when you walk into another bar, and as the bartender recognizes you, he says:

"Hello, there, I haven't seen you for a long time." You say you'll have a Scotch-and-water, and he starts pouring, and the next thing you know after three or four drinks you're blind drunk. He knows you're in the bar business, so he's way overpouring. He knows you like to drink. He wants to be generous to you, but actually he's doing you damage. Drinking is a social thing. When you go into a bar, you go in to drink with other people. Few persons go into a bar with the intention of getting blind drunk. The bartender who habitually overpours is the greatest enemy you can have. Not alone for the house, because he's giving the booze away, but also for the customer.

In this matter, I should add, I am probably one of the worst offenders because I learned the bar business in a dinner house. People who come in these places usually have only one or two drinks before dinner, and when they come in, they want a good, strong drink. They're not going to sit at the bar for three or four hours. So I got into a bad habit of overpouring, which I haven't been able to overcome even yet. Also I think the owner of a place is inclined to overpour because he wants his customers to think that he's a little more generous than he actually is.

One of the policy decisions eliminated by changing times and the permissive society is on dress codes and standards and appearance of the bartender and cocktail waitresses. There are none any more. Oh, I suppose they must keep clean and keep certain vital parts of their bodies covered, but you can't quibble any longer about length of hair or neckties in most places.

I suppose we old-timers look back nostalgically to when the professional bartender wore neatly trimmed hair and an outfit such as a white shirt, black necktie, striped waistcoat, and white mess jacket, but outside of better hotels, clubs, and some restaurants, you just don't see that anymore, and most of your customers—almost all the younger ones—don't want to, either.

I think the owner can insist that he and his employees try to conform to the general dress standards of his neighborhood and customers, though. My place is in a very liberal neighborhood, so I have no standards at all (in dress, that is, or in hair length).

Some of the problems and decisions to be faced in running a bar have been solved simply by the changed attitudes and "morality" of the times.

One of the biggest problems taxing the diplomacy of an owner and bartender used to be how to treat and deal with the

FSB, *femme seule au bar.* Times alone spare you now from having to make any decision. You just treat the woman who comes in and seats herself alone at your bar exactly the same and by the same rules as you would treat any other customer. There should be no variation whatsoever.

Some old-time former men-only bars still do not want or like women in their place. The owner of one of the finest men's saloons in the city, The House of Shields, told his barmen apropos of the ladies and the equal-rights laws:

"You have to serve them, but you don't have to talk to them."

Shields is an institution. No one is going to open a bar these days like it, so just treat women like you treat anybody else.

My wife likes bars and has worked occasionally as a cocktail waitress. She asked to put in a few words about "One Woman's Point of View about Bars."

"Men usually like to go to places where they are recognized, so it's curious that they often don't realize that women have the same feeling. It's nice to walk into a bar and have someone smile and call you by name. After a bad day, especially, it's pleasant when somebody pays attention to you. It gives you a sense of security, as well as a feeling of belonging, when the owner or bartender recognizes and acknowledges you. There are still men who just cannot believe that two women will sit at a bar merely to have a quiet drink and visit with each other. This sort of man thinks you are in there only to see him. Sometimes you can't convince him tactfully and politely that you aren't receptive to his attentions. He may be an ordinarily pleasant fellow whose perceptions are temporarily muddled by too much to drink. It's reassuring to know that the owner or bartender will come to your aid by reinforcing your point of wanting to be left alone. If you refuse the offer of a drink from a man, the bartender will know you don't want to be pestered; if you accept a drink, bar etiquette indicates that you are willing to converse, at least, with the man.

"A bartender's job is to serve drinks and to be as pleasant as he can. He usually knows most of his customers, and most of them know him by name. This gives many women the impression that he's extremely popular and knows everyone. Because of this seemingly universal popularity, and because he is easy going and pleasant, some women will start looking at him with a different eye, mistaking his attention, assuming it is personal, not part of his job. The next thing she knows, she is inviting him over to her house for dinner, or for a drink, or trying to figure a way to get him to ask her out. She often doesn't even question whether or not the guy is available. She figures that nobody who is always so nice to her could be attached elsewhere. This often gives the bartender the false impression that he is the greatest thing invented since sliced bread.

"Because of this, the wife of an owner or bartender must have a good deal of understanding of her man. When a customer, who happens to be beautiful, gives your husband a big hug, then introduces him to three of her best friends, who look even better, you have food for thought, especially when she acts like he was her only friend in the world. You must remember that while you have never seen this 'long lost friend,' nine times out of ten neither has your husband. Even if he recognizes her face, her name has probably escaped him. If you, as a wife or girlfriend of a bar owner, can't accept this as a fact of life in the bar business, you had better plant yourself on a barstool in a pub down the street, or better yet, stay home."

A bartender sometimes will mix the wrong drink for a customer. This is called the "bartender's mistake." Sometimes it is, and sometimes it is the customer's because he inadvertently ordered wrong. One hears often half-jokingly that the bartender "has to" or "gets to" drink his mistakes. Absolutely not. They should be poured out. Never let the ice be scooped out, the drink set aside, then re-iced and served to the next customer who orders that drink. You could easily lose a good customer just to save one drink, and also you don't want to encourage the bartender to make "mistakes" in order to get loaded on your time and booze.

San Francisco is a big union town and 90 percent of the bars are unionized. First of all, you have to get a job, then get in the union. You cannot get in the union first, then get a job. You must be qualified and get a job, then you can get into the union if you want to. But most of the bigger chains that are opening, like Victoria Station, are strictly nonunion, and they're getting away with it because they're doing excellent dollar volume per year. Therefore, the union has no say in the matter, although they're trying to get in. But the pay is low, probably only 50 percent of what a regular union bartender would get. But they hire young kids with practically no experience. I shan't say any more about unions because *whatever* I say, 50 percent of my readers will hate me for it. Passions run high on the subject. Undoubtedly anyone reading this has already formed his unalterable opinion about the role of unions in the bar business, so whatever I were to say would not change anyone's opinion.

Here are a few random but pertinent observations, culled from my experience, which I made in my lectures.

Never make a cash register out of your stomach. You might be offered ten free drinks by customers in the course of a day. Don't take them all in order to ring up 90 cents ten times. Decline most of them politely. If you drink all that is offered you, you will kill yourself or make yourself seriously ill. It's not worth it just to ring up that extra few dollars in gross every day. Virtually no human body can stand up under such a heavy, steady consumption of alcohol. At best, you'll end up in Alcoholics Anonymous.

Bars are a social thing. When a person comes to a new city, the first thing he should do is find either a bar or a church in which to meet people. Also, I recommend joining Alcoholics Anonymous, even if you've never taken a drink in your life. I know a fellow who married two heiresses, both of whom he met through AA.

There are lots of valid and invalid reasons why a bartender may not turn up for work. You should have the names and phone numbers of several persons who know the trade and are likely to be available for part-time or standby duty.

I don't like to have bar stools behind my bar. Sure, the bartender will get tired feet and want to sit down when he isn't busy. However, it looks lax, and many customers are reluctant to ask a bartender who is sitting on a stool behind the bar to get up to fix them another drink, so they just nurse the one they have, or leave, losing you valuable business.

Finally, customers should never be allowed to come behind the bar. It could cause problems. Make this a firm rule, no matter how valuable and trusted the customer may be.

11

Opening Day

Bars can be and are categorized into numerous different types of establishments. No matter how the categorizing is done, it is a generalization and very few bars will fit neatly into one particular category. No two bars, like no two snowflakes, are exactly alike, so lumping them together only serves to give a handy, if somewhat inaccurate, frame of reference. Mooney's Irish Pub, for example, is Irish because I say it is. Probably only one out of a dozen customers in there at any given time was born in Ireland, and maybe only one in four is of Irish descent—the same percentage as that of the United States population as a whole.

My place is also categorized as a progressive music bar because most nights a live combo plays music. Others say it is a hangout for writers and intellectuals. Sure, those types do come in, but they leave promptly when the music starts to play. It is also a rendezvous for longhairs and bohemians. Also it is noted as a tourist trap because it has been mentioned in so many travel magazines.

The guidelines in this book have been laid out to give all the fundamental information for a modest scale saloon. Everything

I say can be multiplied and adapted for a grander operation, but the larger the place, the more numerous the exceptions.

In the general category of size into which I fit, a somewhat larger-than-average metropolitan saloon without food, the owner is usually not only his own general manager but by necessity his own specialist in many of the fields where the larger place hires experts.

An average daily gross revenue of $500 or $15,000 per month would give a sales valuation of $90,000. Costs for such an operation would usually include one bartender on duty, often myself, one or two cocktail waitresses, a swamper, and a part-time accountant.

The big places usually retain a public relations man to flack their names in the papers, especially in the gossip columns. A modest place may also do this, but there are two ways of figuring the expense. Say his fee is $100 per month. You gross $15,000 per month. Therefore, his fee is ¾ of 1 percent, and if he is any good at all, surely his services will bring in more than that in added business. If you look at it the way I do, a net profit on that $15,000 may be $1,000. The PR man's $100 fee is then 10 percent of the net. To break even he would have to increase gross sales $1,500 per month. This is not likely, and, in any event, can never be proved.

The image of my place, to say the least, is blurred, like many of my steady customers. I think this is the norm, not an exception. However, more and more the larger, elaborate, "metropolitan" drinking establishments deliberately try to project a definite image. One of the principal economic reasons for this is the importance of the youth trade, who are capricious in their preferences, or "trendy" as many of them term it. Competition for the entertainment dollar is fierce and drinks are expensive these days.

Most of the huge-volume, elaborate, world-famous operations are a combination bar-restaurant with large staffs of fifty or so employees. They usually employ on that staff or on a consultant basis various experts in accounting, promotion, law, interior design, efficiency, and so on. If you are planning to invest from $250,000 to over $1 million in buying or building such an establishment, you too will be well advised to engage specialists. For one thing, you will probably be envisioning a unique operation, for which a general handbook such as this is merely a starting guide.

In the average, routine establishment, serving snacks, popcorn, pretzels, or hors d'oeuvres is not a gimmick, but it falls into promotion and should be evaluated as such. If the competition serves snacks, you also will perhaps have to. It is thought, also, that serving salty junk food stimulates your customers' thirst, but this is merely a hypothesis. Bars which are attached to restaurants, which we are not discussing, can serve bar food, even excellent canapés, but it is not worth it in a saloon, if you can avoid it and remain competitive.

Most owners will subtract the total price of such offerings from their gross sales figures, and it will be a small percentage. If, however, you are realistic, and subtract it from your net profit, you will find that it is far from negligible. Does anyone really appreciate this stuff? Does it make a determining factor in attracting customers to your place? If you think the answer to either of these questions is yes, by all means offer bar grub, but determine the cost and make sure it pays for itself.

While I do not think much of spending money on advertising or promotion of any sort—popcorn or otherwise—my friend, Frank Harrison, does me one better. Most bars at least have matchbooks printed as a form of advertising. Frank, former proprietor of the Mi Wuk Lodge in the Sierra country above Sonora, not only won't waste money on matches, but actually handed out these with a rather patronizing reverse-sell message on them.

Far away from Mi Wuk, back in the golden years of Hollywood the studio promotion departments tried their best to keep their stars from marrying. They encouraged romances but discouraged matrimony. Their stars were sex symbols, and what good is an unavailable sex symbol? Publicans and bartenders, in a much less local way, are also sex symbols (unless they are of an age, such as I am, to be compared with Walter Brennan or Barry Fitzgerald). Bartenders can be compared to airline stewardesses—they are there.

Safeguard
Pest Control
Guard Your Home with a Professional

I have said that I will not permit my bartenders to make passes at women customers in my place, but what they do off the premises is none of my business, and I don't want to hear about it.

It's widely known around that the principal reason I'm still alive and kicking after fifty-four years of the hardest living is because several years ago I married a nurse matron. She's my lifeline and anyone who knows me at all knows I'll never let go of her. Still I get about three propositions a week from attractive young women. I don't run a swinging bar, either.

I used to have a handsome, personable, young bartender, bit of a poet and writer. One of the town's columnists—witty, well-to-do and vastly erudite—said in a fit of pique: "Bob's no bartender; he's just a sex symbol." I'll swear that Bob never made a first pass at any woman in the bar during the five years he worked for me. We're now being told officially what every barman has always known: Women are every bit as promiscuous as men, given the opportunity.

One of the most successful of San Francisco's old-time bar owners made his bundle on the formula that one attractive young woman by herself at the bar could be counted on to attract an average of six men customers. You can stock your place with Tiffany glass, Brazilian orchids, or Louis XV furniture, but still your most decorative and profitable asset will be pretty girls sitting at your bar. (I most assuredly do *not* mean B-girls or hookers.)

A few years ago one of this town's leading governors was

doing a land office business. He has a sort of weary, blasé charm and the most facile line of gab. He also looks like he needs mothering. He found a woman to do it full time. Six months after he got married his place had to be sold up, and he had to go to work as an employee for somebody else. On the other hand, a pal of mine has owned one of the most popular bars in town for the last ten years. He's had an excellent, steady, high class trade in his fine place smack in the middle of the swinging singles area of town. It's been one of the first places the celebrities head for when they get off the plane. It used to be quite crowded, but not unconscionably so. A year ago he and his beautiful, charming wife were divorced. Now the establishment is so jammed at all hours that you can scarcely get in with a note from the Pope.

None of this will bear logical scrutiny; neither will acupuncture. But both work somehow. If you want to run a singles place, it will be by far the best if you are not married. However, if you are, then hire unmarried bartenders and cocktail waitresses.

Another widely used gimmick is the Happy Hour. I'm dead set against Happy Hours, and it isn't simply because of the sickening coyness of the term. If Happy Hours worked I suppose I could stick the name, but they don't work. They're a desperation measure—sort of a final gasp. A Happy Hour advertises the fact that you're not doing well and need business—any sort of business—badly.

You post notice that between 4:00 and 6:00 P.M. you will sell a drink to one and all for two bits, which is just about the cost of the liquor alone. Obviously you are going to lose money doing this. Where, for example, is the rent money going to come from? The theory is that the cost-conscious consumer is going to come in and partake of these bargains, then hang around after the price goes back to normal and have a dozen more.

There's a place round the corner from mine which has an excellent location and premises. In the eight years I've had my joint, there have been four different names and ownerships of this jinxed location. Every one of them, sooner or later, has run a Happy Hour. Not all the landlords have been amateurs, either. Two, at least, were hard, professional, Italo-American cognoscenti.

The thinking of all of them must have run along these lines:

"That dumb Mick, Mooney, has his dump filled most of the time. What's so special about it? Nothing. Let's cash in and take a bite out of his trade."

Up goes the Happy Hour sign. What happens?

My customers stop in for a couple quick primers, on each of which my competitor loses at least a quarter, then ankle round the corner to my bar. They don't want to be caught in that place when the bailiffs come round again to shut it down.

In life most men are losers. That's the principal reason they drink. To forget the fact that, to themselves at least, they are losers. Why should they drink, then, in a loser bar if they can help it? A truly cost conscious drinker will drink at home, where it's even less expensive than at a Happy Hour. Go into a Happy Hour joint about five minutes before six some evening. What you'll see is everybody there sneaking peeks at his wristwatch to determine whether he has time enough to order another cut-rater before he takes a hike.

It's said that most people are stupid and that television proves it. It's also said that nobody ever went broke underestimating the intelligence of the average American public. Perhaps this is true, but my experience has been to the contrary. Every time I've fallen on my face it was caused by this sort of cavalier underestimation of others' intelligence. Is there anyone around, at liberty, with the price of a drink in his pocket, who really believes that somebody else is going to open a bar in order to sell drinks way below cost out of the goodness of his heart?

No.

Television advertising is patently economically infeasible for a small business enterprise such as a bar. When it is used, it is for the owner's vanity. If you wish to advertise on radio or in the newspapers, it should, if possible, be done on a tradeout basis. That means: You want $100 newsprint space or air time. The publisher or station manager gives you such space or time *at his cost*, not retail price. You give him a chit for $100 worth of drinks *at your cost*.

First, you should check whether this is legal in your locality. (I don't think large, metropolitan media will go for this any longer, but perhaps smaller outlets will.)

I would not purchase time or space in the regular manner. It cannot be pinpointed to a small enough geographic locality and the results cannot be evaluated effectively. Your business is too small and localized to permit such broadside advertising methods.

Still you cannot just sit on your hands and hope the public will beat a way to your door to sample your elfin charm. In a good, broad assumption, your steady, regular clientele will pay your way and make your cushion; your profit will come from your casual drop-in customers. In priority, then, you will want to hook the former first, or as General Motors would phrase it, build Customer Loyalty. This book is concerned with giving quality in *essential* products and service. Promotional inducements might be called *extracurricular* activities. They should provide entertainment and should be self-supporting. They should induce others to join in. The closer you can come to reconciling the two opposites of exclusiveness and inclusiveness, the better any of these programs will be. Here is a short list of some of the most popular:

Softball teams
Picnics and outings
Pool tournaments
Bowling teams
Volleyball teams
Birthday parties
Busses to pro games
Tee shirts
Holiday special events (i.e., St. Patrick corned beef feeds)
Darts matches

Many of these games can be scheduled in intra-bar challenge leagues. That way you get a reciprocating crack at the other bars' clientele as they do at yours. Dart teams have carved their own niche, especially in bars that cater to Irish and Scottish drinkers. Many areas have city leagues. The teams are each sponsored by a bar and compete with one another all the way to playoffs and awards for winners of several divisions.

Some places go as far as purchasing shirts displaying their logo and providing darts for their team. Certainly the rewards are there. The team players and assorted wives, girlfriends, and buddies frequent their sponsor's place often to "practice" and talk about their last victory or plan for the next match. This is a built-in group of customers because naturally you can't shoot darts with a dry mouth. (One word of caution: Some bars don't encourage the game due to hazards like errant, sharply pointed objects hitting their other customers, or the language seemingly required to guide the dart to the triple twenty.)

Bars that have pool tables on the premises can follow a similar tournament approach. The pool table with its quarter-a-game revenue adds up as a means of income. Some bars are able to pay their rent from this extra money alone.

Baseball and touch football games between bars is another promotion that organizes the regulars. This has a couple of obvious drawbacks, namely, that the people are outside playing rather than inside drinking. A further perversity is that the team expects free beer for their exertions in glorifying the name of John's Bar & Grill. You might get some immediate sales increases just after the event when the gladiators are replaying the game, but you might also lose your best customer for a few weeks due to a broken leg.

Another organized sporting event falls into the spectator category. These football or baseball games are watched en masse by your customers, with a reduced chance of physical injury. It works this way. In cities with major league teams, the bar owner buys a block of seats and has the tickets available for customers who want to see a game, but don't have season tickets. Since these events commonly begin around noontime or shortly thereafter on Saturdays or Sundays, the group going to that game begin assembling at your place an hour or so early. They come in to pick up the tickets and since there's a little time, why not have a Bloody Mary or a Fizz? Then, why not have another since it's a long way to the stadium?

A note of caution: Don't hand the tickets out to the people

who bought them during the week for two reasons. Primarily, you're doing this to get them into your place. If they already have the tickets, they are just as likely to sleep late and then head directly to the game from home. Sure, they may have bought a drink when they picked up the tickets, but there is nothing like pre-game drinking to keep the cash register ringing. Also, there is always a percentage of no-shows, so if you collect the money for all tickets spoken for at one time, just prior to leaving for the game, you won't be stuck for the price of several "promised" tickets that you have already purchased with your own hard cash previously. There are always a few customers who get caught up in the revelry who decide then and there to go along, so it usually works out.

Some owners charter busses, the better to assemble their customers and get them to the game and back. If they are good for one or two drinks before, they are in full swing coming back and will generally settle down for a taste before going their separate ways. If it was an especially exciting game, you've got a built-in crowd for the evening.

Other activities range from concerts to fishing trips. All can be fun and provide a social note while they keep business booming. Remember, anyone can buy a bottle and drink at home, but the fun and games and good times are at your place.

How can a house softball team benefit you financially? You can't charge the players a fee to play for you, and you have to foot the bill for caps and jerseys and probably balls and bats. You offer to keep all the uniforms and equipment at your place. They come in for them and probably have a pre-game drink. After the game they come back—with their friends—to dump the stuff off and celebrate or commiserate, as the case may be. Your bar becomes a focus point in their lives. You can be sure that most people in the world are lonely. If they weren't, there wouldn't be any bars in the first place. Casual strangers at your bar will see this camaraderie between these nine guys and their wives and girlfriends (or boyfriends). Even if they can't play softball themselves, they will be attracted, and, vicariously at least, will feel part of the group. The next day down at the shop this four-eyed, butterfingered duffer will say to his mate:

"Well, we squeaked through last night. Tommy Johnson
got a fluke double with two on in the ninth, so we won by one
run."

"Who the hell is 'we'?"

"The gang down at the Drift Inn. We play in the inter-
tavern league every Wednesday night."

This sort of thing is, of course, preposterous in a downtown
bar. The only sort of promotion which might work in a sophisticated locale is to hire a public relations man to flack gossip
items in the local columns. I might go this route in the beginning, but after a few months I would either rely on intrinsic
quality in a downtown place or clear out.

One prime indicator of quality is the length of service of
the personnel. One of the finest old bars in the world is the
House of Shields, across the street from the main door of the
Palace Hotel. They have had a bartender who worked there
continuously for forty-one years and a busboy who was with
them for thirty years. It isn't in the Guinness Book of Records,
but this may be a record. Incidentally, these days you rarely see
bar boys (actually bartenders' assistants) except in places like
this and in hotels and clubs. Economics have practically wiped
out this fine old calling. Moreover, labor-saving devices now
enable the bartender to do most of an assistant's work himself.

As you progressed through the stages of looking for, licensing, and refurbishing your bar, the idea for the blowout that
would be your grand opening probably built in your mind. All
your friends would be there, of course, including those who
helped in one way or another and those that confidently in-
formed you, "It'll never get off the ground." Imagine the surprised look on their faces when . . . but wait a minute. Now
that you're a bar owner, do things the way the people in the
business do. I mean the ones who have been through it before,
maybe more than once, who have learned the proper perspec-
tive. Before the grand opening, how about the Purveyors'
Party?

What's a purveyor? The wholesalers and suppliers who are
providing you with the liquor and glasses and fruit as well as the
napkins to wipe up your spills. The discounts and service they'll

give you in the years to come may make the difference between just making a living or really making a go of it. Sure they're competitive, but there's a difference between merely servicing an account and giving an account extra considerations.

Think of Purveyor's Night in the same light as a wedding reception. You're taking your bar as a bride (perhaps more of a reality than the analogy seems now) and you're about to meet the rest of the family. As with the inlaws (and outlaws) first impressions are important. Don't just dance with the bride, get out and mingle. There's a good reason for that.

As mentioned in Chapter 8 no wholesaler carries a complete line of brand names. Sure, they all have Scotch, but one may have Dewar's and another will have the Cutty Sark. You can be sure that while they are sizing you up as to what kind of person and how large an account you'll be, they'll also be planning how to capture a larger share of the well stock you'll be ordering.

Don't spend too much time with any one person. Of course, they're drinking and eating their own wares that you happen to be paying for, but don't stint and don't slight anyone. That obnoxious fellow who is sloshing a drink on your wife's flower arrangement may be the guy who will save your busy Saturday night by fixing your mixing gun at 8:30 when people are standing three deep at the bar screaming for drinks. He might, of course, be just as obnoxious all the time and hang up on your panicky call, but tonight give him the benefit of the doubt.

Having been to many of these affairs, I can cite an instance or two which may be of help. First of all, it's not just purveyors to be invited to Purveyor's Night. There should be a large sprinkling of your competitors. Other bar owners, bartenders, and cocktail waitresses love to be invited to a really successful party. It should be on a night when these night people can be away from their place and be at yours. Sunday or Monday nights prove successful in San Francisco. These are the nights restaurants and bars close if they are not a seven day a week operation. You can't expect them to be at your place on Friday or Saturday night, the two busiest nights of the week.

If your city is fairly large and has local columnist and TV

personalities, by all means invite them. Don't let them think the
free drinks will continue indefinitely, or you'll be worse off than
if you hadn't invited them. If they develop the habit of having a
few free drinks on you in return for a line or two now and then,
you may be cultivating a bad habit that will hurt you in net profit
later.

Some of your most ardent supporters and good friends will
want to be included even though you may explain the reasons
for Purveyor's Night. They'll be at the Grand Opening but no
one wants to miss out, so invite a few. Your lawyers and
bankers as well as anyone who put up money on your behalf
should be there, too. I have been to a couple openings where the
previous owners attended. They appeared relieved of their
former burden and simultaneously proud as new fathers giving
birth to a new member of the tavern fraternity.

The parties range from a few cold cuts and kegs of beer to
elaborate, catered affairs. It really should follow the guideline
of what you can afford but nice enough not to be an affront to
anyone. One purveyors' party started with lots of food and
champagne, and featured a diminutive but curvaceous waitress. She wore a bikini bottom, a slave bracelet on her ankle
and a wicked, if slightly professional, smile. As she passed
through the groups of people delivering drinks you could track
the sway of her bare bosom by the weaving heads of the men
and the glare of the women. A little bizarre, but certainly a way
of making an impression for the new place and owner. As a
footnote, this effect was diminished by a rather common faux
pas. After a few pleasant hours, the owner allowed customers in
from the street. He may have meant it as a "more the merrier"
kind of move, or perhaps he was trying to make some money to
offset the cost of the evening. In any event, he began charging
for drinks which gave the effect of a crashed party to the invited
guests who soon left. Whatever good impressions achieved
earlier were cancelled out.

I have seen Grand Openings start with friends only, then
the general public is allowed to enter. This seems to work all
right. Another approach is to operate the bar for a few weeks
and then announce the Grand Opening, after a clientele or

following has been established. This also works well and acts as a sort of reward to the regulars.

Have your Purveyor's Night first and the Grand Opening. later. The first party will be good practice, and will give you confidence for your Grand Opening, where the task of building your business really begins.

12

The Basic Drinks

There must be a billion different drinks. Either you have the correct ingredients and can make the drink right or you don't make it at all. To make all the drinks you'd need a bar 500 yards long and twelve bartenders. Still you'd get stuck.

"Sorry, sir, we're not set up to make Mai Tais. I know you don't want one made without fresh pineapple. What's your second choice?" Likely he'll switch amiably to something like bourbon-and-soda.

In this chapter are listed all ingredients for making the basic drinks.

A. Highballs and Cocktails:

1. Vodka (V)

    a. V+r(rocks)
    b. V+r+t(twist)
    c. V+r, olive
    d. V+r, lime
    e. V+r, onion
    f. V, straight
    g. Vodka and *dry* Vermouth
        (1) V-M (Martini)+r

(2) V-M+r+t
(3) V+G+B+r
h. V. lime
i. V. Gimlet
j. V. tonic
k. V. tonic, lime
l. V. tomato
m. V. tomato, lime
n. V. tomato+t
o. V. grapefruit juice (Duber)
p. V. soda
q. V. orange (Screwdriver)
r. V. Coke
s. V. 7-Up
t. V. water
u. V. Collins
v. Salty Dog

2. *Gin (G)*

a. G+r
b. G+r+t
c. G+r, olive
d. G+r, lime
e. G+r, onion
f. G, straight
g. Gin and *dry* Vermouth
    (1) M+r
    (2) M+r+t
    (3) Gibson
h. G. lime
i. Gimlet
j. G+t
k. G+t, lime
l. G. tomato
m. G. tomato, lime
n. G. tomato+t
o. G. grape
p. G. orange
q. G. Coke
r. G. 7-Up
s. Tom Collins
t. G+bitters

3. *Scotch (Sc)*

a. Shot Scotch
b. Sc+r

    c. Sc+r+t
    d. Sc+splash+r
    e. Sc+w(water)
    f. Sc+soda
    g. Sc+splash of soda+r
    h. Sc+Collins
    i. Sc+milk
    j. Sc+coffee
    k. Rusty Nail+r
    l. Rob Roy (RR)+r
    m. Dry RR+r
    n. Perfect RR+r
    o. Sc+ginger ale
    p. Sc+Coke
    q. Sc+7-Up
    r. Sc+sour+r
    s. Sc+Old Fashioned
    t. Sc Mist+shaved ice+t
    u. Stinger (substitute Sc for Brandy)
    v. International Martini

4. Bourbon (B)

    a. B+water (Highball–Low Ball)
    b. 7 High
    c. Coke High
    d. Ginger High
    e. Shot Bourbon
    f. Boiler Maker (straight B w/beer chaser)
    g. B+r
    h. B+r+t
    i. B+r+splash of soda
    j. John Collins+r
    k. Manhattan+r
    l. Dry Manhattan+r
    m. Perfect Manhattan+r
    n. Whiskey Sour+r
    o. Bourbon Mist+shaved ice+t
    p. Old Fashioned
    q. Presbyterian (1 oz. B, equal parts 7-Up & Soda+t)

5. V.O.

    a. V.O.+soda
    b. V.O.+7-Up
    c. V.O.+Coke
    d. V.O.+ginger ale

    e. V.O.+water
    f. V.O.+Manhattan
    g. V.O.+Manhattan, dry
    h. V.O.+Manhattan, perfect
    i. V.O.+Old Fashioned
    j. V.O.+r+t
    k. V.O.+Collins

6. *Seagram's 7 (Repeat for V.O. as above)*

7. *Any Call Bourbon (Repeat for V.O. as above)*

8. *Brandy (Br)*

    a. Br+snifter
    b. Br+Old Fashioned
    c. Br+Manhattan
    d. Br+Manhattan, dry
    e. Br+Manhattan, perfect
    f. Br+7-Up
    g. Br+soda
    h. Br+r+t
    i. Br+Collins
    j. Stinger
    k. Coffee Royal

9. *Cognac*

    Snifter in coffee

10. *Irish (I)*

    a. I+soda
    b. I+r+t
    c. I+hot
    d. I+Manhattan
    e. I+Manhattan, dry
    f. I+Manhattan, perfect
    g. I+Old Fashioned
    h. I+sour
    i. I+coffee

11. *Rum (R)*

    a. R+Coke
    b. R+Collins
    c. R+sour
    d. R+soda
    e. R+water

    f. R+r
    g. R+Toddy
    h. Cuba Libre
    i. Daiquiri

12. *Tequila (T)*

    a. shot T+lime+salt
    b. T+grape
    c. T+soda
    d. T. Sunrise
    e. T+r
    f. T+orange

B. The "Up" Drinks:

1. *Gin-Up*

    a. Martini
    b. M+t
    c. Gibson
    d. Gimlet
    e. Gin Sour: sweet 'n sour, soda, cherry

2. *Vodka-Up*

    a. V+M
    b. V+M+t
    c. V+Gibson
    d. V+Gimlet
    e. V+sour

3. *Bourbon-Up*

    a. Manhattan
    b. Manhattan, dry
    c. Manhattan, perfect
    d. Whiskey Sour

4. *Irish-Up (Same as for Bourbon-Up)*

5. *Brandy-Up*

    a. Br+Manhattan
    b. Br+Manhattan, dry
    c. Br+Manhattan, perfect
    d. Br+sour
    e. Br+Alexander
    f. Stinger

6. *Scotch-Up*

    a. Rob Roy

    b. Rob Roy, dry

    c. Rob Roy, perfect

    d. Sc+sour

7. *Tequila-Up*

    a. Margarita (Triple Sec, lime juice, salt)

    b. T+sour

    c. T+Gimlet

8. *Rum-Up*

    a. R+sour

    b. R+hot

    c. R+hot buttered

    d. Planter's Punch (o.j., lime j., rum, sugar, grenadine, slice of orange, cherry)

Drink Recipes

Whiskey Sour

Equal parts bourbon and sweet 'n sour, add ½ part soda. Blend with regular ice in "milkshake" blender, serve in chilled sour glass with cherry. Slice of orange optional.

Scotch Sour, Brandy Sour, Etc.

Merely substitute "called" name for bourbon and make as a Whiskey Sour.

Daiquiri

Equal parts of light rum and sweet 'n sour. Blend with crushed ice and serve in chilled Daiquiri glass.

Bacardi Cocktail

Same as Daiquiri except add ⅓ oz. grenadine before blending.

Margarita

One part sweet 'n sour, ½ part Triple Sec, 1½ parts tequila. Blend with crushed ice. Pour in chilled Daiquiri glass after rim has been rubbed with a lime wedge and rolled in salt.

Side Car

Same as Margarita except substitute brandy for tequila; sugar for salt on the rim.

Picon Punch

In "Irish" glass pour large dash grenadine, swirling around inside of glass. Fill with ice and pour one oz. Amer Picon. Fill almost to top with soda, stir, and float with brandy. Add lemon twist and serve.

Bloody Mary

In tall glass filled with ice, pour 1 oz. vodka. (*Gin*, tequila, etc. may be substituted for *Gin* Mary.) Add tomato juice, 2 dashes Lea & Perrins, and drop in wedge of lime. Stir well and serve. (Celery stalk makes a good stirrer/edible swizzle-stick.)

Sloe Gin Fizz

Equal parts sloe gin, sweet 'n sour, and soda. Blend with regular ice like a Whiskey Sour and serve in chilled Fizz (Irish Coffee) glass.

Stinger

Equal parts brandy and white creme de menthe over ice. International Stinger made with equal parts Metaxa and Galliano. (Sometimes called a Mediterranean Stinger or Italian Stallion.)

Rusty Nail

Scotch on the rocks with a float of Drambuie.

Brandy Alexander

One part half-and-half (cream), ½ part dark creme de cacao, and ½ part brandy. Blend with crushed ice and serve in chilled Daiquiri glass with straws. (If gin is substituted for brandy, it is called a Gin Alexander.)

Grasshopper

One part half-and-half (cream), ½ part green creme de menthe, ½ part white creme de cacao. Blend with crushed ice and serve in chilled Daiquiri glass with straws.

Golden Cadillac

One part half-and-half (cream), ½ part Galliano, and ½ part white creme de cacao. Blend with crushed ice and serve in chilled Daiquiri glass with straws. (Some places known as a Golden Dream.)

Ramos Fizz

One part gin, 1 part sweet 'n sour, ½ part simple syrup, 1½ parts half-and-half (cream), 2 dashes orange flower water (substitute orange juice), and white of one egg. Blend and serve in chilled Collins glass with straws.

Fizz (Variations)

Same as Ramos, except—Note: only Ramos uses orange flower water; Golden Fizz: use the yolk of 1 egg rather than the white; Silver Fizz: like Ramos except no orange; New Orleans Fizz: use all of 1 egg (except shell), i.e., white and yolk.

Salty Dog

Rim highball glass by rubbing lime around lip of glass and swirling in salt. Now mix vodka and grape juice.

Irish Coffee

In "Irish" glass, put 2 sugar cubes, 1 oz. of Irish whiskey, and almost fill glass with hot coffee. Stir well, then float whipped cream on top of glass.

Coffee Drink Variations

Venetian: substitute brandy for Irish whiskey; Polynesian: substitute ⅔ ounce brandy and ⅓ ounce Kahlua for the Irish. Other variations substitute the liquor of a country for the Irish whiskey. Example: Greek Coffee: Metaxa; Mexican Coffee: Kahlua.

Collins

Fill tall (Collins) glass with ice and pour one oz. gin (for Tom Collins, vodka for Vodka Collins, bourbon for John Collins, etc.), equal parts of sweet 'n sour and Collins mix from "gun," and squeeze and drop in lime wedge. Stir and add cherry and serve with straws.

Harvey Wallbanger

In a Collins or tall glass, pour one oz. vodka and fill with orange juice (Screwdriver) leaving space at the top for a float of Galliano.

Freddie Fudpucker

Same as a Harvey Wallbanger except substitute Cointreau for Galliano.

Cuba Libre

Light rum and Coca Cola with a squeeze of lime.

Black Russian

In a "rocks" glass, pour about 60 percent vodka and 40 percent Kahlua, stir and serve. For a White Russian, pour slightly less with the same proportions and float cream on top.

Tequila Sunrise

In a Collins glass (tall highball) pour one oz. of tequila. Add orange juice and a dash of grenadine.

Old Fashioned

In an Old Fashioned glass ("rocks" glass) put 1½ tsp. of sugar. Add 2 dashes of Angostura Bitters and a splash of soda. Mix well and add ice, 1 oz. of bourbon, stir, add lemon twist and cherry. Slice of orange is optional, but usually done in the East. (Simple syrup may be substituted for sugar for convenience, about ⅔ tsp.)

Coffee Royal

Add one shot (1 oz.) of bourbon to a cup or glass of hot coffee. Brandy, anisette, etc. may be substituted for bourbon.

Hot Brandy

In an "Irish" glass place 2 cubes of sugar. Pour in one oz. of brandy and fill with hot water. Stir well and add lemon twist.

Many good books of drink recipes have been published and are readily available. I'd want to have at least one of them behind the bar as a reference book on how to make the thousands of less popular mixed drinks and cocktails.

13

The Basic Glassware

Until you experience it yourself, it is going to be hard to convince you of the extremely high rate of "shrinkage"—attrition by breakage and pilferage—there is in a bar's glasses.

Mooney's Irish Pub loses an average of one hundred a week. Sure, you will say, the joint is in a disreputable, bohemian neighborhood. I do think, though, that the better the establishment and neighborhood, the higher the glassware theft rate, with excellent hotels and restaurants being the highest and neighborhood bars with a steady clientele the lowest.

You probably won't take my advice at first. I didn't either. When I opened I stocked the bar with beautiful Waterford crystal with an etched shamrock logo, imported from Ireland. My glasses disappeared so fast I never reordered, especially after young ladies boasted to me that they had matched collections of all sizes of my glassware.

It is usually the ladies who steal your glasses, ash trays, and so forth. They are like magpies who steal (or "take as souvenirs") anything small, pretty, and shiny. Some of these girls have even bragged to me about their complete collections of glasses from various fashionable establishments, as well as from my own joint. They don't seem to think of it as theft.

Men often will pack their drinks outside on the pavement, which is illegal and should be prevented when detected, but they usually leave the glass on a nearby sill or step, so some of these glasses are recovered.

(Men, however, steal dice boxes, particularly the fine, expensive leather ones. If the dice boxes are taken to a table, you can kiss them good-by. They are not cheap, so make sure they are used only at the bar.)

Some large places sell their personalized glasses and ash trays. Most men would rather pay for them than face the potential embarrassment of having their women caught swiping these things, but this practice is an awful bookkeeping nuisance because you have created a cash sale item which is almost impossible to account for accurately.

Fewer and fewer bars these days buy beautiful, expensive glasses and accoutrements which are easily portable. I don't know of any way to stop this pilferage. One dandy high-volume youth bar in San Francisco, which started the nationwide craze for light, airy Edwardian conservatory-type bars, posts signs on the doors that anyone stealing glasses will not be permitted to return to the premises. Maybe that is a slight psychological deterrent, but I doubt it.

Most everybody does as I do now: buys the most inexpensive glasses and keeps the variety down to a basic minimum. Remember, also, that you must throw away any glass that is even barely chipped or cracked.

If a glass costs 13 cents each, a loss of one hundred a week would come to $13. You would have to sell over $50 weekly just to cover lost glassware. I strongly suggest your patterning your glassware inventory along the lines of that below.

Basic Glass Inventory

type	quantity*
1-oz. shot	....
2-oz. shot	....

1-oz. (liquor)	
4-oz. rocks or Old Fashioned	2 dozen
5-oz. highball	2 dozen
8-oz. highball (Collins)	2 dozen
4-oz. Whiskey Sour	2 dozen
3-½-oz. stem cocktail	2 dozen
4-oz. stem (Daiquiri)	2 dozen
6-oz. Irish coffee, beer, or fizz	2 dozen
5½-oz. brandy snifter	2 dozen
9-oz. beer	2 dozen
6-oz. wine	2 dozen
2-oz. sherry or port	1 dozen
champagne	1 dozen

*1 case = 2 dozen

You will notice that there is a 1-ounce shot and a 1-ounce liquor. These are the heavy-glass "deceiver" shot glasses with a white line halfway up. The bartender always pours the booze considerably above that line. Because of the refraction of the thick glass and the angle from which he looks down as he pours, the line looks much higher to him. You get what you paid for, but you think you get a lot more.

Here's a word of caution on those large balloon brandy snifters. Cognac is normally the most expensive drink in the house, one case costing about the same as three cases of vodka. This cognac snifter is the easiest glass in the world to overpour. It's not over ice and looks small in that big glass. I'm sure there isn't a bartender in the world who doesn't look twice and then pour more in. Since it's the most expensive booze you have, there's nothing you can do but just lose money on overpouring into these glasses.

Choose the pattern, shape, and size of all your glasses carefully at the outset, because you should stick with it. Otherwise you will end up with a mishmash of ill-assorted glassware that would do credit to a Berkeley commune.

Most bars now serve drinks on bar napkins. Old traditional bars give women napkins, but not the men. In past years in San Francisco, at least, placing a man's drink on a bar napkin was considered a deliberate affront, implying that he was effeminate. In such cases the napkin was called a serviette. These things cost about one-half cent apiece, so they shouldn't be handed out in stacks and wantonly wasted. Each thousand you waste will cost you $5.

The exception in paying a slight premium for your glassware is to buy a brand which gives a guarantee against their rims' chipping. You will certainly save in the long run.

All your glasses should be large enough to accommodate the appropriate drink handily. While it is *au fait* in knowledgeable circles to fill glasses—especially wine glasses—no more than two-thirds of their capacity, this won't go down well in the ordinary bar because many of the customers will think you are shorting them. Don't fill them all the way to the rim, though, because this can be messy. The average tall drink should come up to a quarter inch from the rim of the glass.

Is it necessary to mention that all the glasses (and bottles) on your back bar be kept sparkling clean and free of dust at all times?

14

You've Made Your First Drink

You've made your first drink. You took the order, made it, gave it to your customer, and collected his money. It didn't seem too tough, did it? Now wait a minute. Multiply those actions by, say, a dozen times, adding to it noise, different drink orders coming from different people, and spread it over a wider area. This might confuse you. It probably will at first, but not necessarily. Following are some methods that help to reduce confusion and increase the number of drinks produced in a period of time.

Good methods, usually, are systematic. This takes in everything from your shower-shave-dress in the morning to estimating the number of blue-eyed children that will be born in the month of May in County Cork. The object is to reach your goal in the most efficient, most pleasant or least irritating, and quickest way. Serving drinks is no exception.

Let's start from the standpoint of the waitress serving drinks to customers sitting or standing outside the bartender's effective reach. Her job is to circulate among the customers to gather their drink orders, which usually range from four to ten drinks at a time. If she is an experienced waitress, she will arrange the order in such a way as to make it easiest for the bartender to fill the order.

The waitress' order should take some priority over the orders from customers at the bar. First, she's bringing an order of, say, ten drinks, which is more than the three or four the bartender might get at one time serving his customers up and down the bar. This means more money coming in in a shorter time. Second, it's difficult to remember ten drinks, especially if people are trying to talk to her, or if her customers are moving around so she has to keep an eye on their location. Third, if she's just standing at her station, she's not accomplishing anything. If the bartender is making her order, his customers can see that he is busy and will wait until he can take their order.

By serving the waitress first, you put out more drinks in a more efficient manner and keep more people happy. If you've got more than one waitress, try to stagger the procedure: one waitress' order; two or three bar orders; another waitress' order.

In arranging the sequence of drink orders, there are probably as many ways as there are people in the business. If your bartender and waitresses are experienced and have worked together for any length of time, they have undoubtedly worked out some system. If one or the other is new in the business, they may be able to utilize one of the following methods.

As an example of the latter, in a drink order of six drinks, four have a Scotch base. Thus a Rob Roy, Scotch-on-the-Rocks, Scotch-and-Water, and a Scotch-and-Soda-in-a-Tall-Glass would be called in this sequence despite the fact that a Rob Roy is a stirred drink served up in a stemmed glass; the Scotch Rocks is served over ice in Old Fashioned glass; the Scotch-and-Water in a regular highball glass; and the Scotch-and-Soda in a taller Collins glass. By taking orders in this sort of sequence, the bartender can ice his glasses, setting them in a row on his towel or rubber mat at the pouring station. Then he uses the same one bottle for pouring the base for four drinks. Contrast this with picking up the Scotch bottle several times if the drinks are ordered by glass configuration as is the case when a waitress calls all tall drinks, all rocks drinks, and all the others as separate sequences. Consider the confusion if a waitress called two Scotch drinks, a bourbon drink, another Scotch drink, several miscellaneous drinks, then yet another Scotch drink.

Another method of ordering used by waitresses is ordering "from clear to darker to darkest." Clear drinks using vodka and gin are at the beginning; progressing to Scotch and bourbon; and then to liqueurs, then beers. This works for some people, hence its continued use. It has the advantage of alerting the bartender to which part of his well (or call brand section) he'll use first. Its disadvantage is the possible confusion between, say, a vodka and a gin Martini. The placement on the serving tray will eliminate many errors which might be caused by identical colored drinks and drinks of the same base but with different mixes.

One preferred method for an especially busy cocktail lounge that serves all types of drinks is this: stirred and up cocktails are called first; then rocks, highballs, and tall drinks, followed by blended or shaker drinks, with liqueurs and beer last. This sequence has a time and motion advantage which is important during a rush hour.

To illustrate this system, let's run through a drink order from the beginning. The waitress takes drink orders from three tables of four people, two, and four respectively. To remember, she may match their drinks to the person ordering in ways ranging from their dress, their mannerisms, their faces, or just the order in which they are seated. As she takes each order, she mentally rearranges the drinks into the sequence she will order them from the bartender. In the course of taking the orders, she may come up with duplicate drinks or ones with only slight variations. She rearranges mentally from sequence of the ordering to the type of drink. A Martini each from tables one and three becomes two Martinis, one with a twist, while she groups Scotch or bourbon drinks together according to mix. It's not likely that there will be ten entirely different drinks from ten people, so duplication is common and makes it easier for her to remember what otherwise would be a complex order.

She approaches her serving station, getting the bartender's attention by calling out, "Ordering!" and orders as follows:

"Two Martinis up, one with a twist. Three Scotch-and-Water, make one tall. Old Fashioned, extra sweet, and a Whiskey Sour-on-the-Rocks. Bloody Mary, Grasshopper, and two dark beers."

She should pause between the groups so the bartender can fix the order in his mind. As she orders, he picks up the appropriate glass, fills it with ice, and places on the folded towel. (Stemmed cocktail glasses which have been chilling in the snow will be placed in the mixing sequence in front of him. If the glasses are unchilled, he will put them in the snow to get them cold while he mixes the rest of the order.)

As he sets up the glasses matching the drinks ordered, it can be helpful for him to "image" the finished drink. If he "sees" two Martinis, one with a twist of lemon floating at the top, or the foam of the Whiskey Sour-on-the-Rocks, he won't have to ask for a repeat of the order, and he'll save some time by not having to do a mental scan such as, "Whiskey Sour—that's equal parts of bourbon, sweet 'n sour, some soda, a dash of sugar." He has made the drink before enough times so that the image of a completed drink will trigger his mechanical process involved in the making of that drink.

With all glasses in order in front of him, he begins the mixing. Into a large mixing glass filled with ice he pours a little vermouth from a bottle in one hand and simultaneously pours enough gin for two Martinis with the bottle in his other hand. Next he pours Scotch over the ice cubes in the two highball glasses and the tall glass. He replaces the Scotch bottle and pours the vodka for the Bloody Mary. Leaving the finishing of this drink until later, he makes the complete Old Fashioned while pouring the bourbon into the waiting "milkshake" mixer for the Sour.

The Martinis are chilling in the mixing glass and the Scotches are to be with water, so the short wait giving a small amount of melt from the ice is reducing the amount of water he will add when the remainder of the drinks are finished.

He finishes putting in the ingredients of the Sour, for the moment leaving it, to pour and start the Grasshopper on the blender. While it blends, he opens the two bottles of beer. Placing the beer bottles near the waitress' tray, he returns to add the water to the Scotch, then places them behind the beer. He takes the Grasshopper off the blender, pours it in its tall, wide-stemmed glass and washes out the blender with a quick motion in the sink. He returns the blender to its place and picks up the ingredients for the Bloody Mary. As he is mixing the Mary, the waitress begins to place the drinks on her tray. The bartender hands her the Bloody Mary and returns to the Martinis, giving them several vigorous stirs, then pours them through the strainer into their chilled glasses, and sets them down in front of her tray.

When the waitress transfers the drinks onto her tray, she should place them so that no two glasses touch each other. If they do, and if the tray is wet, the glasses may "waltz" or slide about erratically. Sometimes they waltz right off the tray.

Picking up the milkshake can, the bartender puts it on the mixer and whirs the mixture to a fine froth then pours the drink into the Whiskey Sour glass and places it on the only spot left on the tray. He rinses the can with one hand and reaches for her money with the other. He has mentally totalled up the order. As he turns toward the register, the waitress announces her total, which he checks mentally with his total. Since she must make change for three tables, he breaks an extra ten dollar bill into a five and five ones for her.

There are ten drinks made and sold in the time it would take to get the order, make the drinks, and collect the money from two or three individual customers at the bar.

Regarding garnishes and mixes, many waitress stations are set up so they have a mixing gun as well as "fruit"—lemon twists, olives, cherries, and so on. This way she garnishes the drinks as the bartender makes them. Not only does this save time in production, but it saves confusion in the ordering since she does not have to go into description. Imagine the difference between "Two Martini Rocks," and "Two Martinis-on-the-

Rocks, one takes two olives and an anchovy, and the other takes an olive and a twist."

Agreements should be made between the bartender and the waitress on terminology in order to cut down ordering time and reduce mistakes. For instance, if she calls for a Gimlet, it should be understood it is for one served in a stemmed glass and made with vodka, because that is the way most of the clientele at this particular bar drink them. If the customer wants it otherwise, she will not say simply "Gimlet," but "Gin Gimlet-on-the-Rocks." There are often many variations on a standard drink. Make the plain generic name that of the variation most commonly called for at your bar. If most of your Martini-drinking customers drink them of gin over ice, that is a "Martini" in your parlance. Others are specified, such as "Vodka Martini up."

A beginning bartender won't progress from making one drink at a time to ten in one night. It will take some time for a new man to be able to do this. Your bartenders will accomplish this faster if there is a system.

Finished with the waitress' order, you go back to waiting on your customers at the bar, who are more likely to be ordering single drinks or groups of two or three. Always place a woman's drink on a bar napkin. One spilled drop might ruin her dress.

The basic reason you're in business is to make a profit, so after you serve a drink you smile and ask for the price of the drink. Wait to get the money, then ring it up and give the change. Say, "Thank you." If you set this precedent, your bartenders will pick it up and do exactly the same as you do. If you don't, they won't, and you'll end up not collecting for drinks on each shift. This will mount up to real money fast if you don't always wait to get the money after you serve the drink.

When you open a bar it's a public house and anybody can come in, so you can always expect the worst to happen and hope that it doesn't. Fortunately there are few bars that have fisticuffs or physical encounters. But one thing that can really destroy you in the bar business is losing control of the situation. Normally if somebody is drunk, or out of line or has just had a beef with the old lady he invariably will take it out on a bartender. If you let situations like that get out of hand, you might as well get out of the business. You can be familiar with the customers if you like, but not too familiar. You always treat them with courtesy. A little bit of courteousness goes a long way. It's the easiest thing in the world to call somebody "Sir" instead of "Hey, buddy, what d'you want?" The nicer you are to your customers, the nicer they are going to be to you. They're going to tip you. That's probably half the battle in the bartending business. I know fellows who make $15 to $20 in a three-hour shift, and they're not stealing it. Tipping is like a disease. If one person tips, invariably everybody starts tipping. If you can be nice to just one man and get him moving with the tips, you're going to have a nice day.

Politeness is a prime requisite in earning tips. Note the verb, "earn." Your tips will be greater, also, if you keep in mind the origin of the word, "tip." It is an abbreviation of "To Insure Promptitude." You have to be nice to everybody, no matter who they are, whether they're drunk or whether they're sober. You're nice to them at the beginning. Then you analyze the situation. If you need the person as a customer, you keep him; if you don't, you can give him the message you don't need him as a customer—if you can smell trouble coming around. First impressions usually are wrong. You can see a customer coming in who looks like a bum and he can develop into one of the best customers you ever had in your life. And one of the nicest people, too. It's difficult to analyze anybody who's come in for the first time. You have to be nice at all times, even when you're throwing them out. You say, "Buddy, you're a great guy and I'll see you next week. You are drunk and out of line. Sure, you're upset about something, but everything in the garden's going to be rosy next week. Come on back then."

Two university-educated cocktail waitresses commented on this somewhat formal exegesis of cocktail waitresses' duties. Both of these women write well, so I quote them verbatim. Geri Ribaudo writes:

> Sean,
>   You asked me to recall some experiences I've had waitressing. Although they came freely in conversation, writing them down is a different story, but here goes.

This guy came in and asked what kinds of beer we carry. I told him that we have Coors, Olympia, Bohemia, Ballentine Ale, Guinness Stout, and Miller on tap. So he asks for a Budweiser. Well, here we go again.

I don't serve all people the same way. A young, unexperienced girl might go by rote, but there are degrees of talent and experience in this business just as there are in all other businesses. I don't serve all people in the same manner. Often, after taking an order, I'll return to the table to find the couple engrossed in conversation, with a ten dollar bill lying on the table. I set down the drinks and the change without disturbing the couple. Usually there is a nice tip left when they leave. However, if the guy says 'I'll catch you before I leave,' it's guaranteed no tip.

To break away from Geri's letter, tips are especially important to cocktail waitresses. Their salary ranges from absolutely nothing to very little. The only real money they make is by tips. This is admittedly a rotten way of conducting things. I didn't invent it. I don't like it, but that's the way it's currently done. I don't particularly like the way most things are run in Russia and China, but I understand that it's a crime to offer or take a tip in those countries. They are supposed to get an adequate salary. That I do like. Until we rectify this unedifying situation where a young lady educated in philosophy at the University of California must depend for her living on the largesse of anyone who might drop into the joint, we are stuck with the tip system.

Marijane Pierson also is well educated. She writes:

Sean,
Being a cocktail waitress is very educational. I figure that four and one-half years as a part-time cocktail waitress on top of hanging in bars for fourteen years is the equivalent of a PhD in some behavioral science.

The first lesson I learned was that people group cocktail waitresses in the same category as nurses and stewardesses. You are a woman serving the public and for some ungodly reason men become upset if you don't smile constantly while you are waitressing. As long as you have a smile on your face and they have a drink in their hand, all's right with the world. I think it's connected with their image of woman as servant/mother/mistress. I have been standing in my station after having been burned, kicked, pinched, and goosed, trying to remember fifteen drinks and adding up the prices at the same time and have had some twenty-two year old crew cut Marine order me to *smile*. That's when you understand murder.

Of course, you are working for the money, right? After a few years, you can tell who will tip and who won't. Men who smoke pipes almost never tip. One man who drank Guinness and smoked a pipe never tipped me once in two years. He was very polite and smiled a lot, but he never tipped. He made one of his girlfriends get up out of her seat, so that he could go to the cigarette machine for her so that he wouldn't have to ask me to. One woman he came in with used to leave tips. Needless to say, she didn't come around with him for very long. People who are reluctant to tip or who are worried about the exchange of money always rub their nose with their right forefinger while you are making change, and they mutter a lot. I have found that my tips are better if I place the money on the table or in their hand, rather than leaving it on the tray. The money is not wet and it somehow seems less important.

Tips are not the sum of a cocktail waitress' problems. Geri continues:

Identification is a problem. Electronic games and pool tables attract a lot of underage kids. Most people don't mind being asked for ID, but those who get the most insulted are those who have barely turned twenty-one. One fellow became indignant when I asked him for identification and flung his driver's license at me. When I looked at the date, it proved him to be nineteen years old. I guess he didn't think I'd look at the date, or perhaps he figured I couldn't add.

One slow Saturday night a fairly regular customer came in with his wife. They sat at a table, and I served them each a glass of white wine. After ten or fifteen minutes, the man motioned me over to the table. When I got there, he punched me in the stomach. When I asked him why, he said, "You look sleepy and I thought I'd wake you up." Fortunately, I didn't have my tray with me or I'd have hit him over the head.

The waitress station is prize real estate for hanging around. Everyone wants to stand in it, at it, or around it. Many times I have counted six spaces at the bar with as many people clustered at my station. One night a certain man was constantly in the way. After dealing with him politely, I finally asked, "If I were a secretary, would you sit on my typewriter?" He answered, "Of course not," then remained out of my way.

One night some very drunk people came in. After their

third round, they decided not to pay. I can usually handle this situation fairly well. However, when one of the men started tapping my leg with his foot, I felt the anger rise. I asked him to stop kicking me, whereupon he told me what I could do with myself. I calmly walked back to the bar and told the bartender what had happened. Needless to say, the man was asked to leave. The remainder of the group managed to scrape up the cost of the round, $3.25, in quarters, dimes, and pennies. Don't even ask if there was a tip.

Then, there is the guy who sits next to the waitress station and has to have a blow-by-blow description of what you are doing. Questions like "What's in an Irish Coffee?" "Why do you hold your money that way?" "How can you remember all those drinks at one time?" "Are you the bartender's wife?" And, of course, "What are you doing when you get off?"

A man and his date will walk in the door. I am standing at my station. He looks me straight in the eye, goes to the bar, orders two drinks, and takes them to a table. As I walk by, he exclaims, "Oh, I didn't know there was a waitress here."

I will approach a table of four who have just arrived with, "Hi! Can I bring you anything to drink?" and get back the classic line, "Yes, what do you have?" That's when I turn around and look at a bar with no less than 150 bottles showing. Does he really want me to go through the entire list of possibilities? They'd die of thirst before I was half way through.

I served a gentleman a Black Russian one night and he complained that it was too weak. Not enough booze.

(That reminds me of the time I was in the Rainbow Room atop Rockefeller Plaza in New York one afternoon. In came two extremely respectable tourist ladies. I'll bet they had never been in a cocktail lounge in their lives and only came here for the spectacular view. One lady ordered a Frozen Daiquiri. The other hemmed and hawed for awhile, then ordered "The same thing, please, but make it half strength.")

A group of three people ordered a round of drinks and were upset because I wouldn't take food stamps as payment.

Our poolroom attracts all kinds of people. I enjoy watching the games and everyone seems to enjoy it. This one guy, who was shooting pool, kept ordering his beers through me. After his sixth beer, he apologized for not tipping. He explained that he was on unemployment and couldn't afford it. That one really irritated me.

I work an eight hour shift, four to five nights a week,

adding up usually to forty hours a week. Can you guess how many regulars who come in every night of the week ask me what I really do for a living during the day???

From these accounts it is easy to see that a career of cocktail waitress is not all a romantic bed of roses, although many of the shallower male customers feel that all of these hard-working young women are there merely for their erotic gratification. There are a number of compensations to this job, though, which are not usually found in business offices, some of which are enumerated in the next chapter.

15

On Birds, Dogs, Kids and Other Animals

A friend of mine who owns a Scottish bar has a miniature parrot named "Winston." Like the man he was named after, he has a lisp and is mean as a snake. After you feed him a bag of peanuts, he takes a great delight in trying to chomp off the tip of your finger. Then, like only a parrot, his eyes glaze and he scrunches himself up in a ball and pretends to be asleep, but he is just waiting for an unsuspecting tourist to poke his finger in the cage, whereupon he starts his finger chomping exercise again.

The Health Department turned a blind eye to Winston, who is a favorite of literally thousands of seamen who once or twice a year stop into the bar with goodies from all over the world, first to feed Winston, then as the booze starts to register, to try to antagonize him. The Germans did the same to the original Winston and it's history the way he struck back. At ten o'clock every night Winston used to be set free of his cage. He'd fly around the room chatting with everybody. As near to a human maitre d'hotel as you would ever see, he would miss nobody. It's a marvelous thrill to have a bird sit on your shoulder,

however scant the visit, perched there confidently, ignoring you
individually while scanning the crowd, planning his next flight.

Everything went well for about two years. Then one night
an inspector from the Health Department stopped in to check
out the joint. Who knows the way a parrot thinks? Winston lit
on his glass and calmly pooped in his Bourbon and Soda. That
did it. Winston was cited and all hell broke loose. Litigation was
started. "Get rid of Winston or we'll close your joint down."
There was a hue and cry. It made all the papers. Business
doubled and overnight Winston became a martyr. Douglas Kirk,
a feisty Celtic native of Dundee, started a petition. After an
arduous session with the Health Department, it was decided
that Winston could stay as long as he was confined to his cage.
He just celebrated his twentieth birthday and can still be seen
in the Edinburgh Castle on Geary Street in San Francisco.

Dogs are not legally allowed in barrooms in the United
States. On the other hand, no self-respecting English Protestant
would dream of going into his local after church on Sunday
morning without picking up his dog first. Like the beige
waistcoat, it's the proper thing to do. Public houses in Ireland
welcome children, who are forbidden such places in the United
States. It never ceases to amaze me how beautiful those Irish
kids are with their huge, honest, frank eyes, gorgeous complex-
ions, and scarlet hair. They are as lithe as greyhounds. But as
the Irish grow older they seem to lose their looks. I have a
theory that it has something to do with the climate. In all parts
of Ireland it's not unusual to see a twelve-year-old boy or girl
tending the bar.

Dogs and children are put into the same category in the
United States. They can't go into a bar. Presumably it would
corrupt their morals. However, there is no ordinance which
says you can't take a llama into a bar with you. It was an
exceptionally busy Saturday night the first time I was confronted with this aristocratic looking beast, the pet of a
psychiatrist who had a weird collection of animals, including a
wolf.

Llamas, like camels, spit when they're angry, and they're
deadly accurate. Nothing really bothers me when I'm behind

the bar, but I have to admit that staring at this long-lashed beast, who would make a Revlon ad look pallid, perturbed me, to put it mildly. I didn't know what to do. There was a sixty-five-year-old couple sitting at the bar. They were on their fifth Martini. The llama nudged the lady. She turned around to gaze into the eyes of the long-lashed llama. Very calmly she turned back to her husband and said she thought they ought to leave because she'd had enough. I wouldn't be surprised if she went on the wagon and never mentioned the incident to anybody to this day.

A friend of mine was married to a wealthy oil man from Texas. They had no children so she bought a monkey. This monkey had a lot of class. It would drink nothing but V.O. on the rocks. I experimented a couple of times, trying to ring in some cheap blended bourbon. No dice, the monkey just wouldn't accept a substitute. Later, the situation got out of hand when, immediately after he came into the bar, the monkey would leap across the counter and grab the bottle. He never did figure how to get it open, though. It wasn't unusual for his mistress, on a spending spree, to blow $500 for clothes for her alcoholic pet in Neiman Marcus. He had to be the best-dressed monkey in Dallas.

Turtle racing has been and is a big draw in some bars in Sausalito, California. A bar used to have mouse racing, but the Health Department took a dim view of this sport and it was discontinued. Frog jumping contests drag thousands to Calaveras County, where you can't even get into one of the jammed bars during that week.

Roberts-at-the-Beach, a defunct San Francisco social in-stitution, had a horse for a mascot. Blackie was his name, and his swimming across the Golden Gate with his master, Shorty Roberts, made the place world famous. Two years after it closed, I was mildly interested in buying the place. After all this time, in the space of the thirty minutes I was in there, I had to turn down four phone reservations for parties.

John Wayne told me an amusing story across the bar one night while he was drinking his Bourbon-and-Water. He got a letter from Ireland saying,

Dear Mr. Wayne:

You remember the horse you rode in "The Quiet Man?" He is retired and is now living on my farm in Connemara. I wonder if you would like to contribute towards his keep? He is now seven years old and is in fine fettle.

Wayne took a swig from his glass, gazed at the ceiling and said, "When I rode that horse he was eleven, and that was sixteen years ago."

Finally, how about a chicken playing a piano for a dime? I tried it and it worked. I was approached by a carny. You have to have a lot of respect for carnies because they're outthinking us twenty-four hours a day. You have to be sharp to make a living in the carnival business. This fellow's proposition was that he had a chicken which could play the piano. She plays a tune for a dime and I would get a nickel out of it. How can you turn down a deal like that? The customers laughed their heads off all day long, convinced that I had flipped my wig, but they kept pumping dimes into the machine. It worked this way. When you put the dime in, a light went on. The chicken was programmed to pick the keys of a miniature piano eight times. This released a couple of grains of corn, which were promptly gobbled up. The first day's take was $8.20, of which I made $4.10, one brown egg, and a blast from the Society for the Prevention of Cruelty to Animals for overworking a chicken.

Basking in the limelight seemed to suit her. She was the fattest, healthiest looking chicken I have ever laid eyes on. And one hell of a little piano player.

16

Credit, Tabs, Free Drinks, and Cashing Checks

Giving credit is a sure way for a bar to lose an awful lot of money, and an awful lot of customers. A bar which extends credit will lose probably 50 cents of each dollar of credit given. The type of people who charge drinks in a bar aren't really very stable, otherwise, if they didn't want to lay out ready cash, they would pay by credit card or check. You can figure that half the people who charge drinks sooner or later are going to beat you. You're giving away the liquor and you're probably going to give yourself an ulcer worrying that this man is going to nail you eventually. Half the time you'll never see your money, and there's no way to get your booze back.

Not only do you lose money, but you lose customers, too. Sometimes good ones. When somebody owes you $10, he'll go out and spend $10 in every other bar in the neighborhood (which does not extend him credit), but he won't come in and pay you your ten. It is well known that debtors often think up bogus reasons or rationalizations for disliking their creditors, to justify avoiding them and failing to pay.

A way of politely refusing to give credit, to let the customer down gently, so to speak, is to tell him that you are required by law to pay tax on every drink you serve. If you charge it, you can't pay the tax at the proper time and might get in serious trouble with the state.

Often a customer differentiates semantically between drinking on credit and "running a tab." If you run a tab for one, other customers will observe it and you'll end up having to run a tab for everybody. A senior vice president of a large bank came into a place I was managing in the financial district. It was my first day there. He said that for convenience he wanted to run a monthly tab. I told him politely that our bookkeeping was not set up to accommodate tabs. He was annoyed and let me know that there were two dozen places within blocks where he could drink and that he didn't need my place. I merely asked him politely if I could drop by his bank and set up a tab to draw money every day and pay it back at the end of the month. He laughed and ordered a double Martini over the rocks. He became one of my best customers.

Also, charge for each drink as you serve it. Don't tote them up and let the customer pay when he leaves. This is not as chancy as extending credit, but it does lead to a lot of misunderstandings. Either the customer or the bartender, or both, can forget exactly how many drinks were served, or they may not agree on the number. Often the customer will either walk out honestly forgetting to pay or consciously sneak out to beat you. Remember, your customers are in your place to drink alcohol. Everyone knows that alcohol plays funny tricks with the brain and memory. Disputes over money with somebody who has been drinking never lead to any good will. Also, the other customers hate to have to listen to such disputes. It leaves a bad taste in their mouths.

If the bartender does not collect for each drink right after it is served, a customer might have, say, two drinks, then depart, leaving two dollars on the bar. The bartender will often assume—or talk himself into assuming—that this is his legitimate tip. He doesn't feel that he is stealing, nevertheless payment for the two drinks doesn't find its way into the till, where it rightfully belongs. The fundamental function of a bartender is not making drinks, but collecting the money. There is no point in making drinks if you don't collect the bread.

Do not lend anybody, even your best friends, money from the cash register. If your mother-in-law comes in on the shorts needing some money to buy lunch, give it to her from your pocket, not the register, or in the last resort, write her a check.

If you run a large bar-restaurant, I'd suggest issuing your own credit cards in the standard manner any other sort of company issues its cards.

If somebody you don't know really well wants to cash a check, tell him that you have a short application form which takes about five days to process. If he would care to fill it in, you would be glad to cash his checks and you will tell him what his limit is. If your bartender cashes a check, he should initial the top. If it bounces, it is his responsibility to collect it.

Although a check is a substitute for money, it is not money. All states have enacted statutes making the issuing and passing of bad checks a punishable crime. Since the statutes vary from state to state, it is necessary to consult the statute of your particular state.

In New York the issuing of bad checks is a species of fraud of the grade of misdemeanor. In most cases where you receive a bad check (aside from deliberate and intentional fraud, as where no account exists), it will be dishonored by the bank because of insufficient funds. The salient points of the New York law are: As a drawer or representative drawer, he *utters* a check knowing that he or his principal, as the case may be, does not then have sufficient funds with the drawee (bank) to cover it, and that he intends or believes at the time of *utterance* that payment will be refused by the bank upon presentation. Or he passes a check signed by someone else with the same knowledge. The key word here, of course, is "intent." Usually the person cashing a bad check will claim that he had no intent to defraud, but that he thought it was good, or would be good by the time it was presented.

The New York law, however, has this presumption: When the drawer of a check has insufficient funds with the drawee to cover it at the time of utterance, the subscribing drawer or representative drawer, as the case may be, is presumed to know of such insufficiency.

However, the affirmative defense in any prosecution for issuing a bad check can be that the defendant or a person acting in his behalf made full satisfaction of the amount of the check within ten days after dishonor by the drawee.

I am not trying to be unduly hard-nosed about credit, but merely advising you to standardize your policy with accepted business practice. It is illogical for people to expect lax procedure from an establishment which purveys nonessential commodities such as whiskey and gin, when they would not expect it from a business which sells necessities such as bread and milk. I emphasize, though, using politeness and forbearance in denying these credit requests.

An allied problem comes up with free drinks. Many owners have literally "given away the house," and have gone into bankruptcy because of largesse in standing drinks on the house. It is a costly habit. For each drink you give away, you must sell four *additional* drinks just to break even. Are you going to? Of course not.

As mentioned, sales tax of 6.5 percent must be paid the Board of Equalization on all drinks sold. The board may audit your bar whenever they wish. If you have given away an appreciable amount of liquor and have not paid tax on it, you may be in a sticky position with them. They know how much liquor you have bought and how much you have sold . . . and paid tax on. You *never* want to be on their list of suspects.

In a way, this may be good for you. You can cite this as the reason for never giving away drinks, so a good customer cannot rationally accuse you of being cheap.

Never give an employee the discretion of buying a customer a drink on the house. If you or your bartender give *one*, you will be on a devil's slide; *everybody* will want and feel himself entitled to one.

Savvy bar owners, when they do buy a customer a drink, pay with cash from their own pocket. This is more impressive generosity and it keeps the books accurate. Your cost will be only that of the liquor and mix, that is, not the sales price.

Whatever credit policy you decide on, you should make it consistent and you should make it known. It's difficult and embarrassing to give credit to one person, then to refuse credit to another, sitting down the bar, who has observed the first person receive it.

17

Pricing and Sizing

Many bars' pricing policy is determined merely by what the place down the street is charging. Certainly one has to be competitive with similar places in a similar neighborhood, but this is too unbusinesslike if you haven't made some sort of calculations whether you will make any money simply by charging what seems to be the going price. There is too much luck involved in such a simplistic pricing policy. A better approach is one using standard business formulas. If you aren't making any money, at least you will probably know why.

The fundamental basis of business is cost. Unless you know the cost to you of whatever you are selling, you can never operate in a businesslike fashion. Your mark-up is the difference between the cost of a drink and its selling price. It can be expressed either in dollars or in percentages. When the amount is compared with the wholesale cost, the percentage is the "mark-up on cost." When the amount is compared with the retail selling price, the percentage is the "margin on selling price."

The following illustrations are mark-up calculations and

margin on retail percentages based on a drink that for purposes of illustration costs 35 cents and sells for $1.

$$\frac{\text{Selling Price minus Wholesale Cost}}{\text{Wholesale Cost}} = \text{Mark-up on Cost}$$

$$\frac{\$1.00 - \$.35 = \$.65}{\$.35} = 186\%$$

$$\frac{\text{Selling Price minus Wholesale Cost}}{\text{Selling Price}} = \text{Margin on Selling Price}$$

$$\frac{\$1.00 - \$.35 = \$.65}{\$1.00} = 65\%$$

The margin on selling price roughly equals the gross margin, or the difference between total sales and cost of the liquor. (Cost here is the price paid for the liquor, but not including the cost of fruit, ice, mixes, and so on.) The gross margin must cover your operating expenses and give you your profit. If you estimate that 50 percent of sales must be allotted to cover operating expenses and you wish to realize a 15 percent profit, you must realize a margin on sales of 65 percent.

Multiply the mark-up on cost percentage by the cost of the drink, and adding the result to the cost, you can arrive at the desired profitable price for the drink. This formula converts margin percentages to mark-up:

$$\frac{\text{Margin}}{100 \text{ minus Margin}} \times 100 = \text{Mark-up}$$

You can't go through all this for each of the hundreds of types of drinks you sell, so you make an average and round it off.

A less complicated method, but still far better than just charging what the guy down the street does, because you have no idea where he dreamed up his scale of prices, is to keep your pouring costs down to 25 percent. For each $1,000 worth of liquor you buy, you want gross sales of $4,000. Maybe the competition won't allow you to keep your pouring costs this low.

However, when you have pouring costs much above 30 percent, you may be in trouble.

Three factors determine your pouring costs. The first, the cost of the liquor you buy; second, the price you charge per drink; and third, how much liquor you pour into each drink. The charts on the following pages will give you a handy shortcut in making your calculations.

The magic word which spices all bar owners' conversation is "gross," meaning total sales or revenue. The way people in the business talk, this word is the final end or aim. What is "the gross" *in itself*? Not much unless some of it is retained as net profit. Gross sales in an inefficient operation mean nothing in your pocket, or just a flow of money in and out, with none sticking.

Many owners would do themselves far better if they dwelled a little more on their retained profit and less on "gross" or sheer volume. Too many businessmen, seeing little profit, devote all their effort to increasing sales. This can be self-defeating. If they are losing money on each unit sold, they will probably just lose a larger total if they increase their sales without adjusting their price and expense structure. The bar business can be especially misleading because of the large daily cash flow—not checks, notes, various instruments of some-times invisible credit, but real cash money which can be seen and felt. I reemphasize that it is much too easy to delude yourself into thinking all this money is yours.

An important calculation in measuring your operation's efficiency is "turnover." This is the number of times your bar's average inventory is sold and replaced during the year.

Average inventory is the sum of your inventory on January 1 plus end-of-the-month inventories for the next 12 months, divided by 13. You calculate turnover by these equations:

$$\frac{\$ \text{ Annual Net Sales}}{\$ \text{ Average Inventory at Retail}} = \text{Turnover Rate at Retail}$$

$$\frac{\$ \text{ Cost of Goods Sold in One Year}}{\$ \text{ Average Inventory at Cost}} = \text{Turnover Rate at Cost}$$

Your Cost and Profit Per Drink

● What you take in when you sell a case of twelve <u>fifths</u>

There are 25.6 ounces in a fifth. There are 307 ounces in a case of twelve fifths.

	Drinks in Case of Fifths	When Sold @ 30¢	When Sold @ 35¢	When Sold @ 40¢	When Sold @ 50¢	When Sold @ 60¢	When Sold @ 75¢	When Sold @ 85¢	When Sold @ $1.00
¾ oz.	410	$123.00	$143.50	$164.00	$205.00	$246.75	$307.50	$348.50	$410.00
⅞ oz.	351	105.30	122.85	140.40	175.50	210.60	263.25	298.35	351.00
1 oz.	307	92.10	107.45	122.80	153.50	184.20	230.25	260.95	307.00
1⅛ oz.	246	81.90	95.55	109.20	136.50	163.80	204.75	209.10	246.00
1¼ oz.	273	73.80	86.10	98.40	123.00	147.60	184.50	232.05	273.00
1⅜ oz.	223	66.90	78.05	89.20	111.50	133.80	167.25	189.55	223.00
1½ oz.	205	61.50	71.75	82.00	102.50	123.00	153.75	174.25	205.00

Cost Per Drink

Fifths		Cost Per Drink in Various Sized Glasses (Ounces)					Selling Price Per Drink at 2½ Times the Cost (150% Mark-Up) (Ounces)					Selling Price Per Drink at Triple the Cost (200% Mark-Up) (Ounces)				
Cost Per Case	Cost Per Bottle	¾	⅞	1	1¼	1½	¾	⅞	1	1¼	1½	¾	⅞	1	1¼	1½
$25.00	$2.08	.06	.07	.08	.10	.12	.15	.18	.20	.25	.30	.18	.21	.24	.30	.36
26.00	2.17	.07	.08	.09	.11	.13	.16	.19	.21	.27	.32	.20	.23	.26	.33	.39
27.00	2.25	.07	.08	.09	.11	.13	.16	.20	.22	.28	.33	.20	.24	.27	.33	.39
28.00	2.33	.07	.08	.09	.11	.14	.17	.20	.23	.29	.34	.21	.24	.27	.34	.41
29.00	2.42	.07	.08	.09	.12	.14	.18	.21	.24	.29	.35	.21	.25	.28	.35	.42
30.00	2.50	.07	.09	.10	.12	.15	.19	.21	.25	.30	.36	.22	.26	.30	.36	.44
31.00	2.58	.08	.09	.10	.13	.15	.19	.22	.25	.31	.38	.23	.27	.30	.38	.45
32.00	2.67	.08	.09	.10	.13	.16	.20	.23	.26	.33	.39	.24	.27	.31	.39	.47
33.00	2.75	.08	.09	.11	.13	.16	.20	.24	.26	.34	.40	.24	.28	.32	.40	.48
34.00	2.83	.08	.10	.11	.14	.17	.21	.25	.28	.35	.41	.25	.30	.33	.42	.50
35.00	2.92	.09	.10	.11	.14	.17	.21	.25	.29	.35	.43	.26	.30	.34	.42	.51
36.00	3.00	.09	.10	.12	.15	.18	.22	.26	.29	.36	.44	.27	.31	.35	.44	.53
37.00	3.08	.09	.11	.12	.15	.18	.23	.26	.30	.38	.45	.27	.32	.36	.45	.54
38.00	3.16	.09	.11	.12	.16	.19	.24	.27	.31	.39	.46	.28	.33	.37	.47	.56
39.00	3.25	.10	.11	.13	.16	.19	.24	.28	.31	.40	.48	.29	.33	.38	.48	.57
40.00	3.33	.10	.11	.13	.16	.20	.25	.29	.33	.41	.49	.30	.34	.39	.49	.59
41.00	3.42	.10	.12	.13	.17	.20	.25	.30	.34	.41	.50	.30	.36	.40	.50	.60

42.00	3.50	.10	.12	.14	.17	.21	.26	.30	.34	.43	.51	.31	.36	.41	.51	.62
43.00	3.58	.11	.12	.14	.18	.21	.26	.31	.35	.44	.53	.32	.37	.42	.53	.63
44.00	3.67	.11	.13	.14	.18	.22	.26	.31	.36	.45	.54	.32	.38	.43	.54	.65
45.00	3.75	.11	.13	.15	.18	.22	.28	.32	.36	.46	.55	.33	.39	.44	.55	.66
46.00	3.83	.11	.13	.15	.19	.23	.29	.33	.38	.47	.56	.34	.39	.45	.57	.68
47.00	3.92	.13	.13	.15	.19	.23	.29	.34	.39	.48	.58	.35	.40	.46	.57	.69
48.00	4.00	.12	.14	.16	.20	.23	.29	.34	.39	.49	.59	.35	.41	.47	.59	.70
49.00	4.08	.12	.14	.16	.20	.24	.30	.35	.40	.50	.60	.36	.42	.48	.60	.72
50.00	4.17	.12	.14	.16	.20	.24	.30	.36	.41	.51	.61	.36	.43	.49	.61	.74
51.00	4.25	.13	.15	.17	.21	.25	.31	.36	.41	.52	.62	.38	.44	.50	.63	.75
52.00	4.33	.13	.15	.17	.21	.26	.32	.37	.43	.54	.64	.39	.45	.51	.64	.77
53.00	4.41	.13	.15	.17	.22	.26	.33	.38	.44	.54	.65	.39	.45	.52	.65	.78
54.00	4.50	.13	.15	.18	.22	.26	.33	.39	.44	.55	.66	.39	.46	.53	.66	.79
55.00	4.58	.14	.16	.18	.23	.27	.34	.40	.45	.56	.68	.41	.48	.54	.68	.81
56.00	4.67	.14	.16	.18	.23	.28	.34	.40	.45	.57	.69	.41	.48	.54	.69	.83
57.00	4.75	.14	.16	.18	.23	.28	.35	.41	.46	.59	.70	.42	.49	.56	.70	.84
58.00	4.83	.14	.17	.19	.24	.29	.36	.41	.48	.60	.71	.43	.50	.57	.72	.86
59.00	4.92	.15	.17	.19	.24	.29	.36	.42	.49	.60	.73	.44	.51	.58	.72	.87
60.00	5.00	.15	.17	.19	.25	.29	.36	.43	.49	.61	.74	.44	.51	.59	.74	.88
61.00	5.08	.15	.18	.20	.25	.30	.38	.44	.50	.63	.75	.45	.53	.60	.75	.90
62.00	5.16	.15	.18	.20	.25	.31	.38	.45	.51	.64	.76	.45	.54	.61	.76	.92
63.00	5.25	.16	.18	.21	.26	.31	.39	.45	.51	.65	.77	.47	.54	.62	.78	.93
64.00	5.33	.16	.18	.21	.26	.31	.39	.46	.52	.65	.78	.47	.55	.63	.78	.93
65.00	5.42	.16	.19	.21	.26	.32	.40	.46	.53	.68	.80	.48	.56	.63	.79	.96

This and the following charts are reprinted courtesy of Bin-Merchandiser.

131

Most successful bars average seven stock turns a year. Thus, if your business requires stock valued at $10,000, annual purchases would total $70,000. Beer turnover is higher, but turnover rate for the expensive call brands of liquor is not so high. If you have a lower turnover rate, your bar may be overstocked; a higher rate could mean your inventory is understocked. You should adjust your average inventory in either case. The important point about inventory is to try to avoid loss of sales by being out of a product or demand brand, while at the same time not overstocking it.

Most of the foregoing is textbook mathematical formulae. If you didn't skip over it entirely, it will serve best as a yardstick to measure your actual operation because no bar operates in an abstract, ideal vacuum. The factor of competition largely determines your pricing policies. In the final analysis, you cannot determine your anticipated net profit from any theoretical fixed percentage. It will only be apparent as a result of actual sales, less the total cost of doing business.

Your local competitors may charge less than a reasonable price for some item, forcing you to do the same. On the other hand, you may be justified in charging a higher price because your location is more convenient, or because your decor and atmosphere have distinction, or because of some unique feature you offer, or simply because you have a more attractive personality.

You want to be reasonably sure your prices will attract a profitable clientele. There are profits only when enough sales are made and the cash is in the register. Overpricing will frighten customers away, which means insufficient volume to cover your cost of operation. Underpricing may produce a larger volume, but at the same time a loss in operating profit. The result of continuing either situation will be failure. In all cases the maxim of a successful bar operation is to sell profitably. *Never give away free what you are in business to sell.*

Your Cost and Profit Per Drink

● What you take in when you sell a case of twelve quarts

There are 32 ounces in a quart.
There are 384 ounces in a case of twelve quarts.

	Drinks in Case of Quarts	When Sold @ 20¢	When Sold @ 25¢	When Sold @ 30¢	When Sold @ 35¢	When Sold @ 40¢	When Sold @ 50¢	When Sold @ 60¢	When Sold @ 75¢
¾ oz.	512	$102.04	$128.00	$153.60	$179.20	$204.80	$256.00	$307.20	$384.00
⅞ oz.	439	87.80	109.75	131.70	153.65	175.60	219.50	263.40	329.25
1 oz.	384	76.80	96.00	115.20	134.40	153.60	192.00	230.40	288.00
1⅛ oz.	341	68.20	85.25	102.30	119.35	136.40	170.50	204.60	255.75
1¼ oz.	307	61.40	76.75	92.10	107.45	122.80	153.50	184.20	230.25
1⅜ oz.	280	56.00	70.00	84.00	98.00	112.00	140.00	168.00	210.00
1½ oz.	256	51.20	64.00	76.80	89.60	102.40	128.00	153.60	192.00

Cost Per Drink

Quarts		Cost Per Drink in Various Sized Glasses (Ounces)					Selling Price Per Drink at 2½ Times the Cost (150% Mark-Up) (Ounces)					Selling Price Per Drink at Triple the Cost (200% Mark-Up) (Ounces)				
Cost Per Case	Cost Per Bottle	¾	⅞	1	1¼	1½	¾	⅞	1	1¼	1½	¾	⅞	1	1¼	1½
$25.00	$2.08	.05	.06	.07	.08	.10	.12	.14	.16	.20	.25	.15	.17	.20	.24	.30
26.00	2.16	.05	.06	.07	.09	.10	.13	.15	.17	.21	.25	.15	.18	.21	.26	.30
27.00	2.25	.05	.06	.07	.09	.11	.14	.15	.18	.22	.26	.16	.18	.21	.27	.32
28.00	2.28	.06	.06	.07	.09	.11	.14	.16	.19	.23	.28	.17	.19	.22	.27	.33
29.00	2.41	.06	.07	.08	.10	.11	.14	.16	.19	.24	.29	.17	.20	.23	.29	.34
30.00	2.50	.06	.07	.08	.10	.12	.15	.17	.20	.24	.29	.18	.21	.24	.29	.35
31.00	2.58	.06	.07	.08	.10	.12	.15	.18	.20	.25	.30	.18	.21	.24	.30	.36
32.00	2.67	.06	.07	.08	.10	.13	.15	.18	.21	.26	.31	.18	.22	.25	.31	.38
33.00	2.75	.07	.08	.09	.11	.13	.16	.19	.21	.27	.32	.20	.23	.26	.33	.39
34.00	2.83	.07	.08	.09	.11	.13	.16	.20	.22	.28	.34	.20	.24	.27	.33	.40
35.00	2.91	.07	.08	.09	.12	.14	.17	.20	.23	.29	.34	.21	.24	.27	.35	.41
36.00	3.00	.07	.08	.09	.12	.14	.18	.21	.24	.29	.35	.21	.25	.28	.35	.42
37.00	3.08	.07	.08	.10	.12	.14	.18	.21	.24	.30	.36	.21	.25	.29	.36	.43
38.00	3.16	.07	.09	.10	.12	.15	.18	.21	.25	.31	.38	.21	.26	.30	.37	.45
39.00	3.25	.08	.09	.10	.13	.15	.19	.22	.25	.32	.39	.23	.27	.30	.39	.46
40.00	3.33	.08	.09	.10	.13	.16	.20	.23	.26	.33	.39	.24	.27	.31	.39	.47
41.00	3.42	.08	.09	.11	.13	.16	.20	.24	.26	.34	.40	.24	.28	.32	.40	.48

42.00	3.50	.50	.42	.33	.29	.25	.41	.35	.27	.24	.21	.17	.14	.11	.10	.08
43.00	3.58	.51	.42	.33	.30	.25	.42	.35	.28	.25	.21	.17	.14	.11	.10	.08
44.00	3.66	.52	.43	.35	.30	.26	.44	.36	.29	.25	.21	.17	.14	.12	.10	.09
45.00	3.75	.53	.44	.35	.31	.27	.44	.36	.29	.26	.22	.18	.15	.12	.11	.09
46.00	3.83	.54	.45	.36	.32	.27	.45	.38	.30	.26	.23	.18	.15	.12	.11	.09
47.00	3.91	.55	.46	.36	.32	.27	.46	.39	.30	.26	.23	.18	.15	.12	.11	.09
48.00	4.00	.57	.46	.38	.33	.28	.47	.39	.31	.28	.24	.19	.16	.13	.11	.09
49.00	4.08	.57	.48	.39	.34	.29	.48	.40	.32	.29	.24	.19	.16	.13	.11	.10
50.00	4.16	.59	.49	.39	.34	.30	.49	.41	.33	.29	.25	.20	.16	.13	.12	.10
51.00	4.25	.60	.50	.40	.35	.30	.50	.41	.34	.29	.25	.20	.17	.13	.12	.10
52.00	4.33	.61	.51	.41	.36	.30	.51	.42	.34	.30	.25	.20	.17	.14	.12	.10
53.00	4.41	.62	.51	.42	.36	.31	.51	.43	.35	.30	.26	.21	.17	.14	.12	.10
54.00	4.50	.63	.53	.42	.37	.32	.53	.44	.35	.31	.26	.21	.18	.14	.13	.11
55.00	4.58	.65	.54	.43	.38	.32	.54	.45	.36	.31	.26	.22	.18	.15	.13	.11
56.00	4.66	.66	.55	.44	.39	.33	.55	.46	.36	.32	.28	.22	.18	.15	.13	.11
57.00	4.75	.66	.56	.45	.39	.33	.55	.46	.37	.33	.28	.22	.19	.15	.13	.11
58.00	4.83	.68	.57	.45	.39	.34	.56	.47	.38	.33	.29	.23	.19	.15	.14	.11
59.00	4.91	.69	.57	.46	.41	.35	.58	.48	.39	.34	.29	.23	.19	.16	.14	.12
60.00	5.00	.70	.60	.47	.41	.35	.59	.49	.39	.34	.29	.23	.20	.16	.14	.12
61.00	5.08	.72	.60	.48	.42	.36	.60	.50	.40	.35	.30	.24	.20	.16	.14	.12
62.00	5.16	.72	.60	.48	.42	.36	.60	.50	.40	.35	.30	.24	.20	.16	.14	.12
63.00	5.25	.75	.62	.50	.44	.37	.61	.51	.41	.36	.30	.25	.21	.17	.15	.12
64.00	5.33	.76	.63	.51	.45	.38	.62	.51	.41	.36	.31	.25	.21	.17	.15	.13
65.00	5.41	.74	.61	.49	.43	.36	.64	.53	.42	.37	.31	.25	.21	.17	.15	.13

Here's Your Revenue

Per Fifth

PRICE PER DRINK	Glass Size					
	¾ oz.	⅞ oz.	1 oz.	1¼ oz.	1½ oz.	1¾ oz.
50¢	$17.00	$14.50	$12.75	$10.25	$ 8.50	$ 7.25
60¢	20.40	17.40	15.30	12.30	10.20	8.70
70¢	23.80	20.30	17.85	14.55	11.90	10.15
80¢	27.20	23.20	20.40	16.40	13.60	11.60
90¢	30.60	26.10	22.95	18.45	15.30	13.05
$1.00	34.00	29.00	25.50	20.50	17.00	14.50
$1.25	42.50	36.25	31.88	25.63	21.25	18.13
$1.50	51.00	43.50	38.25	30.75	25.50	21.75
$1.75	59.50	50.75	44.63	35.88	29.75	25.38
$2.00	68.00	58.00	51.00	41.00	34.00	29.00

Per Quart

PRICE PER DRINK	¾ oz.	⅞ oz.	1 oz.	1¼ oz.	1½ oz.	1¾ oz.
50¢	$21.50	$18.25	$16.00	$12.80	$10.65	$ 9.00
60¢	25.80	21.90	19.20	15.26	12.78	10.80
70¢	30.10	25.55	22.40	17.82	14.91	12.60
80¢	34.40	29.20	25.60	20.60	17.07	14.40
90¢	38.70	32.85	28.80	23.18	19.20	16.20
$1.00	43.00	36.50	32.00	25.75	21.33	18.00
$1.25	53.75	45.63	40.00	32.19	26.67	22.50
$1.50	64.50	54.75	48.00	38.63	32.00	27.00
$1.75	75.25	63.88	56.00	45.06	37.33	31.50
$2.00	86.00	73.00	64.00	51.50	42.67	36.00

Drinks Per Bottle or Case

GLASS SIZE	FIFTH	QUART	CASE FIFTHS	CASE QUARTS
¾ oz.	34	43	408	516
⅞ oz.	29	36½	348	438
1 oz.	25½	32	306	384
1¼ oz.	20½	25¾	246	309
1½ oz.	17	21⅓	204	256
1¾ oz.	14½	18	175	206

8 oz. = 1 Half Pint	32 oz. = 1 Quart
16 oz. = 1 Pint	64 oz. = 1 Half Gallon
25 3/5 oz. = 1 Fifth	128 oz. = 1 Gallon

How to Figure Gross Profits

Experience has proven that few businessmen know the difference between *Mark-up* and *Gross Profits*, thus cannot figure profits properly. Keep the following schedule before you and you will find it worth many dollars in the course of a year.

Mark-up—is the percentage of the amount you earn on COST.

How to Figure It—A brand cost you $50.00 a case and sells for $75.00 or $25.00 above your cost. Divide the cost ($50) into your earning ($25) and you will get a percentage of 50% . . . This is your MARK-UP on COST.

Gross Profit—is the percentage of the amount you earn on SELLING PRICE.

How to Figure It—A brand cost you $50.00 a case and sells for $75.00 or $25.00 above your cost. Divide the SELLING PRICE ($75) into your earnings ($25) and you get a percentage of 33⅓. This is your GROSS PROFIT on SELLING PRICE. This means you earn 33⅓ cents on each $1.00 in sales to apply to your expense of operation, which ultimately will show your net profit.

Mark-up	*Gross Profit*
5% added to cost is	4¾% profit on selling price
10% added to cost is	9 % profit on selling price
15% added to cost is	13 % profit on selling price
20% added to cost is	16⅓% profit on selling price
25% added to cost is	20 % profit on selling price
30% added to cost is	23 % profit on selling price
35% added to cost is	26 % profit on selling price
45% added to cost is	31 % profit on selling price
50% added to cost is	33⅓% profit on selling price
55% added to cost is	35½% profit on selling price
60% added to cost is	37½% profit on selling price
70% added to cost is	41 % profit on selling price
80% added to cost is	44½% profit on selling price
85% added to cost is	46 % profit on selling price
90% added to cost is	47½% profit on selling price
100% added to cost is	50 % profit on selling price

Customer Having Company? Use This Guide!

Number of People	Lunch	Cocktail Party	Dinner	Buffet Supper	Evening
for 4	8 cocktails 8 glasses light wine*	16 drinks an hour (first 2 hours) 12 drinks an hour thereafter	8 cocktails 8 glass of wine* 4 liqueurs* 8 drinks an hour during evening	12-16 cocktails 4 liqueurs* 8 drinks an hour during evening	16 drinks
for 6	12 cocktails 12 glasses of wine* 1 Sherry	24 drinks an hour (first 2 hours) 18 drinks an hour thereafter	12 cocktails 12 glasses of wine* 6 liqueurs* 12 drinks an hour during evening	18-24 cocktails 6 liqueurs* 12 drinks an hour during evening	24 drinks
for 8	16 cocktails 16 glasses of wine* 1-2 glasses of Sherry	32 drinks an hour (first 2 hours) 26 drinks an hour thereafter	16 cocktails 16 glass of wine* 8 liqueurs* 16 drinks an hour during evening	24-32 cocktails 8 liqueurs* 16 drinks an hour during evening	40 drinks
for 10	20 cocktails 20 glasses of wine* 2 Sherry	40 drinks an hour (first 2 hours) 34 drinks an hour thereafter	20 cocktails 20 glasses of wine* 10 liqueurs* 20 drinks an hour during evening	30-40 cocktails 10 liqueurs* 20 drinks an hour during evening	50 drinks
for 20	40 cocktails 40 glasses of wine* 4 Sherry	80 drinks an hour (first 2 hours) 72 drinks an hour thereafter	40 cocktails 40 glasses of wine* 20 liqueurs* 40 drinks an hour during evening	60-80 cocktails 20 liqueurs* 40 drinks an hour during evening	100 drinks

*Optional

How Many Drinks from a Fifth Bottle

Whiskey
  16 Highballs
  14 Manhattans
   8 Juleps
  16 Sours
  16 Old Fashioneds

Gin
  16 Tom Collins
  14 Martinis
  16 Fizzes

Rum
  16 Daiquiris
  16 Rum Collins
  16 Rum Coolers

Vodka
  16 Screwdrivers
  16 Bloody Marys
  14 Martinis

Brandy
  16 Highballs

Sweet Vermouth
  28 Manhattans

Cordials
  25 After-dinner
     drinks

Dry Vermouth
  56 Martinis

Champagne
  7 Drinks

Sherry
  16 Drinks

For quarts add 25% to the number of drinks above

Number of Servings in Various Container Sizes

		Liquors	
Number of Bottles		1 oz. Drink	1½ oz. Drink
1 case Quarts		384	256
1 case Fifths		307	204
1 bottle Quart		32	21
1 bottle Fifth		25	17
1 bottle Pint		16	10
1 bottle Tenth		12	8

Wines

Dessert, Appetizer Wine, Quart (32 oz.)—Serves 16 drinks of 2 oz. each.

Dessert, Appetizer Wines, Fifth (25.6 oz.)—Serves 12 drinks of 2 oz. each.

Table Wines, Fifth or Bottle (25.6 oz. or 24 oz.)—Serves 3 to 4 persons.

Table Wines, Half-bottle (12 oz. or 12.8 oz.)—Serves 2 persons.

Champagne, Fifth or Bottle (25.6 oz. or 26 oz.)—Serves 6 to 8 persons.

Champagne, Tenth or Half-bottle (12.8 oz. or 13 oz.)—Serves 3 to 4 persons.

18

Nuisances, Pests, and Trouble

It's going on toward evening on your first day of operation. You've served one hundred drinks and now find you have a couple of obnoxious drunks on your hands. What do you do?

Serving an obviously intoxicated person is a bad mistake. If caught, you are liable for administrative action by the state board, who could suspend or revoke your license. Even worse, you might be liable for a ruinous civil lawsuit under the Dram Shop laws, explained in the section of this book under insurance. Even if you do have insurance protection, it would be a prolonged, nasty procedure, and an astronomical judgment, far exceeding your limits, could be handed against you, wiping you out. Even if you had complete protection, your insurance carrier would probably raise your premiums enormously or cancel your policy. So serving an obvious drunk, even one you know well, is just not worth it.

It is against the law in California to serve an "habitual" or "common" drunkard. This is another regulation which seems to me grossly unfair to the publican. The way the rule reads, this man cannot be served, even if he hasn't had a drink all day. How is the bartender supposed to know the man is a common drunk? Doctors, theologians, scientists, and politicians have been arguing for years about what constitutes an alcoholic. Nobody seems to agree, but the lowly saloonkeeper is supposed to know.

Of course, in most cases the out-and-out common drunkard with his stupefied look, and the obnoxious drunk with his loud mouth are easily spotted. The problem comes in the borderline cases. A customer may come in holding himself very well, very quiet and dignified. He'll order one drink from you and promptly fall apart. He got drunk someplace else and knew his only chance of getting another from you was by holding himself together, if only for five minutes. All he wanted to do was con that one drink from you, knowing that once he got it in his hand you would have a hard time getting it back from him. Unless he is really offensive, you'll probably have to let him finish it, then refuse him further service. I would try to make sure at least one other person in the place noticed the occurrence, just in case the drunk later gets in a smashup. Then you have a witness that he got himself drunk someplace else. If he is coherent, I'd try to find out where he'd been before he got to my place, for my defense in the event anything untoward later happened.

More often than this you may serve somebody who doesn't seem at all intoxicated, but later turns out to have a legally intoxicating blood count. The California Board of Alcoholic Beverage Control outlined to me their position on this matter (which is parallel to their position on serving minors). There can be mitigating circumstances. It boils down to, "Would a reasonable person think he was intoxicated?" There must be negligence before the board will take administrative action. In order for there to be a strong case for a civil suit, there is usually an administrative action by the ABC. You have recourse to an appeal, where you can try to prove that a reasonable person would have acted as you did. If you have reasonable doubt, then do not serve that customer.

To be cut off from further service and asked to leave the premises is called in bar jargon to be 86'd. Since they are public premises, the 86 can rightfully be imposed only for intoxication, illegality, or misconduct, not simply because you don't like the man's looks.

The term may have come from an old waiters' ordering code when food and drinks were ordered by numbers. When the waiter told the bartender that so-and-so wanted a Number 86, it meant he was to get nothing. Another theory is that 86 was the number of some archaic penal code provision.

In today's practice, the 86 is ambiguous. Strictly speaking, it means that the miscreant is barred from the premises for life. Sometimes, though, it means that his drinking privileges are suspended only for a certain length of time, say a week or a month, after which he can return if he mends his behavior. Sometimes it means only that the customer must leave for the present, but can come back the next day or whenever he sobers up. In any event, he is finished for the time being.

Drunks are usually argumentative and irrational. Don't get involved in long discussions why they have to be cut off. Be polite but firm. Don't threaten or cry wolf about refusing them service. Just announce it quietly and do it. Almost always when they know you mean it, they will pack up and leave, not always in very good graces, but they will usually go. Try to do it as inconspicuously as possible and without making a big public issue of it, so their pride won't compel them to make a show of defiance.

The 86 means a customer has been refused service, or as it is sometimes called, thrown out. Nowadays this is used figuratively, not literally. The owner and his bartenders should never get in physical beefs with anyone. Don't come round from behind the bar. Warn the obnoxious drunk that he is cut off. Ask him to leave and come back tomorrow or whenever, but don't put a hand on him. First you say:

"I think you've had enough. Can I call you a taxi?"

If you know him, josh him a little, say that you're not going to contribute anymore to his monumental hangover tomorrow. If he still won't move, then be firm. Request sternly that he leave. Sometimes you must order him to leave. The bartender is king in his own joint, and any seasoned drinker knows that the bartender has the final say on who drinks and who does not drink in his place. By this I refer only to sobriety and propriety. The only persons who are refused service are those who break the law or annoy other customers.

Finally, you make a phony call to the police. Make it openly and loud enough so the pest can hear exactly what you are saying. Ninety-nine times out of a hundred he'll just pack up and leave. Make an actual telephone call to the police only as the last resort. They don't enjoy nuisance calls, or arriving after a drunk has left.

If the pest does hang around but doesn't give the patrolmen any lip, they'll probably just get him out of your place and on his way home. Usually they won't book a man unless he cuts up with them or is really impossible, so you're not really finking on him, rather you are doing him a favor by calling the cops. Sure, the recollection will be painful the next morning, but it won't be nearly the real bad trouble he might have got himself into.

The police are paid to protect us, so we shouldn't take the law into our own hands. Also, if you or your bartender lays on hands, you might be liable for a juicy lawsuit. Whether you're right or wrong doesn't always matter. It will be a bloody, costly nuisance in any event, which does nobody any good. The only exception, when you should intervene or come round the bar, is when men are fighting with fists or weapons so that bystanders are in physical danger.

I like to have the cops in my joint. I get along well with them. They know me, and if I ever needed them they'd get here fast. If anybody wants to commit any mayhem, he'll probably know that some of Mooney's best friends are cops, so he'll do it someplace else.

One night I was having a few friendly snorts at the end of the bar with a couple of friends. Some fellow I don't even recollect having seen before upped to me and offered to poke me in the snoot for being a cheap Mick bastard. I said:

"Friend, look round you. There are at least thirty guys in this bar now. Every one of them is a pal of mine. What's more, two guys down at the other end are off-duty cops. If you really want to punch me in the nose, you've sure as hell chosen the worst place in the world to do it."

He left immediately and quietly. I've never seen him again.

But you can't count on the police being in your place all the time. I did get poked in the nose once. Here's what Herb Caen wrote in the *San Francisco Chronicle* a couple of days later:

> That Sutter St. lawyer who got overloaded at Sean Mooney's Pub Tuesday night and bloodied Sean's nose with a surprise attack is one lucky guy; Mooney has elected to forget it.

It just wasn't worth the trouble. He had to live with himself the next morning knowing that he was the prize horse's ass of the week and that all his friends, if any, knew it.

Probably a retail liquor store needs a weapon such as a pistol or sawed-off baseball bat handy, but don't have such a thing around a bar. The difference is that there are other people in a bar. You should never have a weapon unless you are firmly committed to use it. If you are held up, give them the cash with a smile. Usually the police will pick up an armed robber of a bar within hours. Don't risk your life and that of your customers for such a paltry thing as pride or a few hundred dollars. Most robbers these days are on heroin or some other dope and are legally insane at the time. They are irrational and scared and unpredictable. Don't fool with them.

One night a while ago I was drinking in what is probably the best-managed bar in San Francisco. An obnoxious, drunken stranger was pestering, among others, one of the town's best-known newspaper columnists and one of the leading editors. Bad for business. I signaled the off-duty bar manager, Seamus, who came over and started talking with the fellow. Now Seamus is a pretty stout Dubliner with a pretty hefty paunch. As he argle-bargled with the man, he kept belly bumping him, a bit at a time. He belly bumped him through the front door, down the corridor. The next thing the fellow knew he was standing on the street, alone, and Seamus had never laid a hand on him. No hands, no cops, no violence, no fuss.

Incidentally, it is commonly assumed that Irishmen spend most of their time getting drunk and fighting in bars. The latter half of this, at least, is simply not true in Ireland, where it is a universal rule that fist fighting or physical violence in a barroom

automatically rules you out from re-entering that bar. You can
never return *under any circumstances.* I have never witnessed a
fist fight in a pub in Ireland.

A customer who has been refused service and has been
asked to leave will often claim that you, the owner or bartender,
have no right to do so and will perhaps also further claim that
you are "discriminating" against him. He will be wrong. Our
laws on the matter stem from an English decision of 1834 which
states:

> If a man comes into a public-house, and conducts himself in a
> disorderly manner, and the landlord requests him to go out,
> and he will not, the landlord may turn him out. There is no
> doubt that a landlord may turn out a person who is making a
> disturbance in a public-house, though such a disturbance
> does not amount to a breach of the peace.

It has been held that it is the duty of an innkeeper to accord
protection to his patrons from insult or annoyance. In putting a
stop to the annoyance, he may eject the person guilty of the
offense *and in so doing may use all necessary force.*

The general rule is that the proprietor of a public place of
business, such as a restaurant, is not an insurer of a patron
against personal injuries inflicted by other persons on the premises who are in no manner connected with the business, but is
liable therefore only when he is negligent. However, *American
Jurisprudence, Innkeepers* states, "He is guilty of negligence if
he admits to his place or permits to remain there, as a guest, a
person of known violent and disorderly propensities, who will
probably assault or otherwise maltreat his guests; and he may
be liable in damages for the consequences of such negligence."

Next to drunks, your greatest source of potential trouble
will be minors. Different states have different ages for minors,
but usually it is a person below either eighteen or twenty-one
years of age. Excepting variation in age limits, most states will
have a law similar to California's, which states:

> Anyone who sells or gives liquor to a minor is guilty of a
> misdemeanor. Any on-sale licensee who knowingly permits a
> minor to consume liquor on the premises is guilty of a mis-
> demeanor. A minor who purchases or consumes liquor in a

licensed premise is guilty of a misdemeanor and must be fined at least $100, no part of which shall be suspended.

A licensee or his employees may refuse to serve anyone who refuses to produce documentary evidence he or she is over twenty-one.

Documents regarded as evidence of majority include draft cards, auto operator's licenses, and military ID cards. Proof that the licensee or employee demanded and was shown such evidence and relied upon it shall be a defense in any criminal prosecution or license disciplinary proceeding.

Anyone who furnishes a fraudulent identification card to a minor is guilty of a misdemeanor and so is a minor who uses one to buy liquor. And the minor shall be fined at least $100, with no part suspended. It is unlawful for an on-sale licensee to employ a minor during business hours in the specific area of his place used for the sale of alcoholic beverages. Any minor who loiters in an establishment licensed as a public premise is guilty of a misdemeanor (with the same penalty).

All this is quite clear. When there is any reasonable doubt at all about a customer's age, always ask for ID. If he doesn't have proper identification on him, including a photograph, and if you serve him a drink, you are 100 percent liable. If he hasn't ID, don't serve him.

Very few bars can afford to pay a man the minimum wage to stand at the door to check ID's, so part of the cocktail waitress's job is to check them before she serves anything. Once you get caught serving a minor, you can expect the liquor control board to check your place weekly.

(Note: A minor can never be in an on-sale public premises of the type of license we have been concerned with. A minor, however, can come in an on-sale general bona fide restaurant, but may not drink any alcoholic beverage there.)

In California and most, if not all, other states, excepting Nevada, any form of betting in a bar is illegal. In San Francisco playing dice for drinks is tolerated. It is not in Los Angeles. In Seattle it is allowed to play poker dice on the serial numbers of currency. Even where these forms of wagering are tolerated, the authorities do not permit betting for money with the money on the bar, in the open.

Many places have football pools. Make sure the police will

not kick up if you have one. Most decent places have a pool which pays out 100 percent, merely as a game for the good customers. If you shave the odds to make an operating profit on the pool, the police will probably dislike it.

Never run a book or permit your telephone to be used for placing bets of any sort. What you might make is never worth the risk of losing your valuable liquor license. If you allow professional betting, you run the risk of being labeled a "disorderly house," and the authorities are required to "abate" you, that is, put you out of the business for good.

In San Francisco most owners allow their bartenders to roll poker dice against customers *if the customer requests the game.* Poker, or boss, dice is almost totally a game of chance, if there is no cheating. Liar's dice and other variations are more games of skill, so often the bartender cannot engage in these. It is damn near impossible to *prove* that somebody is cheating, so you can't very well accuse a man whom you suspect. If you have a good reason to suspect anyone, just collect all the dice boxes from the bar on some pretext such as you have a headache and the noise is bothering you. The cheater will get the message. Try to avoid trouble over gambling.

If the police permit dice, remember the customer is wagering the *price* of his drink against the *cost* of your drink.

Vandalism, or malicious mischief, is a problem which you will just have to accept or suffer with. You repair the damage and try to forget it. Otherwise the wear and tear on your nerves and temper will be badly aggravated because this sort of damage is so pointless and unnecessary. Nobody benefits by it, as opposed to theft, say, where the thief hopes to profit. That is understandable; vandalism isn't.

The commonest form of malicious mischief is scribbling on the washroom walls. This nuisance has been around quite a while. The word for it, "graffiti," dates from Roman and Pompeiian times. Obviously, there is no way of stopping it. Customers who get angry at you or just angry in general often will flush a roll of toilet paper in the commode, plugging the plumbing. They also tear soap dispensing fixtures from the wall. For this reason, I don't have these fixtures, but use instead small bars of soap.

Vandals will cut the upholstery of chairs, burn holes in your rugs, and commit other similar unpleasantnesses. I shrug and ponder the stupidity of some people, then have the damage repaired. It's just part of the price you pay for running a pub.

Everyone must stop drinking, all drinks must be taken from the bar, and everybody not employed in the bar must leave by closing time. In California that is 2 AM, and the authorities don't mean 2:01 AM or 2:10 AM. Don't allow any customer to stack drinks prior to closing time and then try to tell you it is okay for him to hang around after closing time because he bought the drinks legally. It is not. All drinks must be cleared off the bar and everybody must clear out. Otherwise they are loitering.

Many bars set their clocks ahead five or ten minutes for obvious reasons. Others ring a bell. The bartender should always give his customers warning that closing hour is approaching along the line of the traditional English, "Time, Gentlemen!" He must make sure the customers leave promptly, and then lock his door.

19

The Next Day

Note: Cashing out and keeping an accurate record of your receipts is a vital part of your business. I'd say that most failures in the bar business originate in lax procedure here. I cash out every morning almost automatically. Everything in this chapter is perfectly clear to me, but, unfortunately, it is almost impossible to explain clearly and simply enough for you to do it yourself right off the bat. I think you can learn cashing out only by doing it yourself. For your first few days in business, you should have either your accountant or an old-timer in the bar business sit at your bar and instruct you in a do-it-yourself course. It's similar to learning how to play tennis. You can teach yourself, but you will probably pick up some wrong habits you can never rid yourself of. It is far better to have a professional instruct you at first, so that your habits, or method, will be properly ingrained from the outset.

Your cash register will play an important part in your future operation. You could collect for drinks and make change out of an old tin box, but besides being more efficient, there's something about a noisy cash register that seems to demand being fed constantly. You can delegate a great deal of authority to your employees, as I do, but you should take the responsibility of cashing out the previous day's receipts yourself.

You should make this an invariable morning routine. If you get into a habit of cashing out each day, after awhile it becomes a normal part of your daily routine to head first for your cash register and start counting the money taken in the day before. You've never seen a Catholic walk into a church without blessing himself first. It's all part of early training and stays with you indefinitely.

All money going in or out of your establishment should pass through your cash register. Memory is fallible, especially in the presence of alcohol fumes. The register is an ingenious and adaptable machine, which will be your best servant, because it will give you a printed record of all your cash transactions. If you don't make your cash out *every* morning, you will probably get your affairs so bollixed up that you won't really even want to know where you stand. By that time you'll be a candidate for the night Greyhound to Tijuana.

The easiest way to keep your daily record is with a plain envelope. Printed envelopes for the purpose are available, but are somewhat involved and are liable to confuse a relief cashier, if you are on vacation or not there for some other reason. Your first step is to count all the silver. All the change remains in the register every day. If the business was good the day before, you'll probably have to add to the quarters, dimes, and nickels remaining in the drawer. On a clean piece of paper you start a column on the extreme *left*-hand side with the figure for the total amount of your change. All money that is going to stay in the register goes in that same left-hand column. This is going to be part of your bank* to start the current day's business.

Next you count the one-dollar bills. For our purposes you may want to have, say, one hundred dollars in singles in the register bank. Put that amount in the left-hand column.

---

*The terminology here is confusing. Your bank in this instance is the money remaining in your register from which you do business, make change, and so forth. Your bank is also the commercial bank where you have your checking account. To make the distinction absolutely clear I'll refer to your register bank and your commercial bank.

Now count the five-dollar bills. Seventy-five dollars in fives ought to be adequate. Enter the $75 in the left-hand column. All other money and checks go in the right-hand column. So:

March 15

Left column	*Right column*
$ 32.50 change	$ 40.00 five-dollar bills
100.00 one-dollar bills	100.00 ten-dollar bills
75.00 five-dollar bills	80.00 twenty-dollar bills
	65.00 checks
$207.50 Total	$285.00 Total

I don't keep any ten or twenty dollar bills in my register bank.

The $207.50 left in the register is your register bank for today's business. You have enough one and five dollar bills, but you are short on change so must add to it. You add $34 in rolls of quarters, dimes, and nickels, making your total register bank $241.50. The $34 can come from one of two places. You can take it out of your gross receipts the day before, or as your accountant would prefer, you deposit the $285 and write a check for the change needed for today's business.

The $285.00 in right column should be deposited in your checking account at your commercial bank and entered in the deposit column in your checkbook. You should keep an accurate running balance in your checkbook at all times. Your commercial bank will send you a statement every month. Balance your checkbook with this statement to ensure accuracy in your account.

All cash payouts should be written on a piece of paper, or a receipt should be in the register in lieu of the cash paid out. Here is what a typical envelope should look like.

March 16

Tape	$240.00
Paid out	
Sugar	1.95
Cream	1.04
	2.99

Cash in register	478.51
Previous day's	241.50
	‾‾‾‾‾‾
Bank (Subtract)	237.01
Paid out (add)	2.99
	‾‾‾‾‾‾
	$240.00

Your cash is accurate today, nothing short, nothing over. This is unusual. Normally it will be off a small sum, usually somewhere between 50 cents and $1.50.

Bank March 17 $235.00

The size of your register bank will depend on the amount of business you think you are going to do. The bank normally will be considerably higher on Fridays and Saturdays.

There are many different types of cash registers. Whatever kind you have when you buy the place will probably have a tab noting the name and phone number of the selling or maintenance company. Phone them and ask for the boss. Tell him you would like to retain the service, but that you are not familiar with a couple of aspects of the machine. He will be happy to send someone out to explain it to you. (If there is no tab attached, then phone the representative of the manufacturer.) With a new register, the selling company will be more than pleased to explain its various functions.

You should learn how to replace the register tape with some facility. If it runs out on you, you can bet it will do so at your busiest time, say six o'clock Saturday night. When green marking appears on the tape, it means you have about enough left for one more day. As soon as I see the green marking come up, I change the tape the first slack time I have.

A register can issue an itemized, mechanically added receipt; it will print separate and total charges on a waitress's checks; and it will accumulate separate totals of various kinds of information for your daily verification.

Your register should have a detail audit strip (the inside tape) which is your basic, printed record of all sales. A machine which merely shows a total won't do. You want to keep each day's tape in your daily envelope. At the end of the month, you give all the daily envelopes to your accountant for verification and processing. The machine may also have an outside tape, which can be torn off with each sale and given to the customer as a receipt. It may also have a slot in which hard cardboard checks may be itemized, although this is usually necessary only in a bar-restaurant.

Here you will complete the third part of inventory control. From your cash register tape, you will know the amount of money you have taken in daily. From your pricing tables, you can determine what the liquor *cost* you. By totaling the ingredients used in making the drinks that have been sold, added to the unused stock behind the bar, you must equal the goods that have been charged to the bar. This added to the stock in your store room is your total inventory. In other words, the bar's inventory must be there in either stock or sales.

Cash sales + Stock inventory = Total liquor purchased and received.

Cashing out is your most vital job each morning, but there are some other tasks which must be attended to. These, like cashing out, can be done after closing the night before, or as outlined here, before opening for business the following morning.

The bar must be swamped out. This means the clean-up or janitorial work. The night bartender is expected to leave the bar tidy, with glasses and ashtrays washed, fruit and juice put in the refrigerator. He locks the cases and secures the premises before he leaves. Still, more intensive cleaning is necessary on a daily basis in an orderly bar operation.

You can do the swamping yourself; hire a swamper (janitor); or engage a reputable, bonded maintenance company (you will have to give them a key to your front door). Whichever method of clean-up you settle for, you should pay special attention to the washrooms, particularly the women's. One visit to a dirty or untidy restroom will often drive a woman—and her escort or escorts—out of your place *permanently*. Neglect of the ladies room is one good easy way to lose valuable business.

If you don't have a female employee to do it, you personally should take a look into this restroom at least once every several hours your place is open for business and set everything that needs it to rights. There is no necessity to elaborate on how a spic and span restroom should appear.

I would say that an adequate ventilating system in both restrooms is essential.

Never run out of toilet paper. That would be almost as bad as running out of ice. It could lose you customers permanently. Check also your supply of soap and towels. Running out of those isn't as critical as running out of toilet paper, but it is a big nuisance to customers.

A woman will be thankful to you, in the case of an emergency, if your restroom has a machine to dispense items of "feminine daintiness." A machine is available which dispenses both the Modess and the Tampax types.

The duckboards should be taken up behind the bar and the area sluiced down thoroughly (hence, the term "swamper"). At least once a week the back bar area should have a good, healthy shot of disinfectant in the swamping water. Everything should be rinsed thoroughly, an operation which is often sluffed off.

All floors should be vacuumed or mopped and the place, generally, should look the way you'd want your living room to look.

You should have your garbage collected as often as possible, preferably every day. In most localities you have to put the cans out on the sidewalk to be emptied. Do this after closing because stale beer stinks to high heaven and other odors, such as stale fruit and whiskey, are far from pleasant. Usually you can't leave the cans standing on the sidewalk during the daytime, so you can put them out only the night before the next scheduled garbage collection.

The swamper should sweep and hose down the front sidewalk every morning. The front windows should be kept clean. Make sure the lights, if any, in your sign all work.

Finally, before you open your doors for the day, replenish the stock of liquor and other supplies behind the bar by bringing what you need in from your store room. After you have been in business for a few days, you'll have a pretty accurate idea of what quantities of what items you'll need. It's much easier to have an adequate stock behind the bar before you open, than to have to keep running to the store room during the hours of business. Now is the time, also, to prepare your handy supply of ice.

At last you are ready to throw your doors open to welcome your happy customers. Chances are, though, that your early customers won't be too happy, especially if you open in the morning.

How many times does a bartender hear those familiar words, "Oh, my God! Never again. I've had the last drink I'm ever going to take." Class-A hangovers combine a ghastly upset stomach, a splitting headache, a throbbing heart, horrible guilt feelings, an empty wallet, and a pocketful of small change. No one yet has died of the whips and jangles, but everyone who has them suspects he might become the first recorded fatality. With these really bad ones, the victim can't remember clearly what he did wrong the night before, but he knows whatever he did must have been perfectly awful. A mallet is pounding his inner skull, and he has a mouth which tastes like the Russian cavalry bivouacked there overnight. He doesn't remember which friend's wife he insulted or where he left his car. A seasoned barkeep has some answer to these problems, and is quiet and patient while listening to the long, doleful spiel.

There is a vast literature written on supposed hangover cures. Probably there is no genuine cure except time and rest, but there are alleviations. The best undoubtedly is a good healthy draught of pure oxygen, but no bar is going to have a tank of this on hand.

Hangovers can be relieved by aspirin or similar pain killers. Many a drinker will pop a couple of aspirins in his gullet before he leaves on his way to the bar. This is more of a preventative than a cure, but it usually results in a less severe hangover.

Practicing medicine without a license is something that all self-respecting barkeeps can be accused of. I have prevented the start of many a bad session of flu by advising a glass of hot water, sugar, Irish whiskey, a healthy twist of lemon, and two aspirins. Then straight home to bed. It works if you take only one. If you try to kill the bug by drowning it in liquor, not only do you finish up sweating and shaking for a few days, but you have to suffer through a monumental hangover to boot.

A large bottle of aspirin is a must behind the bar. A couple of years ago a six-foot-four-inch-tall, bald-headed, black man came into my bar. He drives a cab. His father was one of the all-time great American boxers. It was a Sunday and I had been watching Oral Roberts on the telly. This big man asked me if I could give him six aspirins. I, myself, have taken only about six in my entire life. Astounded, I said, "Six aspirins? Is the whole family sick?" He said no. There were beads of sweat on his forehead and he was obviously in pain. He said he suffered from chronic migraine headaches and took forty aspirin a day. That did it. I decided if Oral Roberts could do it, I'd have a try myself. I grabbed the aspirin bottle, came out from behind the bar, placed my hand on his shoulder, opened the bottle, and with a flourish threw my arms in the air, and let out a roar, "Brother, you and I are going to stamp the Devil out of your head, today, right now." I threw the aspirin on the floor and started jumping on them. He was startled, but sensing my enthusiasm, promptly joined me. We danced together until there was nothing but powder on the floor.

"Your headache is gone, Brother," I yelled with conviction, placing my hands on his head.

He comes in every week, looks adoringly at me. He hasn't had a headache since. He wants to pay my way to New Orleans to cure his niece. He's convinced that I'm a saint.

The bartender is often confronted with the question, "What should I have to get rid of this lousy hangover?" Taking drink to cure drink is called "Having a hair of the dog that bit you." If you take enough, continuing for several days, it will have a pyramiding effect, getting progressively worse, until about all you can do is turn yourself in to a hospital or drunk clinic. Taken in moderation, though, a few hairs can make life bearable until bedtime allows you to get in some effective recuperation.

A beer or two is good, especially for an upset stomach. Stout or ale are better, preferably chilled rather than at room temperature. A Bloody Mary, extra spiced, is about the most popular hangover special. A Ramos Fizz is probably even better. A lot of people want a vodka with either orange or grapefruit juice. That's dandy to quench the Saharan thirst, but it adds one hell of a lot more acid to a stomach already overloaded on acid.

It's commonly thought that the odor of vodka can't be detected on a person's breath. I think it would be more accurate to say that it can't be easily detected. Vodka is just alcohol and water minus the substances which appear in other liquors. A couple of years ago the president of a large corporation circulated this memo to all his sales staff.

"If you must drink at lunch, drink whiskey, not vodka. I would rather have our customers think you are drunk, not stupid."

A vanilla milkshake is good for a queasy stomach. In southern France they prescribe Pernod and bouillabaisse. The notorious French Foreign Legion recommends a rich French onion soup with Gruyere cheese, croutons, and plenty of fresh cracked black pepper. In Paris's swank Relais-Plaza bar, they swear by steak Tartare (raw chopped beefsteak) with plenty of cracked pepper and capers, washed down with a half-bottle of excellent champagne. Doctors, dentists, frogmen, and pilots have access to the best remedy, as stated, fresh oxygen.

The most unusual remedy I ever heard of came from a Liverpool friend who insisted that sexual intercourse relieved him of a hangover. This remedy might be okay for Superman, but for any ordinary barfly it's highly farfetched.

Along with a hangover, you have the accompanying fetid breath. There are lots of chlorophyll lozenges and gums you can buy, but I think that nothing can approach a handful of plain fresh parsley. It is readily available, inexpensive, effective, and natural. It is rich not only in cholorophyll, but also in iron. The next best cure for alcohol on the breath is to chew fresh lemon rind.

By far the most terrible tasting remedy is Fernet Branca.

It's an Italian mixture of alcohol and herbs and root extracts. It has worked, though, since 1845.

Finally, you will always get customers with the hiccoughs. There are many diverse remedies for this affliction. There is a story in Ireland that a recent Pope had the hiccoughs for ninety days. They had specialists in from all over the world to cure him, even an Indian guru. Nothing worked. Finally, the hiccoughs went away by themselves. If the Pope can't get a cure, then who can? I have one which has always worked. I don't know why, but it has. The victim stops up both ears firmly with his little fingertips. With his thumbs he closes his nostrils firmly. Then I feed him an entire glass of plain water. This is a messy procedure, but it's never failed me. Pity they didn't call me over to Rome to try it on the Pope.

Charles McCabe, San Francisco's leading wit, dandy, rake, Whig, essayist, and columnist, came into Mooney's Irish Pub, while this book was being written, with a bad case of hiccoughs. Mooney attempted to pull the above cure for this dread disease. McCabe, who emphasizes that he was born in New York not the Ould Sod, exclaimed indignantly:

"That 'cure' is just another example of your pretentious Irish superstition, Mooney. I can cure this myself without you spilling water down my waistcoat."

He pulled his substantial abdomen taut and held his breath until his face started turning purple. Then he exhaled in a gust. Presto! Damned if his hiccoughs weren't cured. I think the real cure for hiccoughs is to get your mind completely off them, that is, total distraction.

20

Board of Trade

The Board of Trade is a credit adjustment association of downtown merchants. One creditor's complaint can "put you in the Board of Trade." They call you in and tell you you haven't been paying your bills. Usually it is on the complaint of one or more liquor distributors.

The one good thing about going into the Board of Trade is that at least you've got a shot at getting out of trouble. They are going to give you a break if you've got any kind of legitimate reason for staying in business. They'll try to help you. If you tell them, "I know I owe $5,000. I'll pay you $300 a month on it," they'll probably go along with the deal, providing the creditors accept it. It's a terrible shock to be put in the Board of Trade, but if you go back to work and keep your commitments to them, you'll likely have your place back running smoothly in a while. Immediately when you go in the Board, the news is all around the city, so fast that everybody knows it. Automatically nobody will sell you anything, so you're stuck. Once you go in the Board you're on a C.O.D. basis. That is, you must pay cash on delivery for everything on top of paying off your back debt monthly at the figure you agreed with the Board. Hopefully, in no time at all you're on your feet again.

It's terrifying when you go in the Board of Trade, but it's a great feeling when you come out. The Board of Trade, despite its official-sounding title, is not a governmental agency or an arm of the law, and you, as a debtor, are not subject to its will. It is a voluntary adjustment association of creditors, connected with the National Association of Credit Management, who have supplied the list of credit adjustment bureaus in other cities in the United States (see Appendix G).

With only rare and unusual exceptions, a bar owner will be the debtor, or defendant, in any situation involving pecuniary debt (excepting bar bills owed by customers) so you might wonder at the emphasis I place on this Board. It patently represents creditors, who will be your adversaries if you get into debt. My emphasis is because one or more of your creditors might sue you and force you into bankruptcy court. Say you are long overdue with payments to ten different firms. One alone could decide to sue you quickly to get first crack at all your assets. The other nine aren't going to like this at all. This is the *real* reason for the existence of the Board of Trade, not mere Christian benevolence toward debtors. If you are forced into bankruptcy or take shelter in voluntary bunkruptcy, you will lose your business and most likely all your other tangible assets (which may not be distributed equitably among your creditors). By cooperating with the Board you stand a chance of retaining your business and reinstating a favorable credit standing.

The Board declares that it benefits creditors "by providing facilities for prompt and efficient adjustments of the affairs of embarrassed or insolvent debtors . . . by getting creditors together and having them act as a body, thereby preventing precipitate and unwise action by individual creditors and attempted preferences, thus *avoiding numerous bankruptcies*." (Italics mine.)

While designed to benefit the creditors, it can be seen that this will also benefit the debtor. They state this slightly differently, saying that the Board "provides a common meeting place for creditors where they may jointly consider and adjust their debtors' affairs *without court intervention.*" (Italics mine.) This "preserves the businesses of embarrassed but solvent debtors and liquidates insolvent ones expeditiously and economically." "*It* [the Board] *does not handle individual collections.*"

The Board always operates through creditors or creditors' committees which are in full and exclusive control of the cases in their charge. Keeping this in mind, it might be worthwhile to quote in full from their brochure the section, "How Does It Benefit the Debtor?"

> By making it possible for him to meet his creditors out of court and informally, yet giving him assurance of an orderly and fair consideration of his difficulties. By providing him with the advice and assistance of experienced merchants or their credit managers whose money is in his business and whose interest in its preservation is second only to his own. By affording a recognized and responsible medium through which he and his creditors can get together and mutually decide upon terms of settlement as circumstances may warrant. By obtaining for him a release from his obligations without the stigma of bankruptcy, if his business is insolvent and must be liquidated and his failure has been an honest one.

If you can't or don't want to get together with these people, you'd better call in your attorney (if you haven't already done so) because your next dance is going to be a waltz to the bankruptcy court. I take leave of you here because I'm not qualified to give advice on such a tricky legal subject. I can tell you though that dozens of my pals who are now salaried employees behind the plank were at one time, not too long in the past, open-handed, well-beloved owners of popular bars. Most of them are divorced; many read the Racing Form religiously; and almost all of them still love to hand out drinks on the house.

I've covered most of the ways you can land yourself in the soup and how to try to avoid them. One common cause of difficulty, though, I've only touched on. That is partnerships.

A partnership can lead to differences of opinion and animosity in any line of business, but the chances of it are magnified in ours by the omnipresence of liquor. If you and your partners are sober, God-fearing men who follow neither the horses nor strange women you will have no extraordinary difficulties in the bar business. However, if only one partner subscribes to even one of these expensive vices—as would seem likely, given the nature of the majority attracted to this trade—you have potential trouble caused by the dilution of prudence by alcohol, plus the proximity of ready cash.

A reasonably honest bartender won't be likely to skim currency out of the till—with or without leaving an IOU—to finance an evening's revelry with an available young lady left over at the bar, proposing to replace it (the money not the lady) the next day—then forgetting about it. A partner more often will, since, damn it all, isn't it his money anyway?

Again, a partner may have a sick headache each and every morning, precluding him from doing his share of opening the bar.

One can think of all sorts of problems inherent in any type of partnership. Remember, though, that alcohol is not a stimulant. It is a depressant, largely in the sense that it reduces inhibitions; thence the conscience; thence judgment. Small differences between friends and partners can usually be resolved by reason and good judgment, but when these are distorted by the old booze a small difference can become an insuperable problem.

As I implied at the beginning of this book, tolerance is a most desirable trait in anyone who proposes to be in partnership in the bar business. I also stated that partnerships are another form of marriage. I can turn that around here and say that marriage is another form of partnership—quite literally in a community property state such as California.

I can no more give out marriage counseling advice than I can legal advice, but I can say from experience and observation that you would do well to separate your wife from your bar to the greatest degree in your power.

One of the most expensive mistakes you will be likely to make is to have her work in the place in order to save a salary or to keep it in the family. However, there is one thing even worse—having your girlfriend work in the bar. If you do this, you will likely end up standing the price of both a marriage *and* a divorce.

That came, I said, from empirical knowledge. The following is merely an opinion, unsupported by any hard evidence.

Women, by and large, do not like bars.

Sure, you will say, the day of the man's saloon is long past, and most all bars are filled with women. That they are. Still, most women are transient customers and come in for largely different reasons than a man does. Charles McCabe described a good saloon as one frequented by men in search of companionship without intimacy. This is not a strong feminine desire. I'd say that most wives consider their husband's local pub and his pals (and maybe loose women) there as their competition, even enemy.

I could be wrong. Who ever heard of an Irishman who knows anything about women? But give it some thought before you encourage your wife to hang around your joint—on either side of the bar.

Divorce is a costly business, both emotionally and financially. The national average divorce rate is high enough. Surely the rate among bar owners is at least double the general average. I have hundreds of friends and acquaintances who own bars. Offhand I can't think of one of them who is still married to his first wife.

The only time a bar owner profits from divorce is when he has lots of lawyers for customers.

21

Questions and Answers

Whatever else it may be, collaborating with Sean Mooney is never boring. Two days after the inception of this classic handbook, Mooney announced:

"Now all the brain work is done. All you have to do is put it down on paper."

The final part is written dialectically. Green, having spent much of his adult life in bars, considered himself a bit of an amateur expert on the subject.

Mooney, working on the principle that "a little learning is a dangerous thing," set out to prove that "amateur experts" are the worst sort of chumps and suckers ever to come off the pike into the bar business.

"A Methodist who'd never set his bloody foot in a saloon would stand better chance of running one profitably than would the likes of Green," Mooney averred.

Here's why.

Q: Isn't parking a big factor in your bar operation?

A: Sure. It's one of the biggest factors, as it is in all present-day life. That's a prime consideration in choosing your location in the first place. Parking is hopeless in North Beach.

Most of my trade comes on foot or by taxi, but I know that outside of San Francisco and New York, foot trade is negligible except in bars in city business districts. Keep a close eye on parking availabilities when you choose the site for your bar.

Q: Can't you validate parking lot tickets?

A: Not in a strictly bar operation. With a restaurant you should definitely consider validation and valet parking, but you can't do it in a bar. Nor can you rent a parking lot of your own. Everybody would come in for one drink, have his ticket validated and then do all his shopping or drinking in other bars or eating or whatever on your validation.

Q: You mentioned many of your customers using taxis. What should you do about phoning taxis for customers who are leaving?

A: Having a direct telephone line to a taxicab company behind the bar is a good customer service item. The bartender just picks up the instrument. He doesn't have to dial. When it is answered, the bartender merely states the name of his bar. Many taxi companies will be more than willing to install such a phone free if you have the volume to justify it. Find out which cab company usually gives the best service in your neighborhood and contact them. You can tell this by keeping your eyes open and noting the relative numbers of each company's taxis parked and cruising your neighborhood.

Q: Do you have any advice on the subject of telephones in general?

A: You will lose an awful lot of money if you let customers use your business phone for outgoing calls. You can have two instruments behind the bar. One is on such a short cord that a person cannot talk into it, even by leaning over the bar. The second instrument, with a longer cord, has a blocked dial and cannot be used for outgoing calls. When the bartender gets an incoming call for a customer, he asks him to take it on the extension. This is important because the people who usually ask to use your phone are your friends and best customers, just those who are hardest to turn down.

The owner or bartender should be diplomatic about taking

incoming calls for customers. Many bar customers are there just to get away from the telephone. In a bar with steady clientele the bartender often asks so all patrons can hear, "Is everybody here?" to find out who wants to accept them and who doesn't.

The bartender will often know who wants to accept calls and who doesn't. Sometimes he even knows which calls a good customer wants to take, because many good customers seem to get all their calls, and often their mail, care of the bar.

In case of doubt, the bartender should say, "I'll ask if he's here. Will you just hold on a minute?" He covers the mouthpiece with his hand and finds out. Try to avoid yelling out the customer's name, unless he is an actor and enjoys being paged in public places.

Some PR types phone exclusive bars, restaurants, and hotels just to have themselves paged in order to keep their names "in front of the public." Potential clients?

Never give out any information about anybody, employee or customer, on the phone. Either he admits to being there and wants to take the call, or he isn't there. That's the extent of the information you should give out on the telephone.

You should have at least one pay phone, in an enclosed booth, if your space will permit it. Have a pad attached to the wall to keep the scribbling on the walls to a minimum.

A lot of bar owners aren't aware that they may be entitled to a cut of the proceeds of their pay phone. If you have your own separate business phone and if the pay phone is properly located and legitimately open to the public and if you have a sign outside advising that there is a public phone inside and if the phone company thinks it will sustain enough demand, then you should ask them to send a coin consultant out to see you. If your coin phone meets their qualifications, you will be eligible to receive 15 percent of the monthly take. This could amount to a nice bit of change.

Never contribute to telephone solicitations, however worthy or admirable they may sound. Many of these charity solicitations come out of boiler room operations. If you like the sound of the solicitation, ask them to send somebody out to see you in person. If it is legitimate, they will. If it's not exactly on the up and up, nobody will come out to bother you further.

Q: One hears a lot about the prevalence of bartenders drinking on the job. What are your thoughts about that?

A: It goes on a lot. Liquor is handy, and it's easy to sneak a drink, saying it's going to be the only one today, then have another and another. Nobody wants to see a drunk bartender, so that's definitely not permissible. Naturally, an owner would prefer his bartenders not to drink at all, because the owner has to pay for the booze. But where the line is drawn is a matter of house policy. That house policy should be explained before hiring the man. Personally I run a loose ship. I think it's cruel and unusual punishment to make a drinking man work all day around liquor and not let him have a few, within reason. If you were to keep an animal confined in a space roughly three feet wide the Society for the Prevention of Cruelty to Animals would be on your back right away. But a bartender has to do it eight hours a day, five days a week, and there's no society to prevent cruelty to him. I also trust my men. If they're drunk or think they're getting drunk, they always get one of my other men to come in for them. Nobody's let me down yet. But many houses have a firm rule of no drinking on the job whatsoever. Some are so stern that they won't even let a bartender drink in the place on his own time when he pays. It's all house policy.

Q: But a lot of customers order a drink and want to buy the bartender one. What about that?

A: It has to conform to house policy. If that policy is no drinking whatever, the bartender will have to say, "Sorry, sir. Do you mind if I have it later?" The customer will usually understand without further explanation and nod yes. It's usually just a customer's way of offering a tip, anyway. He doesn't want to offer money, so he offers that drink, thinking that the bartender won't have to ring it up and can keep the price of the drink and have it too. That isn't good for the owner, because the customer is giving the bartender a dollar and buying him a drink on the owner at the same time.

Q: What does the owner do about that?

A: Sets down a firm house policy. Mine is, if the bartender takes the drink, he rings it up. If he takes the money for a "later drink," he doesn't ring it up, but he doesn't take a drink on the house, either.

Q: What about women bartenders?

A: Why not? Judge everybody by his personal merits. There's resistance to having a woman bartender working by herself at night. This is usually justified, but not always. The toughest publicans on the Barbary Coast were said to have been Miss Piggott and Mother Bronson. They were both their own bouncers, and they weren't bouncing ordinary office-worker drunks, but the toughest bruisers on the waterfront. Miss Piggott used a bung-starter, and Mother Bronson used her size twelve boots. Ma Bronson once hoisted a gentleman from the floor of her saloon onto the top of the bar with one kick. Miss Piggott gave men whom she disliked a Miss Piggott Special—brandy, whiskey, gin, and liquid opium. When the sucker grabbed his head, Miss Piggott would lean across the bar and let him have it with the bung-starter. There wasn't a cop in Frisco who'd dare tangle with either of these harridans.

Bars aren't as much fun as they used to be in the old days in Frisco. (Johnnie-come-latelies object vehemently to this term. However, this is what the town always used to be called. The rule is: if your grandfather was born here, you call it Frisco.) Miss Piggott had a trapdoor in the floor in front of her bar. Anybody who stood on this trapdoor was a candidate to get it with the bung-starter, be precipitated into the basement, and find himself on the eve of sailing on a nice little voyage under the auspices of some captain like Wolf Larsen to Shanghai, China. It didn't pay for even regulars to get too drunk in this dive, because they could easily get on this trapdoor by drunken mistake and Miss Piggott would take on all comers. Nothing personal, just a matter of business. It's said that it was pretty funny to watch customers come in and skirt this trap, something like watching Charlie Chaplin dance a ballet under the influence.

On the other hand, I used to play the dog racing at White City greyhound track in London. During the war, when there was a shortage of manpower, women were given the jobs of handling the dogs. They were kept on after the men came back. It was found that a woman would not dope or mistreat a dog, while, of course, a lot of men will do almost anything to win—or lose—a race dishonestly. I have noticed a similar trend in female bartenders. They will not cheat you out of money. I have found them to be scrupulously honest. I am sure there must be exceptions, but I've never run across them.

Q: You stated quite positively that the personality of the bartender doesn't influence trade much. What about the personality of the owner?

A: First, you misunderstood what I said. I said that a bartender wouldn't take an appreciable part of your trade with him, no matter how popular he is, if he quits and goes to work at a place more than a very few blocks away. His personality and manner are very important while he is working *in* your place. I also think the character of the owner is one of the most important single factors in the success of a bar. A good owner will set a good tone—"good vibes," if you will. This will attract good employees who in turn will attract a good clientele. A contentious, unpleasant, or dishonest owner will set a poor tone all down the line. There are several types of exceptions, though. Sometimes a disagreeable old man will set up a one-man operation and attract a large following because he is such a "character." Or you can have a guy like Toots Shor, who ran one of the most famous saloons in the world. He built up a reputation for drinking excessively and being nasty and insulting to the customers. Everyone knew, in his case, that this was just a game and that he was an old softie at heart. Most drinkers want to be pals with saloonkeepers. It's a certain cachet of distinction, God only knows why. Perhaps it gives the customer a feeling of worldliness and being in the know. I know I have a lot of drinking pals who wouldn't give me the time of day if I weren't a well-known publican. I don't kid myself that it's my darling personality they adore. It's because I'm Mooney, you know, the Irishman who owns that pub where all those writers and remittance men hang out. Incidentally, I am an American citizen, you know.

Q: You mentioned pourers for the liquor bottles, the "slow pourers" and "fast pourers." Isn't there a "stop pourer," too?

A: Yes. In most busy bars the bartender pours highballs with both hands at once, pouring from the bottle with one hand while squirting in the mix from the gun with the other hand. It's pretty difficult for a customer to know how much liquor he's getting. The stop pourer is a cheating device. He starts pouring the liquor first, a fraction before he starts the gun. The customer sees that a good healthy flow is coming out. Then the gun starts and it's sort of distracting. The bartender puts his finger over a hole on the pourer, cutting off the flow. When he's finished, he adds a little extra touch of the booze. The customer thinks he's getting an extra generous drink, but really he's being shorted. Personally I hate this sort of petty chicanery.

Q: How much time would an owner of a place such as yours expect to put in working at his bar?

A: More than he anticipates! The more hours an owner spends working, the more money he'll make. If he's behind the bar himself, of course, he's saving one salary. No employee can have the interest of the place more at heart than the owner, no matter how good and conscientious the employee. To figure the actual number of hours you have to know the hours the bar will be open; whether you intend to work whole shifts or part shifts, Lots of owners open the place, then leave, and come back to close. It depends whether you're working five, six, or seven days a week. You have the bookkeeping, stock, and inventory work I described. Also it seems that you put in several extra hours each day talking to salesmen. You can figure you're going to be working a lot longer hours than you expected. That's why when a man doesn't much like the business to begin with, he'll end up hating it.

Q: Should you post a visible price list for drinks?

A: The only places that do that are joints near bus terminals or in run-down neighborhoods. But with our present rampant inflation, do make sure all your bartenders and cocktail waitresses know the current daily price of everything. So far, we don't have to pack our currency in wheelbarrows as the Germans had to in the twenties, but those days aren't too far off, the way things are going. A while back I heard my bartender on one shift charge one price for an Irish Coffee. The night man, waiting to come on duty, said he had been charging about 20 percent less. I thought it was somewhere in the middle. The money doesn't matter all that much, but a customer can get the impression that he's being deliberately chiseled, just about the last thing you want said about your place. I keep emphasizing in this book, use one standard for everybody.

Q: On this bartender personality thing. Can't it be overdone?

A: Sure it can. Just as in any business, he can get too big for his boots. Start believing his own publicity. Get to thinking the operation revolves around him as its sun. I mentioned this as one of the big pitfalls for an owner. It happens with bartenders too. A personality bartender can be viewed as a decided asset. On the other hand, some owners consider him a liability. I mentioned Henry Africa's, a most successful, popular operation. He does not want personalities there, just drink technicians. The reason is that he feels that the personality bartender attracts cliques. His pals get special attention and become an "in" crowd. This, Africa feels, sets casual customers off. They feel left out of things. He doesn't want a cliquish store. There's another thing *I* feel strongly about. I'm pretty permissive, but there's one thing I won't tolerate. Bartenders playing Don Juan with the women customers. The women belong to the other customers, or to themselves, *not* to the bartender. It has nothing to do with my personal morals. It's just bad business and sooner or later leads to trouble.

Q: You didn't mention coffee.

A: Coffee is a big item here in California. First there was Irish Coffee, then Italian Coffee, then Mexican Coffee, and I suppose it'll go on until all the nations are exhausted. Plain coffee used to be a give-away item, but it sure isn't now. Coffee is a nuisance in a bar, not only because people want it free, but because it's messy. It also has to be fresh. If your volume of drinks such as Irish Coffee warrants it, by all means carry it. Get in touch with the institutional coffee distributors and make the best deal you can for supplying coffee, with their terms for an automatic coffee brewer, the kind where the coffee comes in a package which you just slip in the machine, not the kind where you have to measure out loose coffee. They'll probably give you, or let you use, the machine free if you agree to buy a stipulated amount of coffee from them. Get a machine which has at least two heating element rings. You will want to use one to keep water hot, just below the boiling point, for toddies and other hot drinks.

Q: You mentioned the need for a mixer and a blender. Why both?

A: The mixer, that milkshake kind, mixes in a circular, horizontal rotation. The blenders mix, chop, and froth the ingredients, including the ice. The two machines are used to make different kinds of drinks because the results of their mixing and blending are different. We use the mixer mostly to whip cream for Irish Coffee. A good example of the product of a blender is a Frozen Daiquiri, which is a kind of sherbet.

Throughout the book I've not used brand names, except where absolutely necessary, that is, for brands of liquor. It wouldn't be fair. I can't say which is absolutely the best. Why do so many people buy only Chevrolets and an equal number buy only Fords? They look and drive the same to me. I can't tell the difference unless I look at the nameplate. I emphasize that when you are buying or leasing expensive equipment, you should try to take along a friend who knows something about it. I don't endorse brand products here.

Q: You mentioned the swiping of ashtrays. Don't the big liquor companies give bars ashtrays, hoping they'll be taken home, as a form of advertising?

A: They used to, before the days of this New Morality, when the pilferage was kept to a reasonable level. Cinzano and Martini & Rossi used to give favorite bars those dynamite, triangular, big ceramic ashtrays, but they don't anymore. The ashtrays cost too much and they go as fast as you set them on the bar. The bar has to buy them now, and for a nice price. Don't have the name of your bar on ashtrays. Maybe having your name on them brings the price up insignificantly, but it also gives the thing a souvenir value a plain one doesn't have.

Q: You touched on trends, but you didn't go into them.

A: I was saving that for last. I once looked up the word. "Trend" actually means a general tendency, and, as such, might extend over a considerable period, maybe even eons, as in the course of a trend in the climate. The way the word is mostly used now, as in "trendy," is more akin to a fad, of transitory duration. If I'd taken up trends, in this meaning, at the beginning of the book, they might be passé here at the end. I have noted several strong trends around here which are probably of more than momentary significance. Many trends start in San Francisco and Los Angeles and gradually wend eastward, so perhaps these haven't been noted clearly in other parts of the country.

The first is youth. There's a demographic reason for this and a psychological reason, but the currently popular bars have a youthful appearance. It's a general phenomenon which I won't go into except to advise you to notice all the middle-aged businessmen wearing long hair, loud clothes, talking current jazzy slang, and driving sportscars. Specifically this manifests itself in bars first by lightness. The new bars have picture windows and good lighting fixtures. They are light and airy. The dark coal-bin cocktail lounge is out. For one thing, with the new permissiveness nobody has to get sexual kicks from necking and feeling in dark lounges. Also the decided trend is to ever-lighter drinks. That light, vodkalike whiskey (actually blended neutral spirits) bombed, nobody knows exactly why, but that's the one exception. The sales of heavy Scotch and bonded bourbon are way off. Everybody knows about the phenomenal rise in sales in vodka. Now tequila is taking off in California. It doesn't taste light to me, but it looks light, and it mixes into tasty drinks such as the Tequila Sunrise and the Margarita. Tequila may be just a fad, but the general popularity of light-colored and light-tasting drinks is a long-term trend.

Along with lightness is spaciousness and comfort. Informality is another allied trend. Live plants are more than a fad. They have a good practical purpose in a bar, too. They purify the air. It's better to hang them from the ceiling than stand

them on the floor. Have them high enough so they won't be used
for ashtrays. Games of semi-skill such as pool and electronic
Ping-Pong and other games have come on strong, but the electronic things seem to be fading already. I think those where you
actually handle the tools will last and those where you activate
an electronic scoreboard will go. The natural will last; the
mechanical and contrived will fail. The latest trend, connected
with these, is dancing—the kind of dancing where two people
actually hold each other. None of this is much of a secret to
anybody who's spent any time in the popular bars in San Francisco, but it might be useful to somebody intending to start a bar
someplace else.

A fairly recent development, or trend, which deserves
comment here is the popularity of wine in bars, at least in
California. Twenty years ago if you'd ordered a glass of wine in
a bar, they'd look you over wondering whether to call the boys
in white to fetch you with a net. (The exception was bars in skid
row neighborhoods where winos drank sweet, fortified wines
such as Port and Muscatel for the sugar sustenance as well as
the price.) Most bars didn't even carry a bottle of dry wine.
Now, I estimate, one-third of the drinks poured at my joint are
wine. In North Beach in general wine must average 50 percent
of the volume.

The United States has been a hard liquor country, so it
is hard to conceive that the history of hard liquor is very short.
In England gentlemen did not take up the habit of drinking brandy after dinner until about one hundred years ago.
Drinking Scotch whiskey caught on only about the time of the
First World War. The lower classes did start drinking gin at the
time of William III, but the upper classes continued with various types of wine until this century.

In Colonial times here the first popular drinks in taverns
were Madeira wine and punches, then later rum. American
whiskeys didn't become popular until about the Civil War when
the saloons became widespread. About this time, the custom of
drinking wine died out in the Protestant majority in this country.

One of the more sensible trends of youth today is eschew-

ing the "get drunk quick" habits of their fathers and grand-
fathers, which has triggered their habit of drinking wine. (It is
also claimed that wine mixes well with marijuana.)

The statistics of pouring wine can be quite interesting to
you. House wine or *vin ordinaire* is purchased by gallon jug. I
buy it by cases of four gallons each. There's a case discount and it
takes up less space. The label claims it is Chablis or Burgundy
or Chianti, or whatever, but really it is either just red or white.
This stuff should be chosen not for positively good qualities but
for absence of bad qualities. In the main you should avoid
brands with a sour or brassy taste. The stuff is blended scien-
tifically so there is great consistency in the taste. The brand I
fancy has about 10 percent of good Napa Valley grape blended
into it. Most of the grapes in this type of wine come from the
prolific, hot San Joaquin Valley and are of low quality, hence
the price—in the case of the stuff I buy—is about at a par with
milk or soda water and less than beer or Coca Cola.

You will notice that most of the bars which have been
around a long time give fair value. Of course, prices vary
because of a number of considerations such as area (rent),
decor, clientele, and so on, but the places which rook you
usually don't last long. They're in the game for a quick killing,
usually based on some gimmick. I suppose that's all very well
given a business ethic of *caveat emptor*, but to be successful at
it you must get in and out quickly. In other words, when you buy
a clip joint proposing to work some gimmick such as topless
waitresses you'd better have the fellow you're going to unload
the business on all lined up the day you open your doors. Wait a
month too long and your gold-plated business opportunity may
become next to valueless.

There is an old saying in the stock market: "The Bull wins
sometimes and the Bear wins sometimes, but the Pig always
loses."

Q: Do you recommend any special way of scheduling
deliveries?

A: I sure do. If at all possible, schedule them all to be made
on one particular day of the week. Set that day aside. You won't
work the bar that day, just take care of deliveries. Also, get the

salesmen into the habit of calling on you that day. Salesmen and deliverymen take up an awful lot of time. Kill all these birds with one stone.

Q: What temperature should you keep the barroom?

A: That's a source of eternal dispute. Women like it warmer, men like it cooler. Older people generally prefer a warm temperature. Many years ago I was in a railway carriage in Switzerland. My companions were an Englishman and a Frenchman. The Englishman would open the window, then in a few minutes the Frenchman would close it. This game went on all the way from Basel to Zurich. Also, years ago, I went into a downtown bar in San Francisco on the coldest, wettest, windiest Christmas Eve I remember in this city. Everybody was sitting at the bar in overcoats, gloves, and mufflers, still shivering. The consul-general of Ireland came in, sat next to me, and ordered a gin-and-tonic. I said to him:

"Excuse me, Pat, but as I understand it, you are charged with promoting the goods and commodities of Ireland here. Why are you drinking that horrible muck instead of Irish whiskey?"

He looked me in the eye and answered with a serious, straight face:

"Sure, I drink Irish whiskey at home, but it's not suitable in this tropical climate here."

So much for the temperature of barrooms. I've mentioned lighting several times. Most current bars are well lighted. Don't forget to have a light over the cash register and under the sink.

Q: What hours should you be open for business?

A: It depends on the traffic. There wouldn't be much sense in keeping a bar in Wall Street open on Sundays. Remember that the rent and insurance and so forth go on whether you're open or closed. However, you have to have enough trade to justify salaries or your time. You can work this out by common sense and observation. But if it's your policy to stay open until midnight, then stay open whether you have any customers or not. People will stop going out of their way to come to your place if they find you closed when you're supposed to be open. I was running a resort hotel in the Mother Lode country a few years ago. At midnight there wasn't a single customer in the bar. The bar manager said he'd had a hard day and thought he'd turn in. I said for him to suit himself, but I was going to stick around because we'd advertised we were open until 2 AM. Sure enough, in about half-an-hour in come fifteen red-jacketed revellers from E. Clampus Vitae, a fraternal order noted for conviviality and openhandedness. They and their wives blew about $90 before closing time. What's more important, they kept coming back. If we'd had the bar closed, I don't think we would have ever seen these big spenders again.

Incidentally, speaking of being open, keep your front door open whenever you can, weather permitting. If a man walks by and is undecided whether he wants to pop in for one or not, chances are he'll come in if the door is open, but pass on by if the door is closed. It's just easier to go in an open door. I've done this many times myself.

Q: I suppose there's a difference in drinking habits the various nights of the week?

A: Sure. Friday is the big night. Saturday night, in San Francisco anyway, is called "amateurs' night." So-called serious drinkers try to stay home Saturday nights. The early part of the week is slack, building up on Thursdays. Saturday night is the biggest volume night, with all the amateurs out. New Year's Eve and St. Patrick's Day are the superamateur nights. People who get drunk on those days can be compared to Catholics who only attend Mass on Easter Sunday. Nights of a full moon bring out a zany crowd. There's a discernable difference in drinking habits. A man who drinks only Scotch-and-Water may drink a Black Russian followed by a Picon Punch when the moon is full. People act crazy, too. I know a lot of bartenders who won't work on nights of a full moon. I don't know if there is any physical relationship or if it is all psychological. I'd guess it's just a convenient rationalization for acting in a peculiar or turbulent manner. Certainly it provides a handy excuse the next morning.

Q: What about expansion?

A: If your place seems too small to handle the big nights, don't be in a hurry to turn an intimate or happily crowded place into a spacious, chilly room. For some reason too much space slows down the drinking drastically. Proprietors have done this, usually with the dismal result of losing rather than gaining business. It's better to turn them away from a packed house than turn them off.

Several theories have been set forth. One popular idea is that distance makes people self-conscious. They feel the people across the room are staring at them. This won't happen in the eyeball to eyeball intimacy of a packed room. One cynic says a crowded place allows vast opportunity for "accidental" brushings and various forms of body contact. Given more space, this would not be tolerated.

Still another view is that you drink in crowded places because it's easier to strike up a conversation. One way is through the vehicle of apology.

"Oh, I beg your pardon, Miss. How could I be so clumsy as to drop cigarette ashes *there* of all places. Did I burn them, uh, I mean, let me buy you another drink, please."

Another problem with expansion is mainly caused by greed. It often starts with the thought, "If I'm making this much with one place, think of how much will be coming in with two places!"

Another cautionary note. Some places do make a big success of expanding to two or more different locations. This takes substantial bankrolling, and nothing can cut into your current profits like trying to build or buy a bigger place. It could be like trying to buy a Lincoln Continental with the money you are saving on gas driving a VW. Don't bet on the outcome unless you are well financed at the outset.

There are some advantages in having more than one place, especially that of purchasing power. If the volume warrants it, you can take real advantage of post offs in well stock. Large lots of twenty or thirty case orders weekly save two or three dollars per case, and wring positively fawning attention from purveyors.

There is also obvious ego gratification for a successful owner handling the reins of a growing concern. But a much smaller percentage will win at multi-expansion than will lose.

Q: Any more helpful hints?

A: I just had to go down to the storeroom to get another bottle of Cognac. Just one bottle, mind you. The reason I was gone so long was because it took me five minutes to find the right key to the room. Look at this ring of keys. How many do you suppose are on this ring?

Q: Looks like about three dozen?

A: That's right. Thirty-three to be exact. And this bunch of keys weighs about a pound. No two locks in this place are alike. If I'd been thinking when I took over the joint and changed the locks, I would have standardized them. Then, I'd be carrying about a half-dozen keys. Not only is this a timewaster and a heavy nuisance, but it's death on my pockets. This ring of keys will wear through any suit pocket I know of in a month. My wife just loves that.

Q: Any final advice, Sean?

A: Yes. Live across the street from your bar. Portal-to-portal from my flat to my bar is 147 paces. I can always get home somehow and I've never had a drunk driving rap in my life. I shudder to see my friends get in their cars and drive way out to hell and gone—or even three or four blocks. I could certainly live more luxuriously someplace else, but not with the peace of mind I have now. God only knows that I've pointed out enough troubles and vexations in this book to suffice anyone. Driving a car after I've had even one or two drinks is a trouble I don't need and can avoid. It's an old, old saying, but so true. Alcohol and gasoline don't mix.

22

The Bright Side

After I've pointed out all the difficulties, vexations, and pitfalls inherent in the bar business, you most likely will ask why anyone at all would get in such a business. I've been in many and have never found one that was a bed of roses. Being a writer sounds like the greatest racket in the world. I thought so until I started trying to write this book. It was a demanding job, I found, and often a headache. After all the work was done, I didn't know whether it would be accepted by a publisher and ever see print or me see a penny out of it. It was by no means the waltz I'd expected it to be when I started. Now that it's printed, I feel good because it was a rewarding experience which came out right—or at least got published.

There also can be many rewards to being a publican, especially if you are successful at it. A century ago there was an amazing success story in the bar business in my town. Two publicans named James Flood and William O'Brien ran a saloon named the Auction Lunch right by the San Francisco Mining Exchange. They picked up so many hot tips on mining stocks that they made a bundle, retired, and became partners with the Virginia City ex-miners John Mackay and James Fair. The four of them became the Comstock Kings, among the richest men in the world. Flood's home on Nob Hill is now the Pacific Union Club, and Fair's the Fairmont Hotel.

This wasn't too bad for a couple of red-necked Irish lads. Respectable men also have done well in the saloonkeeping business. Matthew Vassar was a keeper of an ale house and later also a brewer. With the money he amassed, he founded the first women's college to be conceived as an idea, a manifesto, a declaration of rights, and a proclamation of equality for women.

Liberated women have not been the only benefactors of the purveying of alcoholic beverages. The total alcoholic beverage excise tax collected in California from the end of prohibition to January 1975 alone was $1.779 billion.

Some of the most famous men in American history have been tavernkeepers, including Ethan Allen, Samuel Adams, William Penn, John Adams, Andrew Jackson, and Abraham Lincoln. General George Washington bade farewell to his officers in the Long Room in Fraunces Tavern in New York City in 1783. (This tavern, which opened in 1762, is still open as a public house.) Thomas Jefferson wrote the first draft of the Declaration of Independence in a tavern in Philadelphia called The Indian Queen.

You may view keeping a bar strictly as a way of making a living, which is fine provided it works. It will, I hope, if you have followed the simple precepts in this book. I doubt though if it will give you much satisfaction, viewed in this manner. I daresay that the return of profit is much higher in most other businesses.

Philosophy means the love of truth or knowledge. It is an internally destructive word because none of us knows the visage of truth. On the shallowest level, one is called a philosopher because he utters the shallowest platitudes (as this statement might be classified).

Since no one yet has been able to comprehend absolute truth, we must do with substitutes. We should, I think, try to understand the minds of others and try to put ourselves in their mental place.

This desire, I believe, is the quality which distinguishes the successful publican from the mechanic. Without this quality of attempted understanding, I really do believe a man should not attempt to make a career in the bar business.

Appendix A (1)

Federal Laws
and Regulations*

Taxes. (Occupational or Special Taxes) Here are the annual rates for the occupational or special federal taxes. (This is comparable to the state's annual license fee.) Retail dealer in liquors (spirits, wines, beer) . . . $54.00.

The liquor industry is subject to multitudinous federal laws and regulations, plus two kinds of federal taxes.

The Director, Alcohol, Firearms, and Tobacco Tax Division, Internal Revenue Service, Treasury Department, Washington 25, D.C., is the chief federal official responsible for the administration of the regulations.

Under him are the regional commissioners and assistant regional commissioners with offices in California and the various other states.

The two types of U.S. taxes are the excise tax on distilled spirits, wines, and malt liquors and the so-called special tax (occupational tax) on manufacturers, wholesalers, and retailers.

The excise taxes are payable at the manufacturing level (by the distillers, brewers, and wine growers) and must be paid at least twice a month. Sometimes they are paid weekly or even daily.

The retailer or wholesaler doesn't have to worry about the federal excise tax except to be sure that his merchandise has the federal stamp

---

* Courtesy of BIN-Merchandiser.

affixed indicating the tax is paid. But the occupation or special tax is different. Nearly everyone from the retailer on up must pay it annually on or before July 1 of the fiscal year.

Basic Permit. Basic permits are required by the federal government for those (*except public agencies*) engaged in selling alcoholic beverages to other dealers. Here are the classifications of licensees which must have basic permits: Importers, domestic producers, rectifiers, blenders, warehousemen, wholesalers.

Credit. Federal Alcohol Administration Credit Regulation No. 8 provides a limitation on credit extended to the on-and-off-sale licensees in the alcoholic beverage industry. Generally the extension of credit to a licensee is limited to thirty days.

An extension of credit beyond thirty days is prohibited when it has the effect of tying the hands of the licensee so that he cannot buy from others. In other words, Uncle Sam does not want a wholesaler or producer to get his customers obligated to the point where they are helpless.

After the thirty-day deadline, COD or prepaid deliveries to the licensees are permitted—as long as it doesn't involve any exclusion through inducement, as mentioned above.

Liquor Dealers. Wholesale and retail liquor dealers are subject to special federal taxes and regulations.

Special or occupational taxes are imposed on dealers. A person who pays special tax as a retail dealer in liquors may sell either distilled spirits, wines, or beer, or any two or all three of them.

The following classifications of dealers must pay the tax: Retail dealers, wholesale dealers, retailers in beer, wholesale beer dealers, club licensees, restaurants serving liquor with meals.

Returns are filed on Form 11, with remittance to the District Director of Internal Revenue. A penalty of 5 percent, not to exceed 25 percent, of the tax each month is assessed for failure to file a return.

An extension of time can be granted if reasonable cause for delinquency is presented. Death or serious illness of taxpayer, fire, giving of wrong information by Internal Revenue Office, and so on, are valid reasons.

A tax stamp will be issued by the district director upon payment of the tax. *The stamp is not a federal permit or license, but is merely a receipt for the tax. The stamp affords the holder no protection against prosecution for violation of state law.* The stamp cannot be sold and is not transferable.

A special taxpayer must conspicuously post the tax stamp in his place of business. Retailers must keep similar records and reports.

All distilled spirits, whether domestic or imported, in the possession of wholesalers in containers of a gallon or less must bear either a green or red strip stamp affixed in such a manner as to be broken when the container is opened.

Re-use or refilling of liquor bottles is prohibited.

Penalties (Federal). Wilful failure to pay occupational taxes concerning the liquor industry is punishable by a fine of not more than $5,000 and a prison sentence of not more than two years.

There are thirty-three provisions of the law on penalties, seizures, and forfeitures relating to liquor taxes.

In addition to these laws, the general penalties relating to federal income taxes are applicable to liquor taxes.

For instance, any person who wilfully attempts to evade any federal tax, in addition to other penalties (such as 5 percent a month added to the tax up to 25 percent) is guilty of a felony and subject to a fine of not more than $10,000 or a prison sentence of not more than five years, or both. He must also pay costs of prosecution.

Here are some other ways to get into trouble: Preparing false or fraudulent tax documents, securing a bond under false pretenses, concealing taxable commodities to evade taxes, or concealing records to evade taxes—Fine up to $5,000, prison up to three years, or both, plus costs of prosecution. Filing false returns—fine up to $1,000 or prison up to a year, or both. Failure to keep occupational stamp posted conspicuously—Fine equal to amount of stamp, but not less than $10.

Records and Reports. *Retailers* are required to keep careful records for the federal government.

Each retail dealer must keep a complete record of all distilled spirits, wines, or beer received. Such record shall consist of all purchase invoices or bills covering alcoholic beverages or, at the option of the dealer, a book record containing all of the required information.

Appendix A (2)

Federal Small Business Administration

The Federal Small Business Administration will give you a sixteen-page pamphlet, *SBA Business Loans*, containing easily understood basic information if you write or phone them. SBA has field offices in the following cities:

Agana, GU
Albany, NY
Albuquerque, NM
Anchorage, AK
Atlanta, GA
Augusta, ME
Baltimore, MD
Biloxi, MS
Birmingham, AL
Boise, ID
Boston, MA
Buffalo, NY
Camden, NJ
Casper, WY
Charleston, WV
Charlotte, NC
Chicago, IL
Cincinnati, OH
Clarksburg, WV
Cleveland, OH
Columbia, SC

Columbus, OH
Concord, NH
Coral Gables, FL
Corpus Christi, TX
Dallas, TX
Denver, CO
Des Moines, IA
Detroit, MI
Eau Claire, WI
Elmira, NY
El Paso, TX
Fairbanks, AK
Fargo, ND
Fresno, CA
Greenville, NC
Harrisburg, PA
Hartford, CT
Hato Rey, PR
Helena, MT
Holyoke, MA
Honolulu, HI

Houston, TX
Indianapolis, IN
Jackson, MS
Jacksonville, FL
Jericho, NY
Kansas City, MO
Knoxville, TN
Las Vegas, NV
Little Rock, AR
Los Angeles, CA
Louisville, KY
Lower Rio Grande
  Valley, TX
Lubbock, TX
Madison, WI
Marquette, MI
Marshall, TX
Memphis, TN
Milwaukee, WI
Minneapolis, MN
Montpelier, VT

Nashville, TN	Reno, NV	Sioux Falls, SD
Newark, NJ	Richmond, VA	Spokane, WA
New Orleans, LA	Rochester, NY	Springfield, IL
New York, NY	St. Louis, MO	St. Thomas, VI
Oklahoma City, OK	Sacramento, CA	Syracuse, NY
Omaha, NB	Salt Lake City, UT	Tampa, FL
Philadelphia, PA	San Antonio, TX	Washington, DC
Phoenix, AZ	San Diego, CA	West Palm Beach, FL
Pittsburgh, PA	San Francisco, CA	Wichita, KS
Portland, OR	Seattle, WA	Wilkes-Barre, PA
Providence, RI	Shreveport, LA	Wilmington, DE
Rapid City, SD		

Locate their street address and phone number in your local telephone directory under *United States Government*.

SBA recommends this procedure for new businesses wanting a loan, in seven steps, the first six in writing:

1. Describe in detail the type of business to be established.
2. Describe experience and management capabilities.
3. Prepare an estimate of how much you or others have to invest in the business and how much you will need to borrow.
4. Prepare a current financial statement (balance sheet) listing all personal assets and all liabilities.
5. Prepare a detailed projection of earnings for the first year the business will operate.
6. List collateral to be offered as security for the loan, indicating your estimate of the present market value of each item.
7. Take this material with you to your banker as described in the text.

SBA's General Credit Requirements

A loan applicant must:

- Be of good character.
- Show ability to operate his business successfully.
- Have enough capital in an existing firm so that, with an SBA loan, he can operate on a sound financial basis.
- Show the proposed loan is of sound value or so secured as reasonably to assure repayment.
- Show that the past earnings record and future prospects of the firm indicate ability to repay the loan and other fixed debt, if any, out of profits.
- Be able to provide from his own resources sufficient funds to have a reasonable amount at stake to withstand possible losses, particularly during the early stages, if the venture is a new business.

SBA's application form explains this more fully:

7. RECENT EFFORTS TO OBTAIN CREDIT (For Direct Loan Applicants Only): The SBA is authorized to make loans to business enterprises only when the financial assistance is not otherwise available on reasonable terms. SBA is also empowered to make loans in cooperation with banks or other lending institutions through agreements to participate on an immediate or guaranty basis. Therefore, applicant must furnish the information required below regarding efforts made within 60 days preceding the filing of this application to obtain credit from banks or other sources. Letters declining to extend credit as well as declining to participate with SBA must be obtained from the following lending institutions: (a) The applicant's bank of account; and (b) if the amount of the loan applied for is in excess of the legal lending limit of the applicant's bank or in excess of the amount that the bank normally lends to any one borrower, then a refusal from a correspondent bank or from any other lending institution whose lending capacity is adequate to cover the loan applied for (c) letters from two banks are required if applicant is located in a city with a population in excess of 200,000. These letters must contain date of application, amount of loan requested and reasons for refusal, and be attached to this application.

CREDIT INFORMATION - Applicant expressly authorizes disclosure of all information submitted in connection with this application and any resulting loan to the financial institution agreeing below to participate in such loan or, if none, to its bank(s) of account and (Insert name of other financial institution if desired) _____

PARTICIPATION - Will any lending institution participate with SBA in the loan requested? ☐ Yes ☐ No. If "Yes" institution shall execute Application For Participation or Guaranty Agreement at bottom of page 4.

The regulations governing the Small Business Administration are available from the Office of the Federal Registrar, General Services Administration, Washington D.C. in its *Code of Federal Regulations #13—Business Credit and Assistance*. There is a small charge for this book-sized document. This publication may be obtained from your local Government Printing Office Book Store whose location may be found in your local telephone directory. The SBA has a number of publications available on almost all aspects of running all sorts of small businesses. Some are free and some carry a nominal charge. Some of these could be very useful to you. If you intend to contact the SBA, ask for a list of their publications too.

Appendix B

California—and the Law*

California's basic policy governing the alcoholic beverage control industry is set forth in section 22 of the state constitution.

Here are the principal provisions:

1. The state has exclusive power to license and regulate the industry.
2. But the state or any local public agency is expressly prohibited from engaging itself in the manufracture or sale of alcoholic beverages. Unlike most states, California recognizes the free enterprise system for the industry.
3. Public eating places and public premises may be licensed for sale by the drink and retail stores may be licensed for sale by the package.
4. Alcoholic beverages shall not be sold to persons under 21 years of age.
5. The state Department of Alcoholic Beverage Control has exclusive power to license the industry.

The general policies spelled out in section 22 have remained virtually unchanged in thirty-eight years. This is a tribute to the men who framed the constitutional amendment nearly four decades ago in an

---

* Courtesy of BIN-Merchandiser and California Department of Alcoholic Beverage Control.

191

emotional era following the repeal of Prohibition. It has stood the test of time and no changes are in prospect in the foreseeable future.

There have been only two major changes during this period—the shifting of enforcement from the Board of Equalization to the ABC department and the legalization of sales by the drink at public premises in which minors are prohibited from entering.

Supplementing this constitutional section is the Alcoholic Beverage Control Act. In printed form the act contains more than 200 pages. Much of the language is technical, requiring a legal mind to understand it.

The BIN California Gold Book strives to reduce the ABC Act to layman's language. The principal provisions are explained in simple terms, and according to subject matter in alphabetical order as follows:

Abatement: So-called Bottle Clubs which are not licensed and at which liquor is not sold but at which setups are furnished thereby providing a place for the drinking of liquor may be abated as public nuisances by the attorney general or district attorney.

Accusation: Any person may file an accusation against any liquor licensee. It must be filed with the department in writing and state grounds for suspension or revocation of the license.

Local legislative bodies, chiefs of police, boards of supervisors, or sheriffs may file accusations (depending on whether premises are in city or unincorporated areas) and the department shall call a public hearing and determine whether the license shall be suspended or revoked. If the local authorities certify health and welfare at stake, the hearing must be held within twenty days.

Local authorities must notify the department of any arrest for violations of the liquor regulations and the department must investigate and determine whether the license or licenses should be suspended or revoked.

There is a one-year statute of limitations on violations in the field of fair trade and in many technical matters but a three-year statute of limitations on the more serious charges of disorderly house, B-girls, and the like.

Adulteration: The Alcoholic Beverage Control Act expressly acknowledges that the State Department of Public Health has power to enforce the laws to prevent mislabeling, adulteration, or misbranding of alcoholic beverages.

Advertising: For many years the use of the words *bar, barroom, saloon,* or *cocktail bar* were prohibited on outdoor signs. In the late 1960s and early 1970s the legislature repealed these taboos.

Signs must be used to properly inform the patron of the brand of draught beer coming out of the spigot.

Affidavit of Publication: An applicant for on-sale license shall publish notice of the application in a newspaper of general circulation and file an affidavit of such publication with the department prior to such license being issued.

Age of Whiskey: It is unlawful to sell spirits labeled as whiskey unless the product contains at least 20 percent or more of straight whiskey or whiskeys which have been aged in charred oak containers for four or more years.

Appeals: An appeal of a decision of the ABC Department may be filed with the Alcoholic Beverage Control Appeals Board during a ten-day period following the last day reconsideration can be ordered. This is thirty days after the decision is made. If the department makes its decision immediately, the appeal must be filed within ten days.

Appeals Board: There is in state government an Alcoholic Beverage Control Appeals Board of three members appointed by the governor. The board shall consider appeals from decisions of the Alcoholic Beverage Control Department and its meetings shall be open and public.

Arrests: All state and local enforcement agencies shall notify the department of any arrests for violations of liquor laws. The department shall promptly investigate and determine whether the license or licenses shall be suspended or revoked.

Bar: Use of the word *bar* on outdoor signs is permissible.

Beer: Beer is defined in the law as a fermented alcoholic beverage made with barley, malt, hops, or similar product or combination of products, and includes ale, porter, brown stout, lager beer, small beer, and strong beer. The alcoholic content is limited to 4 percent by weight, but this does not apply to ale, porter, brown malt liquor, and stout.

(Tapping Equipment). Beer manufacturers or wholesalers may furnish tapping equipment to retailers, subject to regulations of department. The equipment remains the property of the supplier. The supplier may service such equipment.

(Tap Signs). Whenever draught beer is sold, tap signs must clearly inform the patron of the brand name.

B-Girls: Permitting anyone to solicit drinks from patrons is cause for a mandatory revocation of the license. The courts have held this penalty is not excessive. It is also against the law to permit anyone to loiter on premises for the purpose of soliciting.

Bona Fide Public Eating Place: This consists of premises in which meals are served. This does not mean sandwiches, salads, or snacks but substantial meals. However, it is not mandatory that food be sold or served with drinks. Convention centers, exhibit halls, or auditoriums, where meals are served, qualify under this definition.

Cocktail Lounge: Use of words *cocktail lounge* in signs advertising premises is permissible. The words *cocktail bar*, banned for many years, also are permissible.

Compromise, Offer In: A licensee faced with a thirty-day suspension or less may petition to make an offer in compromise. The department may examine the situation on its merits, stay the suspension, and accept the compromise. The offer must be equal to 20 percent of the gross sales for the duration of the proposed suspension, but not less than $350 nor more than $2,000.

In the case of retail licensees, the department may accept an offer of 20 percent of the gross business during the term of the suspension which offer must be not less than $100 nor more than $500. Said retailer must not have had any other accusation against him during the prior three years that has resulted in a final decision to suspend or revoke his retail license.

Corporations: Except for big firms listed on the stock exchange, banks, and so on, any corporation holding a liquor license must notify the department of any changes involving ownership of 10 percent or more of the stock. The company's stock register must be available for inspection by the department. Changes in officers or board members also must be reported to the department. Actions by an owner of 10 percent or more of the stock can constitute reason for discipline of the licensee by the department.

Credit: Retailers who do not pay for distilled spirits, wine, or beer by the forty-second day after delivery shall be charged by the wholesaler or manufacterer 1 percent a month on the unpaid balance. If payment in full is not received by the thirtieth day after delivery creditor shall sell only to such retailer for cash. And if the payment of the 1 percent credit charge is not made by the thirtieth day after it is due, the creditor shall sell to such retailer for cash.

Creditors: In any license transfer in which a consideration is involved, the creditors must be satisfied out of the purchase price which must be deposited with an escrow holder. No agreement may be made in the transfer of a license which injures or defrauds the creditors of the transfer.

Criminal Punishment: Anyone selling liquor without a license or otherwise performing acts restricted to licensees is guilty of misdemeanor.

Department: The State Department of Alcoholic Beverage Control was established January 1, 1955, with power to license the liquor industry and enforce the liquor laws. The department is headed by a director under appointment by the governor. He is prohibited from having any direct interest in the industry. He may not even solicit a licensee for the purchase of tickets to any benefit.

These powers came down from the State Board of Equalization under a constitutional amendment. The board retains the power to levy and collect alcoholic beverage excise taxes.

Department of Public Health: The Alcoholic Beverage Control Act leaves expressly to the State Department of Public Health the power to enforce the pure food and drug laws with respect to alcoholic beverages.

Disorderly House: A licensee who runs a disorderly house is guilty of a misdemeanor. Permitting prostitutes to hang about, allowing the presence of drunks and narcotics users, and failing to prevent frequent fights are examples of what leads to a disorderly house.

Dispensing Device: An automatic dispensing device for distilled spirits may be used by on-salers, provided it is locked to prevent refilling of bottles.

District Attorney: Every district attorney and every local peace officer is charged with the responsibility of enforcing the Alcoholic Beverage Control Act.

Elections: There are no longer restrictions against the sale of alcoholic beverages during election hours in California. The final restrictive law on this subject was repealed in 1969.

Employees: Anyone employed to manage an on-sale general licensed establishment must meet the qualifications of a licensee.

Empty bottles: Neither an on-sale licensee nor his employee is permitted to sell, offer for sale, or keep for sale any empty distilled spirits bottle.

Enforcement: The State Department of Alcoholic Beverage Control is vested with broad powers by the constitution to enforce the liquor statutes. However, district attorneys and local law enforcement agencies share in this responsibility. The state Department of Public Health plays a special role by enforcing the pure food and drug laws as they relate to alcoholic beverages.

Examining Books: The department may examine the books or inspect the premises of a licensee.

Exchanges: Any licensee of a public eating place (on-sale) may exchange his license for a public premise license and vice versa. The exchange fee is $100. This must be done at the time of renewal of the license sought.

False Returns and Records: Anyone who knowingly or wilfully files a false report with the department dealing with sales of alcoholic beverages is guilty of a misdemeanor, subject to a fine ($100 to $1,000) or jail sentence (one to six months) or both. Refusal to permit the department to examine the books and failure to keep books similarly are punishable.

Felony Punishment: A felony conviction under the liquor laws is punishable by a fine of not more than $5,000 or a one- to five-year prison sentence or both.

Fines: Violations of fair trade price regulations in connection with sales of distilled spirits to consumers are punishable by fines of suspension or revocation. The fine is $250 on the first offense and $1,000 for each subsequent sale for the next three years.

Former Licensee: A licensee forced out of business by revocation or who voluntarily quits has the right to sell his stock of liquor to other licensees under the rules of the department.

Habitual Drunkard: It is against the law to sell or give liquor to a common drunkard. Anyone who does it is guilty of a misdemeanor.

Hearings: Anyone charged (accusation) with a liquor law violation is entitled to a public hearing. Hearings also can be held on petitions for licenses or on a protest against the granting of a license. The procedures are set forth in the Government Code.

Hours of Sale: Liquor shall not be sold between 2 AM and 6 AM. The day Standard Time changes to Daylight Time (last Sunday in April) and vice versa (last Sunday in September) 2 AM means two hours after midnight of the day preceding the day of the change.

Licenses: Licenses authorizing persons to sell alcoholic beverages are issued by the State Department of Alcoholic Beverage Control. Headquarters: 1215 O Street, Sacramento, California 95814.

Licenses can be renewed at Sacramento headquarters or at any of the department's offices through the state either by mail or in person.

Licenses (Types of):   There are more than 50 types of license for the sale of alcoholic beverages in California.

On-sale General: This type is for hotels, restaurants, cocktail lounges, taverns, and so on, for the service of drinks with or without meals. There are two types, one for bona fide public eating places and one for public premises. The eating place must have facilities for the service of food and must actually serve meals. Minors are prohibited from entering public premises. The public premise need not serve food. These licenses are limited to a population basis. Licensees may restrict their operations to catering activities. Duplicate licenses may be obtained for a room for private parties.

License Limitation: Distilled spirits licenses generally are limited by law.

The number of on-sale general licenses is limited to one for each 2,000 population, or fraction thereof, in the county. The quota for off-sale general licenses is one to 2,500 population.

At the time this law was enacted, a number of counties had in excess of one license to 1,000 inhabitants. The law did not require the cancellation of those in excess of the quota.

The most recent federal decennial or special census is used as the principal guide in allocating the licenses. However, the department, regardless of the census, may issue additional licenses upon a satisfactory showing that the population of a given county has gone up. An applicant for such a license can go before the department and present evidence to substantiate a claim the population has risen.

The exchange of an on-sale general license for a special on-sale license is excluded from the population limitation. The exchange fee is $100.

License Applications: An application for a liquor license must be made on a form prescribed by the department. Pertinent data include name of applicant, names of partnership if the business is a partnership and the names of principal officers if a corporation is involved. The location of the premises must be given. The applicant must state he has had no felony convictions. If he cannot so state, he must enumerate his violations. The application must be verified under oath. The license fee must be paid with the application.

The applicant must post the entrance of the premises with a notice of intention to sell liquor and keep the premises so posted for thirty days. Any applicant for an on-sale license must also publish a notice in a newspaper of general circulation.

The department automatically notifies local authorities (sheriff, district attorney, or chief of police) of an application, and should the authorities protest, a hearing is held. Pending the hearing the license will not be issued. The same goes for an application to transfer a license.

The department may deny a license if an enforcement problem is threatened or if the issuance would add to an undue concentration of licenses. An application may be denied if a showing of public convenience and necessity is not made. These reasons are specified in the law, and the courts have upheld other reasons, such as establishment is in a residential area or applicant has been guilty of acts involving intentional dishonesty (moral turpitude).

License Investigations: The department must investigate applications for licenses and, if a protest is filed, conduct a hearing. A licensed beer and wine wholesaler who applies for a branch license need not be investigated, however. The department must also investigate all liquor law arrests reported to it by local police and determine whether there are grounds for suspension or revocation of a license or licenses. In checking applications, the department must determine whether public welfare and morals are affected, and shall deny applications or transfers where applicants do not qualify. Here are some of the reasons for denial as upheld by the courts: Issuance would create police problem; premise in residential area; applicant guilty of acts involving intentional dishonesty (moral turpitude).

License Protests: Protests may be filed at any office of the department within thirty days from the first date of posting the notice of intention to sell liquor. A protest made by anyone other than an employee of the department or a public officer must be verified.

The department may reject protests deemed to be without merit. Such protests, if pursued by the protestant, can be scheduled for hearing after issuance of license.

License Suspensions and Revocations: The following are the grounds for suspension or revocation of licenses as spelled out in the ABC Act:

1. Continuance of license is contrary to public welfare and morals.
2. Violating any laws involving the adulteration, dilution, misbranding, or mislabeling alcoholic beverages.
3. Misrepresentation of material fact by applicant in obtaining license.
4. Conviction of any public offense involving moral turpitude; conviction under any federal liquor law; or refilling or reusing distilled spirits bottles.
5. Failure to correct objectionable conditions constituting a nuisance after reasonable notice.

Knowingly permitting the sale of narcotics on the premises or permitting employees to solicit drinks from customers are grounds for mandatory revocation.

In disciplinary cases the licensee is responsible for the acts of his employees, the courts have so held.

Food and drug law violations also are grounds for discipline.

The license of any taxpayer is automatically suspended upon cancellation of his bond.

Employment of persons (such as B-girls) to solicit drinks on a percentage basis also is a ground for revocation. (For disciplinary procedures see *Accusation,* and *Hearings.*)

Loitering: It is unlawful to permit or employ anyone to loiter about the premises to solicit drinks from customers. (See also *B-Girls.*)

Minor: Anyone who sells or gives liquor to a minor is guilty of a misdemeanor. Any on-sale licensee who knowingly permits a minor to consume liquor on the premises is guilty of a misdemeanor.

A minor who purchases or consumes liquor in a licensed premises is guilty of a misdemeanor and must be fined at least $100, no part of which shall be suspended.

A licensee or his employees may refuse to serve anyone who refuses to produce documentary evidence he or she is over twenty-one.

Documents regarded as evidence of majority include draft cards, auto operator's licenses, and military ID cards. A person who does not have a driver's license may obtain an identification card from the Department of Motor Vehicles. Proof that the licensee or employee demanded and was shown such evidence and relied upon it shall be a defense in any criminal prosecution of license disciplinary proceeding.

Anyone who furnishes a fraudulent identification card to a minor is guilty of a misdemeanor and so is a minor who uses one to buy liquor. And he (the minor) shall be fined at least $100, with no part suspended.

It is unlawful for an on-sale licensee to employ a minor during business hours in the specific area of his place used for the sale of alcoholic beverages except as provided for entertainment purposes. In other words, the minor can be employed in the dining portion of a restaurant, but not in the bar, or as another example, in the bowling section of a bowling alley, but again, not in the bar.

Any minor who loiters in an establishment licensed as a public premise is guilty of a misdemeanor and punishable by a fine of $100, no part of which shall be suspended.

In accusations involving minors, the department must produce the minor at the hearing unless the licensee waives this requirement. If the minor is unavailable, the department may use a deposition.

Ordinances: The department must recognize valid zoning ordinances which prohibit liquor establishments in certain parts of cities or counties. But any ordinance which bans liquor in the entire city or county is invalid according to court interpretations.

Penalties: Violations of the ABC Act are not subject to criminal penalties. But fines or disciplinary actions may be imposed as follows: First offense—A monetary penalty of $100 or a license suspension not to exceed ten days; Second offense—$250 or a suspension up to thirty days; Third or subsequent offense—A monetary penalty of $500 or a suspension or revocation of license.

Prohibited Activity: The laws and rules contain certain bans against activity of liquor enforcement personnel as owners and operators in the industry.

The ABC Act strictly forbids the director of the department and members of the Alcoholic Beverage Control Appeals Board from profiting in any way from any applicant for a license. They are also forbidden from dealing in insurance covering a licensed premise or in the sale of equipment for use on premise. Subject to removal from office, they are also to refrain from soliciting licenses for the purchase of tickets or for contributions for benefits.

Rule 62 goes much further. It prohibits any employee in liquor enforcement from holding a liquor license. Even after retirement, he must wait ninety days before he can be eligible for a license in the county in which he was employed. This applies to employees of the ABC Department, the Department of Justice (attorney general), or in any sheriff's office or police department. The restriction does not apply to ownership of stock in a corporation listed on a stock exchange or to ownership of stock in a financial institution which obtains possession of a license in a fiduciary (in trust) capacity.

Public Premises: This covers premises which are licensed for the sale of alcoholic beverages by the drink (including on-sale beer) and in which the sale of food is not required. Minors are prohibited from entering such premises.

Publication: An applicant for an on-sale license must within ten days of filing his application cause a notice to be published in a newspaper of general circulation in the city in which the premises are located. If the premises are not in a city, the notice must be in a paper nearest the premises. The notice must give name of applicant and location of premises.

Purpose of Act: The purpose of the Alcoholic Beverage Control Act is to protect the safety, health, morals, and welfare of the people; to promote temperance and to eliminate the evils of unlicensed trafficking in liquor. It is the intention of the legislature that the liquor laws will be enforced strictly, honestly, uniformly, and impartially.

Reinstatement of Automatically Suspended License: A license is automatically suspended if the taxpayer loses his bond or is delinquent in taxes. The license is automatically reinstated once a valid bond is filed or the delinquent taxes are paid, as the case may be.

Any taxpayer who loses his license under this regulation is entitled to a hearing. There must be five days' notice of the hearing.

Rules and Regulations: The Alcoholic Beverage Control Act conveys upon the department the power to issue rules to supplement the law. These rules have the same force as law, and a violation thereof subjects the licensee to the same penalties (suspension or revocation) invoked for violation of the ABC Act itself.

Serial Numbers: It is a misdemeanor crime to tamper with serial numbers, stamps, or other markings required by the federal government on alcoholic beverages until the contents are disposed of.

Signs: An on-sale licensee may not have a sign advertising liquor outside his premises which exceeds 720 square inches. The words *bar, barroom, saloon, tavern,* and *cocktail lounge,* long taboo, are now legal.

No signs shall be obnoxious, gaudy, blatant, or otherwise offensive and may not obstruct the view of the interior of the premises from the street.

Substitution of Brands: A bartender or anyone who without telling the customer substitutes another brand for the one called for is guilty of a misdemeanor.

Tax Delinquency: The department may refuse to renew or transfer a license or issue a new one if the applicant is delinquent in taxes due the state or local government. This includes liquor taxes, sales taxes, personal income taxes, bank and corporation taxes, unemployment taxes, or unsecured property taxes.

Tied-House Restrictions: Manufacturers, wholesalers, wine growers, rectifiers, and so forth, are strictly prohibited from:

Owning any interest, directly or indirectly, in an on-sale license, or off-sale general license.

Time: A liquor license must be put to use within thirty days after its issuance. Otherwise it becomes null and void.

Title of Act: Most of the state laws affecting the industry are found in Division 9 of the State Business and Professions Code. This division is officially known as the Alcoholic Beverage Control Act. It is published in pamphlet form (containing some of the related statutes) and is obtainable by writing the State Department of Alcoholic Beverage Control, 1215 O Street, Sacramento, California 95814.

A copy may be obtained also by writing the Documents Section,

General Services, P. O. Box 20191, Sacramento, California 95820 and enclosing $2.70 for each Act and 1970 Supplement, including tax and postage.

Universities: For about eighty years in California it was against the law to sell alcoholic beverages within certain limits (ranging from one to three miles) of university campuses and prisons. Recognizing the automobile age and the state's fast growing population, the legislature in 1959 modified this restriction as being obsolete. Issuance of liquor licenses to bona fide eating places in the vicinity of campuses is now permissible and under the complete control of the ABC Department which has adopted a rule establishing generally a mile zone around each campus. In these zones licenses are issued only to restaurants and hotels which do not cater to students.

In 1965 the legislature further relaxed this policy by permitting sales by wholesalers, manufacturers, and so on, to the so-called dry zones. The law now allows a caterer to serve alcoholic beverages in a dry zone in conjunction with the service of meals.

Whiskey: Whiskey is defined as distilled spirits under state law. This means an alcoholic beverage obtained by the distillation of fermented agricultural products, and includes spirits of wine, whiskey, rum, brandy, and gin, including all dilutions and mixtures thereof.

Wine: Bottled wine means wine put up in containers of a gallon or less. Bulk wine is that which is packaged in containers larger than a gallon or is transported by pipeline or shipped in tank cars.

Wine is obtained from normal alcoholic fermentation of the juice of sound, ripe grapes or other agricultural products containing natural or added sugar or any such alcoholic beverage to which is added grape brandy, fruit brandy, or spirits of wine, which is distilled from the particular agricultural product or products of which the wine is made and other rectified wine products and by whatever name and which does not contain more than 15 percent added flavoring, coloring, and blending material and which contains not more than 24 percent by volume, and includes vermouth and sake, known as Japanese rice wine.

A wine gallon contains 231 cubic ounces.

ABC Rules and regulations*

What It Means: The Alcoholic Beverage Control Act, containing the main body of law affecting the industry, is a product of the legisla-

---

* Courtesy of BIN-California Gold Book.

ture: Supplementing these laws are the rules and regulations of the State Department of Alcoholic Beverage Control. The ABC Act can be changed every year during regular legislative sessions, or at special sessions if called by the governor for that purpose. The rules and regulations are more flexible and can be changed by the department at any time, with proper notice and hearings. Licensees must obey both the laws and the rules.

Most of these rules are quite technical. If you intend to open a bar in California, I would suggest subscribing to BIN-California Gold Book to get a copy of the fuller text.

Advertising: (Misleading Advertising): No licensee shall disseminate any advertising statement with respect to price, kind or type of alcoholic beverages which is untrue or misleading.

Beer Prices: Minimum retail prices of beer by the containers, pack, or case may be filed by the brewer or importer. In other words, beer minimum prices are optional with brand owner, but mandatory for distilled spirits. Rule 90 is similar to Rule 99: notice of fifteen days is required on the original posting of prices, notice of forty-five days is required on price changes. A brewer who drops minimum prices cannot restore them for ninety days.

As in the case of distilled spirits, the state is divided into two trading areas where different prices can be maintained. The southern area consists of Santa Barbara, Ventura, Los Angeles, Orange, Riverside, San Bernardino, Imperial, and San Diego counties. The rest of the state consists of the northern area.

Beer Labeling Requirements: Draught beer or beer sold in bottles or cans shall not exceed an alcoholic content of 4 percent by weight. This does not apply to beer for export or to ale, porter, brown stout, properly labeled as such.

Ale, porter, brown stout, or malt liquor of less than 4 percent alcoholic content by weight must be so labeled. And only such labeled products can be sold by on-sale beer licensees.

Beer Tapping Equipment: Manufacturers may furnish retailers certain tapping equipment and service and repair same.

Hostesses, Topless: These rules ban solicitation of drinks by hostesses (B-girls), and topless waitresses, lewd entertainment and movies. At this writing the subject matter is under review by a panel of three federal judges in Los Angeles.

Licenses: (The ABC Department's regulations covering licenses are found mostly in Rules 55 to 81. These, of course, are supplementary to the state laws covering licenses and are summarized in Chapter 2 dealing with the Alcoholic Beverage Control Act.)

On-Sale General Seasonal Licenses: An on-sale general seasonal license may be issued only for a bona fide eating place or sports facility in a recreational area where the demand is warranted by public convenience and necessity. This generally means summer or winter vacation resorts. Sports facility includes golf courses of at least nine holes and ski grounds with chair tow or lift.

No seasonal licenses shall be issued for more than nine months out of the year.

Seasonal licenses may be transferred from person to person or premises to premises, provided foregoing requirements are met.

State, county, or district fairs are ineligible for seasonal licenses unless they obtained licenses prior to adoption of this rule.

A seasonal licensee must operate during the same season each year unless, with the department's permission, he shows there is a change in season of maximum patronage.

The standard of public convenience and necessity is met if the seasonal population increases to the point existing licenses cannot satisfy the public demand. But no license shall be issued if the number of permanent and seasonal licenses exceeds one per 2,000 adult population. The one per 2,000 ratio need not apply in remote areas where vacationers would be forced to travel long distances to obtain beverages.

Fingerprinting of Licensees: Every licensee and the officers of every corporate licensee must have their fingerprints taken by the department if they have management responsibilities. These prints are taken at the time of making application.

The husband of a married woman who seeks a license also must submit his fingerprints, unless his absence from the state makes it impossible. The wife of a married man who seeks a license must be fingerprinted if she is to work in the business.

Manager Defined: An employee shall be deemed a manager subject to qualifications of a licensee (see *License Qualifications*) if he has power to hire and fire, enter into contracts for purchase of equipment and supplies, disburse funds and to make policy decisions.

Qualifications of a Manager: An on-sale licensee must notify the ABC Department within fifteen days of the employment of a manager. The manager must be fingerprinted. The department must investigate the qualifications and approve or reject the proposed manager.

Application by Married Persons: If the business is community property, a license may be issued either:

1. In the husband's name if the wife takes no part in the business;

2. In the name of both;
3. In the name of the wife, if it is impractical for the husband to participate in the business.

If the business is not community property, the license will be issued to either husband or wife as the case may be, provided documentary evidence is submitted establishing separate ownership.

Transfer of Licenses: Limited licenses may be transferred from person to person, and premises to premises within the same county. Other licenses also are transferable from premises to premises anywhere within the state.

No new original on-sale license issued after June 1, 1961, other than one for beer alone, and no on-sale license transferred from county to county, may be exchanged for public premise license without showing of public demand.

The transferor must file the application for transfer in writing in duplicate on department forms. The transferee also must make an original application for the license to be transferred.

The transferee must pay the transfer fee.

In the absence of a temporary permit, the transferor is responsible for the conduct of the business until the transfer is completed.

An administrator or executor of an estate may initiate a transfer, supporting it with a certified copy of letters testamentary or letters of administration. Similarly the guardian of an estate of a licensee may execute a transfer.

But the transferee must be acceptable to the department. The trustee or executor, and so on, may grant an option to the transferee for ninety days or less, provided the purchase price is refundable should the department find the transferee unacceptable.

In the event of death of a partner, a surviving partner or partners may initiate a transfer.

A trustee of a bankrupt estate or the receiver of the estate of a licensee may execute a transfer.

If no estate is involved, a surviving spouse may file a transfer application.

(The ABC Act contains further detailed regulations concerning transfers. See *License Transfers.*)

License Limitations: Under state law, on-sale general and off-sale general licenses are limited.

Restrictions on Government Owned Premises: This rule makes it clear that a person or corporation which has a license on public premises, such as an airport or municipal auditorium, cannot dispose of said license by transfer and re-obtain one for the public premise—licenses on such public premises being exempt from population quotas.

Off-Sale General License Restrictions: No original off-sale general license shall be issued to the holder of an on-sale general license, unless the department is satisfied the on-sale and off-sale businesses are physically separated and that the operations will be conducted in a bona fide manner.

Law Enforcement Personnel Not to Hold Licenses: Employees of the State Department of Justice, the Department of Alcoholic Beverage Control, employees in any district attorney's office, sheriff's force, or police department may not hold a liquor license or have an interest in the business. This does not apply to ownership of stock in a corporation listed on the stock exchange, or ownership in a financial company which has an indirect interest in the liquor business. The rule does not apply to persons holding a license as an executor, administrator, or guardian.

Nor does it apply to a peace officers' association holding a club license.

License Reinstatement After Revocation: A licensee who loses his license by revocation for failure to renew may within six months file an application for reinstatement. He must pay the annual fee, plus a penalty of $50 or an amount equal to the annual fee, whichever is lesser. An investigation is then made by the department and if it is determined there is good cause for the failure to renew, the department shall reinstate the license. In the meantime, the licensee must not operate his business.

Premises Under Construction: No on-sale general license issued for premises to be constructed or under construction shall actually be delivered to the licensee until the premises are finished and ready to operate.

Licenses may be transferred to premises in process of construction and the certificate held by the department until the premises are completed and ready for operation.

Surrender of License on Closing of Business: Any licensee who closes up for more than fifteen days must within the next fifteen days surrender his license to the department. If he fails to do so, the department may seize his license. The relinquished premises may be relicensed by the department. Surrendered licenses are cancelled if not put to use within a year. Extension of one year period can be granted by ABC Department on good cause under specified circumstances.

Premises Where License Previously Denied: If a license application for a particular premise is denied, another application cannot be filed for a year unless the conditions which caused the denial no longer exist.

On-Sale Beer License: An on-sale beer license will not be issued for any premises for which any other type of license is issued and vice versa.

Employment of Minors in Public Premises: Licensees of a public premises may employ or use the services of any minor, eighteen or above, as a musician, entertainer, or in any other capacity during business hours in any portion of said premises.

Warning Notice: Holders of on-sale general, on-sale beer and wine licenses, or on-sale beer for public premises must post a sign, not less than 7 by 11 inches in size, reading: "No Person Under 21 Allowed." The sign must be at or near the entrances and visible from the outside. Lettering must be at least an inch high. A similar sign must be posted inside.

Notice of Suspension: Whenever a licensee is ordered to suspend the sale of alcoholic beverages, he must conspicuously post both inside and outside the premises a sign 2 feet long and 14 inches wide and which reads:

NOTICE OF SUSPENSION
Alcoholic Beverage Licenses Issued
For These Premises Have Been
Suspended by Order of the
DEPARTMENT OF ALCOHOLIC
BEVERAGE CONTROL
For Violation of
Alcoholic Beverage Control Act.

Invoices: Every sale or delivery of alcoholic beverages, except beer, from one licensee to another must be recorded on a sales invoice. They must be accessible for examination by employees of the ABC Department.

The invoices must contain complete data—name and address of purchaser, date of transaction, kind, quantity, size, cost (together with discount), place of delivery, and so on.

California Alcoholic Beverage Tax Laws*

Administration and Enforcement: The State Board of Equalization is designated as the agency to collect and enforce the excise taxes on alcoholic beverages.

---

* Courtesy of BIN-California Gold Book.

Alcoholic Beverage Control Fund: All liquor taxes, interest, and penalties are to be paid to the State Board of Equalization which deposits them with the state treasurer to the credit of the Alcoholic Beverage Control Fund.

Bond: Every taxpayer must file a bond with the board to guarantee payment of taxes, penalties, or other obligations under the liquor tax laws. The amount of the bond is fixed by the board and must be twice the taxpayer's estimated monthly tax. It must never be less than $500. The taxpayer may deposit cash instead of a bond. The state treasurer must reimburse the board from these individual deposits to meet any specific tax delinquencies certified by the board. The board shall notify the State Department of Alcoholic Beverage Control in event a taxpayer's bond is cancelled or in event he is delinquent in his taxes. Since most of the taxes are paid by wholesalers, manufacturers, and so forth, these provisions seldom apply to retailers.

Collections: The alcoholic beverage taxes are paid on or before the fifteenth of each month with the board of Sacramento by distilled spirits taxpayers, beer manufacturers, wine growers, and beer and wine importers. Forms with which to file the returns and pay the taxes are provided.

If for some reason the taxes are not paid, the board has many weapons with which to force collection. It may bring court action, in which case the attorney general will represent the board. In any such suit the board's showing is prima facie evidence the tax is due. The board may merely file a certificate with the county clerk stating taxes are due and the clerk must immediately enter a judgment against the taxpayer. An abstract of this judgment may be recorded with the county recorder and the penalty set forth in the judgment constitutes a lien on the taxpayer's property. The lien is good for five years and may be extended and is also a valid lien on property acquired after the recording of the judgment.

The board may issue a warrant for the enforcement of the lien. This means any sheriff, marshall, or constable can levy the lien and sell the taxpayer's property if necessary.

Whenever a tax is delinquent, the board also may seize real or personal property of the taxpayer and sell it at public auction. Written notice of the sale of at least ten days must be given. If the sale brings in more than is necessary to meet the delinquencies, the board shall return the excess amount to the taxpayer.

The board may notify debtors of the taxpayer, whereupon they shall not transfer such debts without the board's permission.

The state may use any or all of these remedies. It does not have to stick with one. In the case of insolvent taxpayers, the state's claim for taxes has priority over virtually all other creditors.

Deficiency: If the board is dissatisfied with the amount of tax paid by a taxpayer, it may compute the tax on the basis of information available. If it is found the taxpayer was underpaying due to negligence, a 10 percent penalty shall be added. If fraud is involved, the penalty is 25 percent. Interest also is added. The board must give the taxpayer written notice of its determination. Except for fraud, a notice of determination must be given within three years. In case of failure to file a return, the notice must be given within eight years. The taxpayer may petition for a redetermination and have a hearing.

Evidence of Sale: It is presumed in the law that any beer removed from bonded premises or wine removed from bonded premises has been sold in this state by the beer manufacturer or wine grower unless satisfactory proof is offered the beverages are otherwise disposed of (exported, sold to another manufacturer, or otherwise exempt from taxation).

It is also presumed that distilled spirits acquired by a taxpayer have been sold in this state unless there are specified conditions showing the beverages are exempt.

A similar presumption applies to imported beer and wine.

Interest: When the board makes a deficiency assessment, interest of ½ of 1 percent a month is charged on the amount of tax due. The same rate applies on taxes assessed by the board if the taxpayer fails to file a return.

The board may grant a taxpayer a thirty-day extension of time on his regular tax payments, but he must pay an annual interest rate of 6 percent from the time his tax was due.

All taxes not paid on the date due bear an interest rate of ½ of 1 percent per month until paid.

In the event a taxpayer wins a judgment for a refund of taxes, interest shall be allowed him at 6 percent a year on the amount illegally collected.

Interest of ½ of 1 percent a month is allowed on any overpayment of tax.

Jeopardy Determination: If the board believes collection of a tax is jeopardized by delay, it may make a jeopardy determination and order the tax paid immediately. If not thereon paid, interest (½ of 1 percent a month) and a penalty (5 percent) apply. The taxpayer may within ten days petition for a redetermination but must put up security covering the tax.

Limitation Period: Any prosecutions for violations of penal provisions of the law must be commenced within three years after the offense occurs.

A claim for a tax refund must be filed with the board within three years. If disallowed, the taxpayer may file a suit.

Local Taxes: Cities, counties, or local subdivisions are prohibited from imposing taxes on alcoholic beverages.

Offenses: Violations of the liquor tax laws are specified as follows: Failure to keep records, false returns, tax evasion, diversion of industrial spirits or wine to beverage use.

Filing false returns is punishable as a misdemeanor—fine of $100 to $1,000 or six months' jail sentence or both.

Tax evasion and diverting tax-free liquor to beverage use are felonies. The punishment is a fine up to $5,000 or prison sentence from one to five years, or both fine and sentence.

Payments: Liquor taxes are due monthly, and each taxpayer must file a return with the board by the fifteenth of each month covering taxes for the preceding month. The board may grant a thirty-day extension, but interest is added at 6 percent. Taxes otherwise not paid on time bear interest at ½ of 1 percent a month. A penalty of 5 percent of the amount of the tax also is added for late payment.

Penalties: For late payment of taxes—5 percent of amount of tax.

For failure to file return —$5. But this will not be added to the 5 percent penalty (above) if the 5 percent exceeds $5. If failure is due to negligence the penalty is 10 percent and if due to fraud 25 percent (added to the 5 percent).

Failure to pay taxes as determined by board following failure to file return—10 percent of the amount due.

When the board, dissatisfied with taxpayer's return, makes a deficiency determination—10 percent if deficiency due to negligence; 25 percent if due to fraud (plus interest).

Records: The board has the right to inspect the books of persons selling, manufacturing, transporting, or warehousing alcoholic beverages.

Anyone who refuses to keep books or permit the board to inspect his books or who makes false records is guilty of a misdemeanor. The punishment is a fine of $10 to $1,000 or six months in jail or both fine and jail.

Redetermination: If a taxpayer is dissatisfied with amount of taxes as determined by the board, he may petition for a redetermination within thirty days. He may have a hearing. The board may increase or decrease the tax, but may increase it only if it asserts a claim for an increase in advance. The final amount determined is due and payable at once, and if not paid a 10 percent penalty is added.

Refunds: If the board determines any taxes are overpaid, it shall certify the amount to the state board of control. If the board of control approves, the amount can be credited on any amounts due from the taxpayer and the balance refunded. A claim for the refund must be filed with the Board of Equalization within three years. Failure to file the claim within this period is a waiver of all demands against the state. Interest is allowed on overpayments except those made intentionally or through carelessness.

If the board of control rejects a claim or fails to act on it within six months, the taxpayer may file suit in court within 90 days. However, no injunction may be obtained to prevent the state from collecting any taxes sought.

Failure to bring suit constitutes a waiver of rights.

A court judgment for the taxpayer shall be credited to any taxes due, the balance to be refunded.

Interest at 6 percent is allowed on a judgment.

Rules and Regulations: The board has power to adopt rules and regulations to enforce the tax laws.

Taxes: The tax rates on alcoholic beverages are explained in the sections dealing with various types, but are repeated here in the general category of taxes as follows:

Beer—$1.24 for every barrel containing 31 gallons. This is 4 cents a gallon.

Wine—Still wines containing not more than 14 percent of absolute alcohol by volume, 1 cent per wine gallon and at a proportionate rate for any other quantity.

All still wines containing more than 14 percent alcohol by volume, 2 cents per wine gallon and at proportionate rate, and so on.

Champagne, sparkling wine, except sparkling hard cider, whether naturally or artificially carbonated, 30 cents per wine gallon.

Sparkling hard cider, 2 cents per wine gallon.

Distilled spirits—$2 per gallon.

California Alcoholic Beverage Tax Regulations*

These regulations are issued under the board's power to collect and enforce taxes on the alcoholic beverage industry. In the following pages is a summary of the regulations. Most of the answers to problems

---

* (Issued by the State Board of Equalization, Sacramento, California)

which might come up on the day-to-day operations of a licensee are contained. However, this is not complete. If specific information is needed on any of the technical details, a copy of the regulations may be obtained by writing to the Beverage Tax Division, State Board of Equalization, 1020 N Street, Sacramento, California, 95800.

Records: General. Every licensee liable for payment of taxes based upon the sale of alcoholic beverages shall keep complete and accurate records of all transactions in alcohol or alcoholic beverages.

All records shall be kept and maintained in the licensed premises of the taxpayer in this state, unless permission has been granted by the board to keep and maintain the records at some other location.

Every licensee required to file reports shall retain copies of all such records by which employees of the board may verify such reports.

All records required by law or rule and regulation to be kept by any licensee, shall be kept and preserved for a period of three years.

Failure to keep and maintain records and copies of reports will be considered as evidence of negligence or intent to evade the tax, and will result in the imposition of appropriate penalties.

Invoices: Contents. Every sale or delivery of alcoholic beverages, except beer, from one licensee to another must be recorded on a sales invoice, whether or not consideration is involved. Invoices must be readily accessible for examination by employees of the board.

Other California Laws on Alcoholic
Beverages Penal Code Sections*

Sales Near Universities, Prisons, Veterans' Homes: Under the well publicized section 172 of the Penal Code the sale or giving away of alcoholic beverages is prohibited within certain distances of universities, state colleges, prisons, veterans' homes, et cetera. The state capitol and its grounds also are covered.

The distances range from 1,900 feet from a state reformatory to 3 miles from the University of California campus in Berkeley. However, the law specifies one mile for most campuses.

All of the above does not apply to beer or 3.2 percent wine, porter, or ale.

And the extension of boundaries of the mentioned facilities does not require existing licenses subsequently brought into the "dry" zones to move.

---

* Courtesy of BIN-California Gold Book.

Further, under section 172e, the department is authorized to license bona fide eating places within these limits.

Gambling: Anyone who possesses or operates slot machines or other coin-operated gambling devices faces a fine from $100 to $500 or up to six months in jail or both fine and jail. A bookmaker or anyone who permits his place to be used for bookmaking or registering bets faces a county jail or prison sentence from thirty days to a year.

Public Nuisance: Once a place is ordered abated as a public nuisance, the continuation of its operation after due notice constitutes a separate offense every day thereafter.

Adulteration: Anyone who fraudulently adulterates or dilutes liquor or who sells it is guilty of a misdemeanor. A retailer who produces a written guarantee of purity from the person from whom he purchased adulterated or diluted goods shall not be convicted.

Drunkard: Selling liquor to a habitual drunkard or to one who is legally incompetent or insane is a misdemeanor.

Hours of Sale: It is a misdemeanor to sell alcoholic beverages between 2 AM and 6 AM of the same day.

Adulteration, Misbranding: A food or beverage is deemed to be adulterated if it contains injurious, poisonous, unsafe, or diseased substances; if it is produced under insanitary conditions; if the container is composed of any poisonous or deleterious substance.

Other forms of adulteration include: Use of substitute substances, concealment of damage or inferiority, use of uncertified coal tar or use of mineral oil.

Misbranding includes: False and misleading labels, selling in the name of another food, and offering an imitation without so labeling it.

An advertisement of a food shall be deemed to be false if it is false in any material particular.

Wherever there is a conflict between the ABC Act and the health and safety code over advertising, the ABC Act controls.

The manufacture, selling, or keeping for sale adulterated or misbranded foods is prohibited.

No person shall sell, offer for sale, or keep for sale distilled spirits in any package which has been refilled or partially refilled.

Possession of adulterated or misbranded food is evidence of a violation.

Judgment Against License Prohibited: A license to sell alcoholic beverages, or any other business or professional license issued by the state, is not subject to execution to satisfy a judgment. A levy can be made against your wages, personal and real property, money, et cetera, but NOT against your license. However, the court may appoint a receiver to take possession of the license and sell it to satisfy a judgment.

Business and Professions Code. Discrimination: Every licensee, except a club licensee, is subject to disciplinary action by the department if he refuses to service a person on the basis of race, color, sex, religion, ancestry, or national origin.

Appendix C

Brief Highlights from Laws of Other States*

I had intended to append a precis of the various state legalities and statutes and regulations. Then, I waded through those of California alone, which are 270 pages of impenetrable legal prose. What I would have ended up with, since the regulations in all the fifty states are different, is a 13,500 page unreadable encyclopedia. This is a practical handbook, not an omnibus compendium.

Practically, then, I suggest you write to DISCUS* and buy their synopsis of legal qualifications governing the sale of alcoholic beverages in the fifty states. In some states, counties, and municipalities you just can't sell booze at all, and that's that, legally.

That handbook gives charts and graphs which anyone with a clear head can understand. However, if you decide that you are getting serious about buying a bar, then you will need fuller information about laws and regulations. You should then pay a personal call on the governing body in your state. The names and addresses of all these control boards are given in Appendix D.

If my experience is any guide, they will be friendly, informative, and willing to oblige any civil applicant. They know they are dealing

---

* Summary of State Laws and Regulations Relating to Distilled Spirits, Distilled Spirits Institute, Inc. (DISCUS), 1132 Pennsylvania Building, Washington, D.C. 20004, $7.50.

with a potential publican, not a metaphysical attorney, so they will give you an understandable rundown on their rules. They hope to be collecting taxes from you, so it is to their benefit to let you know the facts and to encourage you. Nevertheless, they must be precise and discreet, so I would spring several hundred bucks and engage a lawyer familiar with this business to sit down with me and explain the hard facts. There's an old saying in the business that "the first loss is the best loss." In other words, you might be reluctant to pay some fellow three or four hundred dollars to chat with you for a few hours. But it might save your shirt later.

I had thought, when I started writing this book, that you could put up a few dollars and get all the answers. But by now you know that there are simply too many variables in the business. If I had tried to be magisterial and comprehensive, it's almost a certainty you would not have got this far in your reading.

Perhaps this sounds like a cop-out (and I'm not sure it isn't) but Benjamin Jowett, Master of Balliol College at Oxford, said that an education is not imparting facts but teaching you where to find the facts if you need them.

Basically, you will find three distinct legal philosophies in the sale of alcohol: prohibition, state monopoly, and free enterprise. The Constitution of the United States leaves the control up to the states. Some of the states subdivide it further and leave it up to local option by county or township.

The liquor control acts of the fifty states of the union must have been written by Laurel and Hardy. In Oklahoma, for example, bars and almost everything else are PROHIBITED. However, sale of 3.2 percent beer is allowable in package stores to "Male—21, Female—18, Other—21." I wonder how many mustangs and rattlesnakes get to be 21?

In New Mexico the entire act was declared unconstitutional. However, unconstitutional or not, "prices must be as low as in any other state or D.C."

Nevada is undoubtedly the most civilized state in this regard. In most categories Nevada says "no restrictions." But dear old New Mexico says that you may import without tax any "reasonable" quantity of liquor by an adult. Probably tequila.

In Nebraska you have to pay cash for a drink except in a club to members. (I did not invent this syntax.) If this has not yet been declared unconstitutional, it probably will be if the Supreme Court reads this book.

In Colorado a wholesaler may give a bar owner "napkins, coasters, menu sheets, ash trays, lamps, and so forth and may sell certain others: glasses, clocks, picnic coolers, matches, and paper cups, and material of negligible value."

In Michigan here are the restrictions on advertising, and I swear on the hand of the Holy Ghost that I didn't make this up. "No offer prize in contest, referring to deceased President, Holy Days, depiction Santa Claus, Xmas trees or gifts at fireplace, association with juveniles, nor use words 'Easter,' 'Noel,' 'Christmas,' 'Yule,' etc." One can detect the fine Italian hand of the Vatican here.

I know a fellow here in Frisco, an excommunicated Jesuit priest, who just went banco in a bar operation. He's now studying for his real estate license and has the scheme to sell bars to attorneys as tax losses. If it takes a year for an ordinary person to get hung up on one of these laws, an attorney should be able to do it in three months.

Before they wrote all these laws, Stan and Ollie starred in a classic movie called *Another Fine Mess*. Here are some more highlights from the screenplay.

The United States of America has a keystone philosophy of free enterprise and competition. We claim to be opposed to the concept of state control and monopoly. However, the following states control and monopolize the sale of alcoholic beverages.

Alabama	Ohio
Idaho	Oregon
Iowa	Pennsylvania
Maine	Utah
Michigan	Vermont
Mississippi	Virginia
Montana	Washington
New Hampshire	West Virginia
North Carolina	Wyoming

You cannot run a bar in North Carolina, West Virginia, Kansas, and Oklahoma. In Tennessee you cannot buy a drink in a bar after noon on Sunday, but you can buy a bottle all day. Probably they figure you'll lug the bottle with you to Evensong.

There is an appendix in the DISCUS book which informs you of the "States in Which, and Conditions under Which, Distilled Spirits May Be Sold in Miniature Containers Other Than Trains, Planes, or Boats."

Presumably somebody got, or is getting, rich off this Pecksniffery. What it leads to is the exact 180 degree opposite of what it piously and purportedly intends. Anyone, not a lawyer, confronted with all this illogic, will throw up his hands and say, "Ah, what the hell. I'll do it my own way and see if they catch me." If you do this, then you're playing right into *Their* hands. I emphasized that They will know what you are doing. You can't keep it a secret. Then They have the sword hanging over your head; any time They want to bring it down, They can.

You are playing on their field with their ball, so you have to beat them by their own rules. All these bureaucrats are collecting taxes from you, so they want to keep you in the game. They don't want to rule you out unless you give them flagrant provocation. I can't think of an easy, legal way to make a living. There are manifold aggravations in the bar business, but there are also great pleasures, mainly, as I said, recognition, which to me is an earthly joy.

I attended a service managers' convention at the General Motors Training School in Beavertown, Oregon. They were discussing employee relations. They passed out a questionnaire to all the dealers and service managers. It said: "What is the most important consideration of employment to your mechanics?" It listed about twenty alternatives. All the dealers checked compensation first, that is, wages and monetary benefits. The dealers continued with pensions, working conditions, union benefits, and so on.

General Motors had also circulated this questionnaire to thousands of mechanics. By far, an overwhelming majority of the mechanics said that their most important job consideration was: Recognition.

Finally, I would advise you—before you buy your bar—to wade through the official acts and regulations of your state. It will be heavy going but you will find all sorts of traps and pitfalls to avoid gracefully.

Appendix D

Addresses of State Regulatory Bodies

Liquor Control Agencies*

Alabama
Alabama Alcoholic Beverage Control Board
607 Administrative Building
P. O. Box 1151
Montgomery, Alabama 36102

Alaska
Alcoholic Beverage Control Board
860 MacKay Bldg.
338 Denali Street
Anchorage, Alaska

Arizona
Department of Liquor Licenses and Control
1602 West Jefferson
Phoenix, Arizona 85007

Arkansas
Department of Alcoholic Beverage Control
National Old Line Building
Little Rock, Arkansas 72201

City of Baltimore
Board of Liquor License Commissioners
113 American Building
Baltimore, Maryland 21202

---

* Courtesy of California Department of Alcoholic Beverage Control.

Colorado	Liquor Licensing Authority 486 Capitol Annex Building 1375 Sherman Street Denver, Colorado, 80203
Connecticut	Liquor Control Commission Room 562, State Office Building Hartford, Connecticut 06106
Delaware	Delaware Alcoholic Beverage Control Commission P. O. Box 1789 Wilmington, Delaware 19899
District of Columbia	Alcoholic Beverage Control Board Room 201, District Building 14th and E Streets, Northwest Washington, D. C. 20004
Florida	State Beverage Department of Florida Tallahassee, Florida 32304
Georgia	Alcohol Tax and Control Unit Department of Revenue 516 State Office Building Atlanta, Georgia 30334
Hawaii	Liquor Commission of the City and County of Honolulu 1455 South Beretania Street Honolulu, Hawaii 96814
	County of Hawaii 25 Aupuni Street Hilo, Hawaii 96720
	County of Maui Wailuku, Hawaii 96793
	County of Kauai Lihue, Hawaii 96766
Idaho	Idaho State Liquor Dispensary P. O. Box 959 Boise, Idaho 83701
Illinois	Illinois Liquor Control Commission 410 Centennial Building Springfield, Illinois 62706
	188 West Randolph Chicago, Illinois 60601

Indiana	Indiana Alcoholic Beverage Commission 911 State Office Building Indianapolis, Indiana 46209
Iowa	Iowa Liquor Control Commission State Office Building 300 Fourth Street Des Moines, Iowa 50319
Kansas	Office of the Director of Alcoholic Beverage Control 10th Floor, State Office Building Topeka, Kansas 66612
Kentucky	Department of Alcoholic Beverage Control 404 Ann Street Frankfort, Kentucky 40601
Louisiana	Department of Revenue State of Louisiana Baton Rouge, Louisiana 70821
Maine	Maine State Liquor Commission State House Augusta, Maine 04330
Maryland	Alcoholic Beverages Division Room 310, State Office Building Annapolis, Maryland 21401
	Alcoholic Beverages Division Room 308, State Office Building West Preston Street Baltimore, Maryland 21201
Massachusetts	The Alcoholic Beverage Control Commission State Office Building 100 Cambridge Street Government Center Boston, Massachusetts 02202
Michigan	Liquor Control Commission 506 South Hosmer Lansing, Michigan 48904
Minnesota	Liquor Control Commissioner 80 State Office Building St. Paul, Minnesota 55101
Mississippi	State Tax Commission Jackson, Mississippi 39201

Missouri	Department of Liquor Control State Office Building Jefferson City, Missouri 65102
Montana	Liquor Control Board Front and Lyndale Avenues Helena, Montana 59601
Nebraska	Nebraska Liquor Control Commission State House Lincoln, Nebraska 68509
Nevada	Nevada Tax Commission Cigarette and Liquor Tax Division New State Office Building Carson City, Nevada 89701
New Hampshire	State Liquor Commission Storrs Street Concord, New Hampshire 03301
New Jersey	Division of Alcoholic Beverage Control 1100 Raymond Boulevard Newark, New Jersey 07102
New Mexico	Division of Liquor Control Bureau of Revenue P. O. Box 1540 Santa Fe, New Mexico 87501
New York	Executive Department, State Liquor Authority Division of Alcoholic Beverage Control 270 Broadway New York, New York 10007
North Carolina	North Carolina Board of Alcoholic Control Old Health Building P. O. Box 9613 Raleigh, North Carolina 27603
North Dakota	Liquor Control Division Office of State Treasurer Capitol Building Bismarck, North Dakota 58501
Ohio	Department of Liquor Control 33 North Third Street Columbus, Ohio 43215

Oklahoma	Oklahoma Alcoholic Beverage Control Board 210 Northeast Fourth, Room 100 Oklahoma City, Oklahoma 73104
Oregon	Oregon Liquor Control Commission 9201 S.E. McLoughlin Blvd., Box 22297 Portland, Oregon 97222
Pennsylvania	Pennsylvania Liquor Control Board Northwest Office Building Capital and Forster Streets Harrisburg, Pennsylvania 17124
Rhode Island	Department of Business Regulations Liquor Control Administration 49 Westminster Street Old Industrial Trust Building Providence, Rhode Island 02903
South Carolina	Alcoholic Beverage Control Commission 1710 Gervais Street Columbia, South Carolina 29202
South Dakota	Department of Revenue State Capitol Building Pierre, South Dakota 57501
Tennessee	Department of Revenue War Memorial Building, Room 103 Nashville, Tennessee 37219
Texas	Texas Liquor Control Board 201 East 14th Street Sam Houston State Office Austin, Texas 78711
Utah	Utah Liquor Control Commission 1625 South 8th West Salt Lake City, Utah 84101
Vermont	Department of Liquor Control State House Montpelier, Vermont 05602
Virginia	Virginia Alcoholic Beverage Control Board 4th and Grace Streets P. O. Box 1395 Richmond, Virginia 23211

Washington   State Liquor Control Board
                            General Administration Building
                            P. O. Box 1189
                            Olympia, Washington 98501

West Virginia   West Virginia Liquor Control Commissioner
                            2019 E. Washington Street
                            Charleston, West Virginia 25305

Wisconsin   Department of Revenue
                            State Office Building, Room 1000
                            Madison, Wisconsin 53702

Wyoming   Wyoming Liquor Commission
                            1740 Pacific Avenue
                            P. O. Box 538
                            Cheyenne, Wyoming 82001

Appendix E

Excerpts from New York State Dram Shop Act

Precis of the General Obligations of Law of the State of New York, Section 11-101, *Compensation for Injury Caused by the Illegal Sale of Intoxicating Liquor.*

1. Any person who shall be injured in person, property, means of support, or otherwise by any intoxicated person, or by reason of the intoxication of any person, whether resulting in his death or not, shall have a right of action against any person who shall, by unlawful selling to or unlawfully assisting in procuring liquor for such intoxicated person, have caused or contributed to such intoxication; and in any such action such person shall have a right to recover actual and exemplary damages.

2. In the case of the death of either party, the action or right of action given by this section shall survive to or against his or her executor or administrator, and the amount so recovered by either wife or child shall be his or her sole and separate property.

3. Such action may be brought in any court of competent jurisdiction.

4. In any case where parents shall be entitled to such damages, either the father or mother may sue alone therefor, and recovery by one of such parties shall be a bar to suit brought by the other.

To maintain an action under Section 11-101, the following factors must be present:

1. An intoxicated person.
2. Injury or damage either (*a*) caused by the intoxicated person or (*b*) arising out of the intoxication.

3. Defendant seller whose illegal sale or furnishing of the liquor caused or contributed in whole or in part to the intoxication.

4. Plaintiff victim of the injury or damage.

It has been held that Section 11-101 must be read in conjunction with Section 65 of the Alcoholic Beverage Control Law which prohibits the sale for which Section 11-101 affords the remedy. Section 65 of the ABC Law provides:

Section 65, *Prohibited sales*

No person shall sell, deliver or give away or cause or permit or procure to be sold, delivered, or given away any alcoholic beverage to

1. Any minor, actually or apparently, under the age of eighteen years.

2. Any intoxicated person or to any person, actually or apparently, under the influence of liquor.

3. Any habitual drunkard known to be such to the person authorized to dispense alcoholic beverages.

Neither such person so refusing to sell or deliver under this section nor his employer shall be liable in any civil or criminal action or for any fine or penalty based upon such refusal, except that such sale or delivery shall not be refused, withheld from or denied to any person on account of race, creed, color, or national origin.

Appendix F

Trade Press Directory*

ALASKA BEVERAGE
 ANALYST
2403 Champa Street
Denver, Colorado, 80205
Tel: (303) 266-3277
Allen Bell, Editor and Publisher
Vicki Bane, Man. Editor
Mariette Bell, Ad. Mgr.

ALCOHOLIC BEVERAGE
 EXECUTIVES'
 NEWSLETTER
115 W. Sunrise Hwy.
P. O. Box 263
Freeport, L.I., New York, 11520
Tel: (516) 379-8531
Central U.S. Office:
2121 Douglas, 68102
P. O. Box 3188, 68103
Omaha, Nebraska
Tel: (402) 422-1795
Patricia Thibodeau Kennedy,
 Editor and Publisher

ANNUAL DIRECTORY OF THE
 WINE INDUSTRY
703 Market Street
San Francisco, California, 94103
Tel: (415) 392-1146
Philip Hiaring, Editor and
 Publisher

ARIZONA BEVERAGE
 JOURNAL
3302 North Third Street
Phoenix, Arizona, 85012
Tel: (602) 266-2408
Sylvia D. Diamond, Publisher

BAR-SERVER HANDBOOK
488 Madison Ave.
New York, New York, 10022
Tel: (212) 758-5620
Robert A. Amato, Publisher
Allen Schwartz, Editor

---

* Courtesy of Beverage Industry News.

BEVERAGE BULLETIN
8447 Wilshire Blvd.
Beverly Hills, California, 90211
Tel: (213) 653-4445
Herbert B. Granas, Editor and
    Publisher
Max J. Kerstein, Administrative
    Assistant
Neona Ward, Assoc. Editor
Mrs. Ann Granas, Assoc. Editor

BEVERAGE DEALER &
    TAVERN NEWS
6338 W. Roosevelt Rd.
Oak Park, Illinois, 60304
Tel: (312) 848-1680
William Cepak, Sr., President
    and Managing Editor
William (Bill) Cepak, Jr., Editor

BEVERAGE INDUSTRY NEWS
    BIN-MERCHANDISER
    BIN-CALIFORNIA
    GOLDBOOK
703 Market Street
San Francisco, California, 94103
Tel: (415) 986-2360
Southern California Office:
11332 Weddington St.
N. Hollywood, California, 91601
Tel: (213) 769-3643
LeRoy W. Page, Publisher
Timothy Guiney, Editor

BEVERAGE MARKET &
    PRODUCTION
51 Dowing Street
New York, New York, 10014
Tel: (212) 243-2200
Robert C. Rhodes, Editor

BEVERAGE MEDIA
251 Park Avenue, South
New York, New York, 10010
Tel: (212) 677-3300
Philip Slone, Publisher and
    Editor
Max J. Slone, Co-Publisher &
    Adv. Director

BEVERAGE RETAILER
    WEEKLY
250 W. 57th Street
New York, New York, 10019
Tel: (212) 582-1370
Joseph Matzner, Publisher
Robert A. Wilson, Adv. Director

BUCKEYE BEVERAGE
    JOURNAL
P. O. Box 499
Columbus, Ohio, 43216
Richard V. Baxter, Publisher and
    Editor
June B. Brand, Assoc. Editor

CALIFORNIA WINELETTER
P. O. Box 70
Mill Valley, California, 94941
Tel: (415) 781-1132
C. H. van Kriedt,
    Editor-Publisher

COLORADO BEVERAGE
    ANALYST
2403 Champa Street
Denver, Colorado, 80205
Tel: (303) 266-3277
Allen Bell, Editor & Publisher
Vicki Bane, Man. Editor
Mariette Bell, Ad. Mgr.

CONNECTICUT BEVERAGE
    JOURNAL
2529 Whitney Ave.
Hamden, Connecticut, 06518
Tel: (203) 288-3375
Roy Lawson, Publisher
Gloria C. Sherwood, Editor

FLORIDA RESTAURANT &
    BEVERAGE GUIDE
4919 Melrose
P. O. Box 18323
Tampa, Florida, 33609
Tel: (813) 877-2206
Homer Daniels, Publisher and
    Editor
Cletia Daniels, Assoc. Editor

ED GIBBS COMMENTS
445 W. 23rd Street
New York, New York, 10011
Tel: (212) 243-7941
Ed Gibbs, Editor

HAWAII BEVERAGE GUIDE
305 Royal Hawaiian Ave., 96815
P. O. Box 853, 96808
Honolulu, Hawaii
Tel: (808) 923-3983
Esther Smith, Editor and
    Publisher

IMPACT WINE & SPIRITS
    NEWSLETTER
280 Park Avenue
New York, New York, 10017
Tel: (212) 661-2980
Marvin R. Shanken, President
Leslie K. Taylor, Editor

ILLINOIS BEVERAGE
    JOURNAL
One LaSalle Street
Chicago, Illinois, 60602
Tel: (312) 263-5680
James E. O'Brien,
    Publisher-Editor
Phil Bleecker, Managing Editor
James E. O'Brien, Jr., Editor and
    Adv. Mgr.
John T. O'Brien, Editor

INDIANA BEVERAGE
    JOURNAL
Atkinson Sq., Suite G-1
2511 E. 46th Street
Indianapolis, Indiana, 46205
Tel: (317) 545-5262
Richard V. Baxter, Publisher and
    Editor
June B. Brand, Associate Editor

FRANK KANE'S WEEKLY
    LETTER
15-02 College Point Blvd.
College Point, New York, 11356
Tel: (212) 359-3335
Morris Nissman, Editor

KANSAS BEVERAGE NEWS
P.O. Box 1677
150 No. Rock Island
Wichita, Kansas 67201
Tel: (316) 263-0107
Betty A. Paige, Publisher
Charles Walters, Jr., Editor
Dorothy Pond, Ass't to Publisher

KENTUCKY BEVERAGE
    JOURNAL
100 E. Main Street
Frankfort, Kentucky, 40601
Tel: (502) 223-1621
Farnham F. Dudgeon, Editor and
    Publisher
Mike Bennett, Managing Editor

LICENSED BEVERAGE
    JOURNAL
2917 Bruckner Blvd.
Bronx, New York, 10461
Tel: (212) 881-4733
Norman Bogart, Editor

THE LIQUOR HANDBOOK
488 Madison Avenue
New York, New York, 10022
Tel: (212) 758-5620
Robert A. Amato, Publisher
Clark Gavin, Editor

LIQUOR STORE MAGAZINE
488 Madison Avenue
New York, New York, 10022
Tel: (212) 758-5620
Robert A. Amato, Publisher
Dan Hect, Editorial Director
Allen Schwartz, Editor

MARYLAND-WASHINGTON-
    DELAWARE
    BEVERAGE JOURNAL
2 East 25th St.
Baltimore, Maryland, 21218
Tel: (301) 235-1716
Washington Office:
2653 Connecticut Ave., N.W.
Washington, D.C., 20008
(202) 234-6559

Wilmington Office:
919 Market Street
Wilmington, Delaware, 19801
Tel: (302) 655-6353
Thomas W. Murray, Publisher
Anna N. Pumphrey, Editor
Earl Goldstein, Washington Rep.
Ed Golin, Delaware Rep.
F. Louis Brown, Production Mgr.

MASSACHUSETTS
   BEVERAGE JOURNAL
Bodwell Street
Avon Industrial Park
Avon, Massachusetts, 02322
Tel: (617) 471-7750
David R. Shir, Publisher
Emmanuel Rempelakis,
   Managing Editor

MISSOURI BEVERAGE
   JOURNAL
4504 Excelsior Blvd.
Minneapolis, Minnesota, 55416
Tel: (612) 920-7711
Gary Diamond, Publisher

NEBRASKA BEVERAGE
   ANALYST
2403 Champa Street
Denver, Colorado, 80205
Tel: (303) 266-3277
Allen Bell, Editor and Publisher
Vicki Bane, Managing Editor
Mariette Bell, Ad. Mgr.

NEW JERSEY BEVERAGE
   JOURNAL
1180 Raymond Blvd.
Newark, New Jersey, 07102
Tel: (201) 623-3535
Harry Slone, Publisher and
   Editor

NEW MEXICO BEVERAGE
   ANALYST
2403 Champa Street
Denver, Colorado, 80205
Tel: (303) 266-3277

Allen Bell, Editor & Publisher
Vicki Bane, Man. Editor
Mariette Bell, Ad. Mgr.

NORTHWEST BEVERAGE
   JOURNAL
4504 Excelsior Blvd.
Minneapolis, Minnesota, 55416
Tel: (612) 920-7711
Gary Diamond, Publisher

OKLAHOMA BEVERAGE
   NEWS
P.O. Box 1677
150 No. Rock Island
Wichita, Kansas 67201
Tel: (316) 263-0107
Betty A. Paige, Publisher
Charles Walters, Jr., Editor
Dorothy Pond, Ass't to Publisher

PATTERSON'S CALIFORNIA
   BEVERAGE GAZETTEER
422 Wall Street
Los Angeles, California, 90013
Tel: (213) 627-4996
Owen A. Sloan, Managing Editor
No. California Office:
925 Harrison St.
San Francisco, California, 94107
Tel: (415) 826-1443
Bill Murray, Assoc. Editor,
   No. California

RHODE ISLAND BEVERAGE
   JOURNAL
603 Hope Street
Providence, Rhode Island, 02906
Tel: (401) 351-3878
Aaron A. Bilgor, Publisher
Edith G. Bilgor, Editor

SOUTHERN BEVERAGE
   JOURNAL
13225 S. W. 88th Ave.
P. O. Box 1107
Miami (Kendall), Florida, 33156
Tel: (305) 233-7230
Marvin Levin, Publisher

John Hiser, Editor
Raymond Feldman, Ass't to
  Publisher

STATEWAYS MAGAZINE
488 Madison Avenue
New York, New York, 10022
Tel: (212) 758-5620
Robert Amato, President
Dan Hect, Publisher

TAP & TAVERN
117 S. 13th Street
Philadelphia, Pennsylvania,
  19107
Tel: (215) 925-5188
Morris C. Nissman, Publisher

TEXAS BEVERAGE NEWS
922 Neil P. Anderson Bldg.
411 W. 7th Street, 76102
P. O. Box 71, 76101
Ft. Worth, Texas
Tel: (817) 336-4663
Walter H. Gray, Publisher

THE VINEYARD VIEW
Bully Hill Rd., R.D. 2
Hammondsport, New York,
  14840
Tel: (607) 868-4814
Nancy Dorwart, Editor

WINE MARKETING
  HANDBOOK
488 Madison Avenue

New York, New York, 10022
Tel: (212) 758-5620
Robert A. Amato, Publisher
Clark Gavin, Editor

WINE MERCHANDISER
488 Madison Avenue
New York, New York, 10022
Tel: (212) 758-5620
Robert A. Amato, Publisher
Dan Hecht, Editorial Dir.
Allen Schwartz, Editor

WINES & VINES
703 Market Street
San Francisco, California, 94103
Tel: (415) 392-1146
Philip Hiaring, Editor and
  Publisher

THE WINELETTER
P. O. Box 70
Mill Valley, California, 94941
Tel: (415) 388-2578
Charles van Kriedt,
  Editor-Publisher

WISCONSIN BEVERAGE
  JOURNAL
606 West Wisconsin Avenue
Milwaukee, Wisconsin, 53203
Tel: (414) 276-5856
Herbert D. Zien, Editor and
  Publisher
Nora A. Zein, Office Mgr.

Appendix G

Credit Adjustment Bureaus

ALBUQUERQUE, NEW MEXICO
Albuquerque Association of
Credit Management
P.O. Box 30108 Station D
(8420 Lomas, N.E.)
Albuquerque, New Mexico
87110
505-265-5875

AMARILLO, TEXAS
Wholesale Credit Association,
Inc.
P.O. Drawer 1820
(912 Taylor Street)
Amarillo, Texas 79105
806-374-2823

ATLANTA, GEORGIA
Georgia Association of
Credit Management, Inc.
1330 West Peachtree Building,
N.W.

Atlanta, Georgia 30309
404-892-8211

BALTIMORE, MARYLAND
Baltimore Association of
Credit Management, Inc.
6600 York Road
Baltimore, Maryland 21212
301-377-4222

BILLINGS, MONTANA
Montana Association of
Credit Management
P.O. Box 1395
(#16, 1015 Broadwater 59102)
Billings, Montana 59103
406-252-3454

BOSTON, MASSACHUSETTS
New England Association of
Credit Executives, Inc.
77 Summer Street
Boston, Massachusetts 02110
617-542-2131

---

* Courtesy of National Association of Credit Management,
475 Park Avenue South, New York, NY 10016.

BUFFALO, NEW YORK
Credit Management
Association of
Western New York
210 Delaware Avenue, Suite
202
Buffalo, New York 14623
716-854-7018

CHARLOTTE, NORTH CAROLINA
NACM - Carolinas Unit, Inc.
P.O. Box 4482
(1311 East Morehead Street)
Charlotte, North Carolina
28204
704-334-8655

CHATTANOOGA, TENNESSEE
NACM - Cherokee Unit
P.O. Box 21403
(5511 Brainerd Road 37411)
Chattanooga, Tennessee 37421
615-894-9571

CHICAGO, ILLINOIS
Chicago-Midwest Credit
Management Association
P.O. Box 7369
(315 S. Northwest Highway,
Park Ridge, Illinois 60068)
Chicago, Illinois 60680
312-696-3000

CINCINNATI, OHIO
Cincinnati Association of
Credit and Financial
Management
707 Race Street Building - 4th
Floor
Cincinnati, Ohio 45202
513-241-3841

CLEVELAND, OHIO
NACM - Northeastern Ohio
666 Euclid Avenue - Room 606
Cleveland, Ohio 44114
216-781-0710

DALLAS , TEXAS
Dallas Association of
Credit Management, Inc.
P.O. Box 47807
(1515 Viceroy)
Dallas, Texas 75247
214-637-3753

DAYTON, OHIO
Dayton Association of
Credit Management
1006 Harries Building
Dayton, Ohio 45402
513-228-6124

DENVER, COLORADO
The Rocky Mountain
Association
of Credit Management
789 Sherman Street
Denver, Colorado 80203
303-222-4713

DES MOINES, IOWA
NACM - Iowa Unit, Inc.
1119 High Street
Des Moines, Iowa 50309
515-244-5284

DETROIT, MICHIGAN
NACM - Eastern Michigan
19016 Woodward Avenue
Detroit, Michigan 48203
313-368-0710

EL PASO, TEXAS
Tri-State Credit Association
P.O. Box 3247 - Station A
(812 N. Piedras Street 79903)
El Paso, Texas 79923
915-566-1635

EVANSVILLE, INDIANA
NACM - Tri-State Area, Inc.
223 S.E. Eighth Street
Evansville, Indiana 47713
812-425-2651

FORT WORTH, TEXAS
NACM - Fort Worth Division
P.O. Box 7115
(3000 E. Belknap-Riverside
State Bank Building - Suite 311)
Fort Worth, Texas 76111
817-838-8377

GRAND RAPIDS, MICHIGAN
NACM - Western Michigan,
Inc.
48 West Fulton Street
Grand Rapids, Michigan 49502
616-459-3371

HARTFORD, CONNECTICUT
NACM - Northern Connecticut
Div.
410 Asylum Street, Room 237
Hartford, Connecticut 06103
203-525-4421

HOUSTON, TEXAS
Houston Association of
Credit Management, Inc.
P.O. Box 3388
(1302 McGowen Street)
Houston, Texas 77001
713-659-2511

INDIANAPOLIS, INDIANA
Indiana Association of
Credit Management
130 East New York Street
Indianapolis, Indiana 46204
317-632-4444

JACKSONVILLE, FLORIDA
NACM - North Florida Unit,
Inc.
221 East Adams Street
Jacksonville, Florida 32202
904-355-9581

KANSAS CITY, MISSOURI
Kansas City Wholesale
Credit Association
3119 Gillham Road

Kansas City, Missouri 64109
816-931-7115

KENILWORTH, NEW JERSEY
New Jersey Association of
Credit Executives
504 Washington Avenue
Kenilworth, New Jersey 07033
201-272-9191

KNOXVILLE, TENNESSEE
NACM - Knoxville Division
709 North Broadway
Knoxville, Tennessee 37917
615-546-0452

LOUISVILLE, KENTUCKY
Louisville Credit
Management Association, Inc.
P.O. Box 1062
(116 West Market Street 40202)
Louisville, Kentucky 40201
502-583-4471

LUBBOCK, TEXAS
Lubbock Association of
Credit Management, Inc.
P.O. Box 3125
(3708 Avenue Q 79412)
Lubbock, Texas 79410
806-744-4521

MEMPHIS, TENNESSEE
Memphis Association of
Credit Executives, Inc.
P.O. Box 4728
(1906 Madison Avenue)
Memphis, Tennessee 38104
901-726-4505 or 725-4141

MILWAUKEE, WISCONSIN
NACM - Wisconsin, Inc.
P.O. Box 11695
(3575 N. Oakland Avenue)
Milwaukee, Wisconsin 53211
414-964-5600

NEW ORLEANS, LOUISIANA
New Orleans Association of
Credit and Financial
Management
P.O. Box 30609
(633 Carondelet Street)
New Orleans, Louisiana 70190
504-523-1701

NEW YORK, NEW YORK
New York Credit and Financial
Management Association
71 West 23rd Street
New York, New York 10010
212-924-0100

NORFOLK, VIRGINIA
Tidewater Association of
Credit Management, Inc.
711 Law Building
Granby and Plume Streets
Norfolk, Virginia 23510
804-623-4339

OAKLAND, CALIFORNIA
Wholesalers Credit Association
of Oakland
P.O. Box 2176
(7700 Edgewater Drive - Suite
501)
Oakland, California 94621
415-632-1100

ODESSA, TEXAS
West Texas Association of
Credit Management, Inc.
312 West 4th Street
Odessa, Texas 79761
915-332-0779

OKLAHOMA CITY, OKLAHOMA
NACM - Oklahoma Division
P.O. Box 60626
(1717 West Main)
Oklahoma City, Oklahoma
73106
405-235-1341

OMAHA, NEBRASKA
NACM - Nebraska-Western
Iowa Unit
2962 Harney Street
Omaha, Nebraska 68131
402-342-2480

ORLANDO, FLORIDA
NACM - Central Florida Unit
P.O. Box 2746
(367 North Orange Avenue
32801)
Orlando, Florida 32802
305-425-8613

PHOENIX, ARIZONA
Wholesalers Credit Association
of Arizona, Inc.
P.O. Box 1987
(811 North Third Street 85004)
Phoenix, Arizona 85001
602-252-8866

PITTSBURGH, PENNSYLVANIA
The Credit Association of
Western Pennsylvania
908 Penn Avenue - 5th Floor
Pittsburgh, Pennsylvania 15222
412-281-6822

PORTLAND, OREGON
Oregon Association of
Credit Management, Inc.
937 S.W. 14th Avenue
Portland, Oregon 97205
503-226-3531

ROCHESTER, NEW YORK
Rochester Credit and Financial
Management Association, Inc.
P.O. Box 915
(19 Prince Street 14607)
Rochester, New York 14603
716-654-9100

ST. LOUIS, MISSOURI
St. Louis Association of
Credit Management

P.O. Box 1910, Bechtold
  Station
(4679 South Grand Boulevard
  63111)
St. Louis, Missouri 63118
314-832-4800

SALT LAKE CITY, UTAH
  Inter-Mountain Association
  of Credit Men
  P.O. Box 151306
  (49 W. Malvern Avenue)
  Salt Lake City, Utah 84115
  801-487-8781

SAN ANTONIO, TEXAS
  NACM of Texas, Inc.
  P.O. Box 1113
  (214 Dwyer Avenue)
  San Antonio, Texas 78294
  512-225-7106

SAN DIEGO, CALIFORNIA
  San Diego Whole Credit
  Men's Association
  110 West C Street
  San Diego, California 92101
  714-239-8191

SAN FRANCISCO, CALIFORNIA
  Board of Trade of San
  Francisco
  989 Market Street
  San Francisco, California
  94103
  415-421-6302

SEATTLE, WASHINGTON
  NACM - Western
  Washington-Alaska
  P.O. Box 21966
  (212 Virginia Street 98101)
  Seattle, Washington 98111
  206-624-2400

SIOUX CITY, IOWA
  NACM - Interstate Division
  605 Frances Building
  Sioux City, Iowa 51101
  712-255-8915

SPOKANE, WASHINGTON
  NACM - Spokane Division
  P.O. Box 2606 - Terminal
  Annex
  (North 1710 Calispel 99205)
  Spokane, Washington 99220
  509-326-2550

SPRINGFIELD, MASSACHUSETTS
  NACM - Western
  Massachusetts
  Division, Inc.
  P.O. Box 1362
  (1537 Main Street 01103)
  Springfield, Massachusetts
  01101
  413-785-1581

TAMPA, FLORIDA
  National Association of Credit
  Men
  Florida Gulf Coast Unit
  P.O. Box 22827
  (4601 West J. F. Kennedy Blvd.
  33609)
  Tampa, Florida 33622
  813-877-9457

TOLEDO, OHIO
  NACM - Northwestern Ohio
  640 Phillips Avenue
  Toledo, Ohio 43612
  419-476-4426

WASHINGTON, D. C.
  Credit Management
  Association of
  Greater Washington, Inc.
  620 Washington Building
  Washington, D. C. 20005
  202-347-8400

WICHITA, KANSAS
  Wichita Association of
  Credit Management, Inc.
  P.O. Box 455
  (575 West Douglas 67203)
  Wichita, Kansas 67201
  316-263-1257

Index